Frontispiece courtesy Lensmen Ltd.

DE VALERA
AND HIS TIMES

Edited by
John P. O'Carroll
and John A. Murphy

Cork University Press
1983

First published in 1983 by
Cork University Press, University College, Cork

British Library Cataloguing in Publication Data

De Valera and his times.
1. De Valera, Eamon   2. Ireland — Politics and
government — 1910-1921
3. Ireland — Politics and government — 1922-1949
4. Ireland — Politics and government — 1949-
I. O'Carroll, J.P.   II. Murphy, John A.
941.7082'2'0924   DA965.D4

ISBN 0-902561-26-X

Printed in the Republic of Ireland by Tower Books,
86 South Main St., Cork

Preface

The papers which comprise this volume were read at a conference held in University College, Cork, October 1-3, 1982 marking the centenary of the birth of Eamon de Valera. The conference was sponsored jointly by the Department of Irish History and the Department of Social Theory and Institutions.

The editors wish to express their thanks to the President of University College, Cork, Prof. Tadhg Ó Ciardha for the considerable support provided by the College towards both the conference and the preparation of the proceedings for publication. They also wish to thank the Committee of Cork University Press, and particularly its Secretary, Mr. Donal Counihan, whose day-to-day assistance proved invaluable. Finally, the editors thank Ciaran McCullagh, Joe Ruane, Monica Jefferies and Teresa O'Flynn of the Department of Social Theory and Institutions, and Charlotte Wiseman of the Department of Irish History, for their advice and assistance, and Miss M. Collins and the staff of the Secretarial Centre for their dedication in the preparation of the typescript.

Errata

Page 56, line 27, *for* quivalent, *read* equivalent.

Page 107, line 31, *for* people will be able to exactly, *read* people will be able to do exactly.

Page 114, *passim, for* Whittaker, *read* Whitaker.

Page 140, line 22, *for* paralel, *read* parallel.

Page 146, line 28, *for* sited, *read* cited.

Page 154, line 35, *for* reign, *read* rein.

Contents

Abbreviations

AC	Appeal Cases
CO	Colonial Office
DE	Dáil Éireann, Official Debates
GC	Government Committee
ILRM	Irish Law Reports Monthly
IR	Irish Reports
ITUCLP	Irish Trade Union Congress and Labour Party
NLI	National Library of Ireland, Dublin
PRO	Public Record Office
PRONI	Public Record Office Northern Ireland, Belfast
RP	Resident Magistrates Papers
SPO	State Paper Office

The Career of Eamon de Valera
1882-1975

A Summary

1882   ✓ 14 October, born New York.

1885   ✓ Brought to Ireland to live at Bruree, Co. Limerick.

1888-1898   ✓ Educated at National School, Bruree and Christian Brothers' School, Charleville.

1898-1903   ✓ Secondary education continued at Blackrock College, Dublin. University education in Dublin.

1903-1916   ✓ Teaching and lecturing in mathematics in various institutions.

1910   ✓ Married Sinéad Flanagan.

1913   ✓ Joined Irish Volunteers.

1916   ✓ Commandant 3rd Battalion, Dublin Brigade, Irish Volunteers in Easter Rising. After Rising, death sentence commuted to penal servitude for life.

1917   ✓ Returned home from imprisonment in England.
11 July, won East Clare by-election for Sinn Féin.
26 October, elected President of Sinn Fein at Ard Fheis.
27 October, elected President of Irish Volunteers.

1918   Led anti-conscription campaign. Again interned in England. At General Election, December 1918, returned unopposed for East Clare and defeated John Dillon in East Mayo.

1919   Escaped from Lincoln Prison. Elected Príomh-Aire (President) by Dáil Éireann.

1919-1920   In United States, sought financial aid and moral support for, and official recognition of, the Irish Republic.

1921   Re-elected by Second Dáil as President of the Irish Republic. Accepted invitation by Lloyd George to Anglo-Irish conference in London, but was not a member of the Irish delegation. Subsequently, rejected 'Articles of Agreement for a Treaty between Great Britain and Ireland'.

1922   After Dáil approved Treaty (7 January), de Valera resigned as President, and failed narrowly to be re-elected. In June, on outbreak of Civil War, joined Republican army.

1923   In May, supported cease-fire call to anti-Treaty forces.

1925	Condemned the copperfastening of Partition, following the collapse of the Boundary Commission.
1926	Founded Fianna Fáil.
1927	Ended abstentionist policy towards the institutions of the Irish Free State. Entered Dáil Éireann with Fianna Fáil deputies, and became leader of the opposition.
1932	Fianna Fáil formed Government.
1932-1948	De Valera in power, first as President of the Executive Council and then (from enactment of new Constitution in 1937) as Taoiseach.
1932-1938	Anglo-Irish tension: Economic War: 1937, new Constitution. The international dimension: De Valera active in League of Nations.
1938	Anglo-Irish Agreements: End of Economic War and return of 'Treaty ports'.
1939	On outbreak of war, Irish neutrality affirmed.
1940	De Valera's government rejected British promise of Irish unity in return for Irish involvement in war.
1944	De Valera rejected 'American note' requesting expulsion of Axis representatives from Dublin.
1945	Reply to Churchill's end-of-war criticism of Irish neutrality.
1948	Replaced by Inter-Party Government. Leader of the opposition. Visited USA, Australia, India. Spoke against partition.
1951-1954	Taoiseach again.
1954-1957	Once more in opposition.
1957	Began last period as Taoiseach.
1959	Elected as President of Ireland.
1966	Re-elected President for second term.
1973	Retired to private life.
1975	29 August, died, seven months after death of Sinéad (7 January).

Introduction

The aim of the conference at which these papers were presented was a scholarly re-appraisal of the life and times of Eamon de Valera. At the planning stage it was felt that the insights of various social scientists should supplement those of the historians in order to provide a more rounded view of the subject. In the event, the great majority of the contributors were historians, but a unique inter-disciplinary flavour was provided by the contribution of papers from the fields of political science, law, folklore and sociology.

Rather than trying to attempt the impossible task of covering all aspects of the de Valera age, the organisers allowed the conference to develop, as it were, around the contributors. The published proceedings, therefore, make no claim to comprehensiveness but it is hoped that the individual papers will help to throw new light on the various facets of the subject. The cultural, political and social origins of the movement spearheaded by de Valera are examined in a number of papers. Other aspects which are explored to a greater or lesser extent include the leadership structure; the relationship between opposing elites; the creation and adaptation of ideology; the nature of ties between leadership and rank and file; the wider question of the inter-relationship of politics to the economy, society and culture; and finally, the impact of the leadership on the evolution of the formal structures of the state.

It will be seen that several contributors consider de Valera in the round while others concentrate on his attitude to specific national issues and on his relationship with particular groups and institutions, and this explains the sequence in which the papers are published here.

It should be recorded that in the course of the conference several contributors drew attention to the poverty and inadequate availability of political source material in Ireland. It is significant that the conference felt itself especially indebted to Maurice Moynihan's excellently edited collection of de Valera's speeches and statements. All otherwise unattributed references are to this source.

J.P. O'Carroll.

John A Murphy

The Achievement of
Eamon de Valera

John A. Murphy

When Eamon de Valera died on 29 August 1975 there was much official eulogy and some caustic criticism.[1] The criticism was a response to the expected obsequiousness of the eulogy. It was not a good time to appraise de Valera fairly. He had long outlived his own generation during a time of bewildering change. He was out of the public mind when he died, it was only 'the shade of that which once was great' that had passed away, and funereal pomp was simply the ritual formalisation of something seemingly already over and done with. The public becomes bored even with the greatest of patriots when they live too long and when they die in their beds, at least in their own beds.

Seven years afterwards the climate is remarkably more propitious for an assessment. The peculiar irritations of that belated funeral time have disappeared. We may consider our subject in an atmosphere of academic calm. There is no disturbing after-presence, as there was with Parnell in the manner of his fall and death. Research on the de Valera age has advanced apace and fresh material is available, though regrettably not de Valera's own papers, as yet. The lapse of seven years provides at least an interim perspective. As we view the de Valera period through the lens of our own preoccupation, the man and his times appear to have a relevance which was perhaps obscured in 1975. The issues of his day, in different form admittedly, continue to exercise us almost a quarter of a century after he left active politics. These issues include the attitude of this State, its government and its citizens towards Northern Ireland; the ability of government to influence the economy and to create employment; the extent to which the Constitution and the laws should embody the moral code of the majority denomination; the degree of the State's sovereignty in international affairs; and the continuing, if greatly changing, policy of neutrality.

Even in death de Valera's inveterate opponents and their descendants are still reluctant to cede him his place in history. The occasional sour note has been struck during this centenary, and there are still those who choose to believe their own propaganda that de Valera started the Civil War. It is as well, then, to begin any discussion by reiterating the obvious: Eamon de Valera is the most significant figure in the political

1

history of modern Ireland. This is a statement of incontrovertible historical fact, and it does not necessarily involve a laudatory judgement. Nor is it a ranking in order of the nationally meritorious, a putting down of other people's heroes, a disparagement of Pearse's rarefied idealism, Connolly's revolutionary fire, Collins's swashbuckling pragmatism. If there were no other reasons for de Valera's importance, he was at the centre of political life in this country for forty-three years, not including the fourteen-year period as President. We have here a span of political power and influence virtually unparalleled in contemporary Europe and in Irish history.

Mere longevity, however, or political survival after the manner of the Abbé Sieyès, does not in itself add up to achievement. De Valera's prolonged career was, not surprisingly, a very chequered one, and there are parts of it which represent the very opposite of achievement. The initial successes in the heroic period of 1917-18, the donning of the Parnell mantle, the lively administrations of the 1930s, the adroit handling of neutrality, — these are to be contrasted with the mistakes of the American tour in 1919-20, the fatal blunder in not leading the Irish delegation to the Treaty talks in 1921 (subsequent sagacious explanations[2] notwithstanding), the fumbling and agonising from Treaty split to Civil War, and the sterile anti-partitionism of the late 1940s. Such a pattern of light and shade can no doubt be discerned in the careers of the politically great elsewhere.

The first achievement, then, was to preside with an astonishing flair and assurance (for such a political tyro) over the resurgent nationalist movement of 1917-18. Trailing clouds of 1916 glory (but by no means anxious to repeat the performance), de Valera skilfully orchestrated the popular anti-conscription mood and reaped the political reward, as he was to do with the neutrality policy many years later. His political acumen, in eclipse in the Civil War period, was once again evident in the mid-1920s when he deployed skill and patience in disengaging himself from the I.R.A. and in retreating from the cul-de-sac of Sinn Féin. Indeed, if we take together de Valera's move away from 1916 militarism to the constitutionalism of elections in 1917 and 1918, his break with abstentionist and extra-parliamentary Sinn Féin in 1926 and the stern, if professedly anguished, steps against the I.R.A. in the 1940s, we can say that not only did he epitomise at the outset of his career the ambivalence of constitutionalist and violent traditions in Irish nationalism but that he also bridged them, and finally and firmly asserted the supremacy of the civil over the military tradition, the constitutional principle over that of physical force, and majority rule over the-people-had-no-right-to-do-wrong assertion. To his critics who might with apparent good reason point out that de Valera's conversion to parliamentary democracy was a disastrously belated one, it might be responded that the civilians among the anti-Treatyites could claim that they had never wavered in their allegiance to Dáil Éireann and that their position was really an affirmation of parliamentary legitimacy, the crucial point in their view being that the jurisdiction of the lawful parliament of the Republic had been usurped by a puppet pro-Treaty parliament.

Among the indisputable achievements of Eamon de Valera was the direction and the development (others dug the foundations) of the political party that quickly was to become the largest and most dominant in the State, and in many ways, as its members claimed, as much a national organisation as a party. I have written elsewhere[3] that the

> reconstituted Sinn Féin in 1917 was never [de Valera's] creation in the sense that Fianna Fáil was. It was Fianna Fáil that enabled him to realise his potential as a political leader and that brought about his transformation from uncertain amateur to skilled professional. Sinn Féin was never his *team*, its elements were disparate and its programme was not one of his making. With Fianna Fáil, he literally came into his own.

Let us take as read the spectacular achievement of the completion of the constitutional revolution in Anglo-Irish relations, and move on to the successful policy of neutrality in World War II. The Anglo-Irish agreements of 1938 were popularly regarded as a triumph for de Valera and characteristically exploited for election purposes by Fianna Fáil. The return of the British-held naval bases was the *pièce de résistance* of these agreements though it may have been less a matter of 'Dev getting back the ports' than a British decision that they weren't worth the bother and risk of holding on to them.[4] At any rate, the scene was set for the Irish decision to remain neutral, though the chances of success of such a policy were slim.

In the course of to-day's intermittent debate about defence and security, and the occasional kite-flying about membership of a military alliance, a disparagement of wartime neutrality is frequently included. Such criticism is generally ill-informed and ignores the particular historical circumstances of the period. It is significant that the two authors who have written full-length studies of the neutrality policy have no doubt that formal neutrality was the only feasible course for the State in 1939.[5]

For de Valera, neutrality was necessary for three main reasons. First, it was the supreme expression of national sovereignty. Secondly, it was the only feasible policy while partition lasted. Finally, and following on his direct observation of the collapse of League of Nations sanctions and of the principle of collective security, he believed that small states should resolve that they would not become the tools of any great power, and that they will resist with whatever strength that they may possess every attempt to force them into a war against their will.[6]

In contrast to the rationale advanced by latter-day advocates of Irish neutrality, the 1939 policy was seen as a positive isolationist virtue. Neither had it any pacifist connotations as can be seen from the above passage and as was evident from the seriousness with which tens of thousands of ordinary citizens prepared themselves to make any invader pay dearly for the violation of their country's sovereignty.

It is also worthy of note that neutrality was not, for de Valera at any rate, an expression of anti-British feeling, and this was attested by Sir John Maffey, the British minister.[7] In de Valera's view, England's difficulty was no longer Ireland's opportunity. From the time he made his 'Cuban' proposal in 1920, his constant position was that a free Ireland would never allow itself to be used by an aggressor against Britain, and this attitude he maintained throughout the war. In April 1938 he asserted that he had

> always said that in my view an independent Ireland would have interests, very many interests, in common with Great Britain. In providing for our defence of our own interests, we would also of necessity be providing to a certain extent for British defence of British interests.[8]

As the war proceeded, neutrality as the hallmark of sovereignty became more and more emphasised. De Valera was increasingly aware of its valuable cohesive force as a builder of national morale. The policy also gave him the opportunity to project himself, as he had done during the anti-conscription campaign in 1918 and tried to do at the time of the Boundary Commission *débâcle*, as the leader not just of a party or faction but of nationalist Ireland as a whole. Partition as a cause of neutrality tended to become almost a secondary consideration and the June 1940 British cabinet promise of a united Ireland in return for Irish involvement in the war effort was turned down by the Irish government. There are various explanations for this — the awareness of the fatal price John Redmond had paid for his collaboration in World War I, the improbability that the promise could be delivered and the almost academic nature of the offer in the context of a seemingly imminent German victory. But the really fundamental reason for looking this peculiar gift horse in the mouth was that neutrality, not the reunification of Ireland, was now the supreme national value. As the most crucial test of the sovereignty of the State, neutrality could not be abandoned even for a united Ireland. Maffey rightly observed in October 1939 that 'the creed of Ireland to-day was neutrality. No government could exist that departed from that principle'.[9] As de Valera put it to David Gray in April 1940, 'we could never bargain with our neutrality'.[10] And it was with some heat that he also told Gray that neutrality was 'not for sale'.[11]

The truth is that during Eamon de Valera's long period in office, he was fundamentally concerned with the interests of the State he ruled rather than the hypothetical united Ireland which *appeared* to preoccupy him all his life and especially when he was out of office. Neutrality was the supreme measure of this concern for the State. The policy may have begun as an *ad hoc* response to a particular situation and on 29 September 1939 he dismissed the 'theoretical, abstract idea of neutrality'.[12] But the concept of neutrality underwent a rapid evolution and in his 1941 St Patrick's Day message to the United States, it seems to have reached the status of an ideology. The relevant statement[13] is worth quoting at some length.

Americans who seek to understand the reasons for our attitude need only study Washington's declaration of neutrality in 1793 and his letter to James Monroe in 1796. Some twenty years ago, when, in the cause of Irish freedom, I addressed many public meetings in the United States, I pointed out that the aim of the overwhelming majority of the Irish people of the present generation was to secure for Ireland the status of an independent sovereign state which would be recognised internationally as such and could pursue its own life and develop its own institutions and culture in its own peaceful way outside the hazards of imperial adventure — if possible with its neutrality internationally guaranteed like the neutrality of Switzerland. A small country like ours that had for centuries resisted imperial absorption, and that still wished to preserve its separate national identity, was bound to choose the course of neutrality in this war. No other course could secure the necessary unity of purpose and effort amongst its people, and at a time like this we heed the warning that the house divided against itself shall not stand. The continued existence of partition, that unnatural separation of six of our counties from the rest of Ireland, added in our case a further decisive reason.

Note the almost casual addition of partition as 'a further' reason. The final word to be said on the neutrality issue is that it shows Eamon de Valera to have been, in fact though not in verbal protestation, the Twenty-Six-county leader *par excellence*. In directing the neutrality policy, he helped to shape and stabilise the State, more than any other figure in post-independence Ireland.

Writing in 1975,[14] Professor Emmet Larkin made this statement about the relationship of Church and State in de Valera's time:

De Valera's real achievement in Church-State relations, however, cannot be fully appreciated if it is not understood that while he has done much to make the Irish state more confessional, he has also prevented it from becoming any more clerical.

In this view, de Valera inherited from Parnell a clerical-nationalist consensus which recognised a division of jurisdiction between Church and State. 'De Valera's own political greatness', says Larkin, 'certainly owes much to his understanding of the dynamics of this system of politics by consensus'. Thus he acknowledged the prerogatives of the bishops in the sphere of public morality and legislated accordingly in such areas as contraception, continuing censorship and regulation of dance halls. In addition, of course, the rights of the Church in the always crucial area of education were recognised. The 1937 Constitution gave a formal and explicit expression to the confessionalisation of the State.

But, says Larkin, de Valera determined the exact limit of episcopal rights and maintained the State's authority within the consensus. Thus, bishops who criticised the 'economic war' policy were studiously ignored; de Valera refused to be hustled into outlawing Communists at home or supporting the Franco regime in Spain, and he cared not at all for ecclesiastical sensibilities when he condemned the Italian invasion of Ethiopia and advocated the entry of the USSR into the League of Nations. Moreover, his government censored an episcopal pastoral for allegedly being in conflict with the neutrality policy. Most importantly, the de Valera administration rejected Catholic proposals for the vocational reorganisation of the State since it would essentially undermine ministerial responsibility and the prerogatives of a democratically-elected government. Thus were episcopal pretensions held in check, a correct balance between Church and State maintained in the consensus, and the State prevented from becoming clerical while becoming increasingly confessional.

Larkin's thesis, it may be said, provides a helpful framework for de Valera's dealings with the Catholic Church, but it omits a number of factors and does not adequately explain his own quite complex attitude to the whole religious and ecclesiastical scene, not does it allow for the fact that much of the time he played this game by instinct.

The good impression de Valera had made on the bishops during the anti-conscription campaign of 1918[15] was undone during the Treaty split and Civil War and he found the position brought about by the joint excommunication of October 1922 personally and politically distressing. However, he was by no means alienated from the Church since he never lost the contacts and friendships he had earlier made with churchmen. His message[16] of 'dutiful homage' to the Pope to be conveyed by the unsuccessful peace emissary, Mgr Luzio, reminds us of a very important fact about Eamon de Valera in this context of Church-State relations, and that is his life-long piety. Not alone was he brought up in the faith-and-fatherland tradition like thousands of others but he had a strong religious faith matched by a deep sense of devotion. There was, moreover, something ecclesiastical and priestly about his persona, and an element of the preacher in his bearing, his attire and his rhetoric. His speeches to the people of Ireland tended to be secular sermons. If a bishop is called 'a father in God', then de Valera was a kind of 'father in Ireland', and his paternalism was the counterpart of the prevailing clerical paternalism of the age. Though relations with individual churchmen (Bishop Fogarty of Killaloe, for example) might be strained, de Valera was very much at home with the clergy, mixed with them on terms of equality and enjoyed a day out at an episcopal consecration just as much as one of his political successors would do at a Munster hurling final.

De Valera, then, as an individual and as a politican throughout his career was more than usually well disposed to the Catholic Church, and was always ready to seek a *modus vivendi* with it at times of crisis, as he did when rehabilitating himself in clerical eyes after the Civil War and when allaying episcopal suspicions over health legislation in 1953. There is no doubt that his personal piety and his friendship with some clerics helped overcome the intense hostility[17] of many priests to de Valera and his new party as they moved, first into the Dáil and then into government. He also lost no opportunity of affirming[18] and demonstrating that Fianna Fáil was as Catholic as, if not more so than, their opponents, and whatever anti-clerical elements existed within the party were kept well under control.

Yet Larkin is right in pointing to the demarcation line within the consensus. De Valera and Fianna Fáil were quite independent of the clergy who, in contrast to the eras of O'Connell and Parnell, had no place in a secular organisation with a secular policy, largely uninfluenced by the contemporary fashion for Catholic sociology.[19] A recent work has even suggested that 'the emergence of Fianna Fáil was a major secularising event in Irish life'.[20] One point may be made without undue cynicism: Fianna Fáil anxiety to establish its Catholic credentials faded according as its electoral strength grew, and the challenge to vocationalism came at a time when it was securely established in power.

The distinction between the clerical and the confessional State is a much finer and more difficult one than would appear from Larkin's argument. It is not always easy to see where and why Eamon de Valera drew the line between Christ and Caesar: at least the historian finds it particularly difficult to read de Valera's mind here. Perhaps the line was blurred or crossed now and then. At times, de Valera appears to be the simple son of the Church, making filial noises on behalf of a Catholic nation. This is the approach on his accession to power in 1932 in his message to the Pope, in the welcome to the Papal legate at the Eucharistic Congress in the same year, in his visit to Rome during the Holy Year of 1933 and in his 1935 St Patrick's Day broadcast to the

United States in which he said 'Ireland is still a Catholic country'.[21] His compliance with the rigid instructions of the Church is seen at its most dependent and puerile on the occasion of former President Douglas Hyde's funeral in July 1949 when de Valera observed the Catholic rule of not attending Protestant services and meekly waited outside St Patrick's Cathedral. In matters such as these, he was truly, in Shaw's disparaging description of the average Irish Catholic, 'a child before his Church'.[22] His opposition to the appointment of a Protestant librarian in Co. Mayo in 1931 was another example of a particularly restrictive Church influence, though it should be added that poor Miss Letitia Dunbar-Harrison's misfortune was that she was not a heretic only but exclusively English-speaking as well.[23] De Valera's public reaction twenty years later to the 'mother-and-child' scheme *débâcle* was an unedifying example of political expediency and fence-sitting, and those who would ascribe olympian statesmanship to his solitary remark on the occasion of the great debate in the Dáil[24] ('I think we have heard enough') are either ingenuous or blinkered.

On the other hand, de Valera regarded himself as the equal of the Church when he was about the State's business and the bishops acknowledged and respected, sometimes perforce, his total independence within his own jurisdiction. It is this healthy respect that explains the relative success of his government in grasping the prickly nettle of the health services. In addition, there were some spirited displays of opposition on his part to bigotry and privilege. At the 1943 Fianna Fáil Ard-Fheis, he criticised, without naming it, the Knights of St Columbanus, stating that it was 'absurd' to have 'an organisation for the protection of Catholic interests' 'where ninety-three per cent of the people are Catholics'.[25] In the summer of 1957, in the twilight of his political career and in his last years as Taoiseach, he made a magisterial condemnation of the Fethard-on-Sea sectarian boycott which had received the support of, among others, the formidable Bishop Browne of Galway. De Valera's statement in the Dáil on the matter pulled no punches, and he referred to the boycott as 'ill-conceived, ill-considered and futile', 'unjust and cruel', and a 'deplorable affair'.[26]

When the new Constitution was being drafted, the article on religion gave de Valera more anxiety than anything else in the document. How could the claims of the Catholic Church and the just rights of other churches be reconciled? The Irish version of the official biography puts de Valera's dilemma in a revealing phrase: *'conas a réiteodh sé an dualgas a bhí air a chreideamh san aon Eaglais fhíor a fhógairt ach gan éagóir a dhéanamh ar mhionlaigh, agus gan deacrachtaí a mhéadú'.*[27]

There were those in Fianna Fáil who, remembering episcopal hostility during the Civil War, found the confessional provisions of the

Constitution and the 'special position' clause hard to swallow, or so they later said. But even for the mildly secularist members of the party what real choice was there? The government believed it was vital that the Constitution should be adopted, as an affirmation at home and abroad of Irish independence and sovereignty, and if its safe passage was to be secured the risk of alienating the goodwill of the Church could not be taken. In 1936-37, Fianna Fáil, only a few years in power and rather apprehensive about facing the electorate after a turbulent period in office, simply could not cock a snoot at the Catholic Church, even if it had wanted to. Besides, as de Valera put it when piloting the measure through the Dáil, the 'special position' clause simply recognised a sociological fact.

> There are 93% of the people in this part of Ireland and 75% of the people of Ireland as a whole who belong to the Catholic Church, who believe in its teachings and whose whole philosophy of life is the philosophy that comes from its teachings . . . If we are going to have a democratic State, if we are going to be ruled by the representatives of the people, it is clear their whole philosophy of life is going to affect that, and that has to be borne in mind and the recognition of it is important.[28]

Was this a characteristic piece of casuistical reasoning, designed to stifle the still small voice of republican conscience? The secular republican voice was a very weak one in Fianna Fáil, and it was easily muffled by the demands of *realpolitik*.

Given all the constraints of the period, however, the clause on religion was a relatively liberal one, or so it was regarded at the time. The various Protestant leaders in the State had no fault to find — or more accurately, no fault to express — with the specific recognition accorded to them in Article 44, and de Valera ignored the clamour from the Catholic right for an unequivocal constitutional acclamation of the Catholic Church as the true Church of Christ. The recognition of the Jewish communities may be regarded as generous and enlightened in a period when anti-Semitism was murderously rampant in much of Europe and acceptably fashionable elsewhere.

Nevertheless, Mr de Valera's liberal attitude towards the non-Catholic denominations — and under this we may include his generosity to Trinity College — sprang more from a sense of fair play and justice than from a deep ideological conviction that Protestant, Catholic and Dissenter were all absolutely and equally entitled to the common name of Irishman. In this connection, his perception of Ireland as a Catholic nation was crucial.

When Eamon de Valera departed from active politics in 1959, he left Irish society very much as he found it. Though there was, even then, a general improvement in living standards since 1932, the structure of

Irish society remained virtually unchanged. Despite the high-sounding phrases in the Constitution the sources of national wealth remained either neglected or exploited for private gain. Class-consciousness was perhaps even more rampant than when de Valera came to power, according as the nationalist and populist consensus waned. The greed and acquisitiveness which had long been distinguishing features of the ambitious town and rural classes (and which we have been deluded into regarding as only a recent growth) still flourished. Social injustice and social callousness still reigned in Catholic Ireland. The high ramparts of privilege walled in the citadel of higher education, ramparts only nominally and occasionally breached by the fortunate few who were beneficiaries of lamentably scattered and inadequate scholarships.

In 1957, the year in which Eamon de Valera was returned to power for the last time, unemployment reached a peak of 78,000 and the unemployed were coldly comforted by miserably minimal social welfare payments. In the same dark year of 1957, the country lost 54,000 of its young people, the worst year of an emigration haemorrhage that was a national humiliation.[29] This admission of national failure was all the more stark set against the predictions of national prophets and philosophers in the decades before independence that a free Ireland in charge of her own resources would end emigration for good. 'No longer shall our children, like our cattle, be brought up for export', promised a confident de Valera soon after he first came to power.[30] The splendid promise remained bitterly unfulfilled, and the fine phrase perished. Indeed, the comparison with the cattle trade proved unfortunate and ill-chosen: those caught up in the great emigration tide to England during and after World War II might well angrily reflect that in the manner of their going they too were part of the livestock export trade. The animal parallel was heightened by the conditions of the boats, the preparatory sulphur bath and the purchase of the two-shilling-and-sixpenny travel permit which was bitterly regarded by some emigrants as not only the value their country had placed on them but a mean tax extracted by a government unable to give them a living in their own land.

'The hungry sheep look up and are not fed'. The whole socio-economic area was one of minimal achievement for Eamon de Valera. 'I never regarded freedom as an end in itself', he claimed in the Dáil on 29 April 1932, 'but if I were asked what statement of Irish policy was most in accord with my view as to what human beings should struggle for, I would stand side by side with James Connolly'.[31] Though these were expedient things to say since he was dependent on Labour party support at the time (his remarks came during a Labour party motion on unemployment), there is no reason to believe that he did not mean them. Yet the evidence from his career as a whole is that he never gave any real thought to the ideas of James Connolly. De Valera, like so many of his comrades in Fianna Fáil, had no socio-economic philosophy to speak of. He was heir to the woolly amalgam that constituted the mainstream of Irish nationalism at the turn of the century and he had no revolutionary theory of society, as a Marxist would have. And there is some substance in the Marxist view that liberals, social democrats and populists never change society because of the absence of a philosophical commitment.

But there was another, more personal and perhaps more fundamental reason why de Valera never transformed Irish society. 'He had', as I have written elsewhere,[32] 'no burning passion to redress social inequities'. Or to put it in a graphic colloquialism, he had no fire in his belly. On the face of it, this is very strange. After all, he grew up in an agricultural labourer's cottage, endured hardship and fatigue in receiving his early education, and advanced his scholastic career only because he pushed himself to win exhibitions and scholarships. But he never seems to have railed against social and educational privilege and whatever about his later profession of rapport with James Connolly, his nationalist ardour was military-cultural-political rather than social. Perhaps it was that the Coll family was more rural petit-bourgeois than rural proletarian and that the class struggle was more muted in Bruree than in Dublin. Perhaps it was a matter of personal temperament, a particular cast of mind, a religious or philosophical acceptance of the existing order, the quietism of the scholar and the pedant. At any rate, there was a total absence of the rage, the *saeva indignatio*, that characterised Connolly and even Pearse, and it is a hugely important factor in helping to explain the passivity, the resignation, the defeatism of de Valera's Eire. 'The hungry sheep look up and are not fed'. They asked him for bread and he gave them, if not quite a stone, stale constitutional and cultural crusts.

A later age has chosen to ridicule de Valera's arcadian idyll, as enunciated *par excellence* in his St Patrick's Day 1943 speech.[33] It is an *aisling* that is now too easy to caricature but it should be remembered that the evocation of a frugal pastoral utopia was not peculiar to Eamon de Valera, though perhaps he gave it a more rarefied expression. Other products of the Irish-Ireland movement, including the pragmatic Michael Collins, shared the vision of an Ireland remade in the image of Knocknagow. It is not, however, the naivete and the sentimentality of the concept that are to be faulted: though the speech was addressed to nostaligia-charged Irish-American listeners, a domestic Irish audience in 1943 would not have regarded it as wildly romantic. Shorn of its forest-of-Arden verbiage, de Valera's speech crystallised the still pervasive nationalist feeling that the future of Ireland lay in a revitalised countryside, a theme sketched by Collins in the bits and pieces he has left to us. The real criticism is not of de Valera's vision but the almost total failure to do anything practical to achieve it. Instead of exploiting for the common good the rich resources of land and sea, he presided over the depopulation of a poverty-stricken rural Ireland.

The reconstructed nation of the *aisling* was also to be Irish-speaking, and this was the main burden of the famous St Patrick's Day 1943 address. In Michael Collins's necessarily brief exposition of his own political philosophy, the notion looms large that Gaelic civilisation could be restored in some form after independence. De Valera's commitment to the revival of the Irish language (however that might be defined) was sincere, intense and life-long. Again, it was not, in the days of Sinn Féin resurgence and before the Civil War, a hopelessly unattainable objective, but de Valera was fated to suffer the progressive disappointment of witnessing during his lifetime the gradual disappearance of a residual Irish-speaking Ireland. No one man and no one political party could have halted or reversed the complex phenomenon of language decline but it did not help the *cúis* that de Valera's concept of Gaelic culture was a rather narrow and pedantic one: 'he never succeeded in infecting even his admirers with his enthusiasm perhaps because it took the form of a rather bookish Gaelic League devotion and was divorced from the harsh realities of social and economic life in the Gaeltacht areas',[34] and, we might add, from the richness of the literature and the earthiness of the living Gaelic tradition. It is significant that his interest lay rather in such matters as language standardisation and dictionaries. His schoolmaster-ish love for Irish was uncongenially linked in the minds of many of his followers with his disapproval of such facets of modern popular culture as jazz, and his puritanism in respect of drink, though the latter was more apparent than real and faded with the passage of time.

In a conference which focusses largely on the career of a single political leader, the danger is ever present that we may lapse into the quaint heresy of the Great Man interpretation of history. In the last analysis we cannot quantify de Valera's exact contribution to, or responsibility for, historical processes. The continuing decline of the Irish language and the total lack of progress towards the goal of Irish unity are to be largely explained in terms of historical forces which would have been at work even if de Valera had never existed or if he had been executed in 1916. Yet one must note his individual failure to promote in any meaningful way the aim of Irish unity, as distinct from talking about it — his apparent failure, indeed, to comprehend what was involved. In this field — in this fourth green field — we have to note not only a lack of achievement but a *damnosa hereditas* of myopia to his successors.

The Great Man interpretation of history has, of course, a certain validity if kept within limits. The total style of the dominant political leader must have some influence, if only by example, on the society he leads. In this connection, we may note that de Valera's celebrated virtuosity in the world of formula and symbol had an obverse side. In the exposition of the concept of external association, in justifying the taking of the Oath, in defining though not designating the State as a republic, de Valera deployed elements of prevarication and casuistry which had a moral-theological counterpart in the jesuitical pronouncements of the question-and-answer pages of contemporary ecclesiastical journals. To say the least of it, the unprepossessing national penchant for deviousness was not offered an exemplary counter-model by Eamon de Valera.

It may be objected that it is unfair to arraign a political chief before the bar of history for failing to achieve that which he never claimed to be able to achieve. It is a fact, nevertheless, that de Valera was presented to the people as a man of destiny, a new Parnell, an *ath-Mhaois* (Tomás Ruadh Ó Súilleabháin's description of Daniel O'Connell). This was exemplified by the exploitation of his personality at election times. He was the party's most valuable stage prop and their star turn, and his appearance was stage-managed to perfection. The long black cloak with the silver clasp, the theatrical epiphany on horseback, the aura of enigma, austerity and even slight exoticism — all were intended to convey the overwhelming sense of destiny attached to a man whose 'hundred best sayings' were collected and published as early as 1924.[35] There is no reason to believe that de Valera demurred at this image, or rejected its implications, or did not actively promote it.

It is in the light of this deliberately cultivated mystique that we must consider his greatest failure. If civil war, partition and poverty in the 1920s made a desert out of the promised land of independence, the appearance of Fianna Fáil led by Eamon de Valera held out the hope that there was a second chance to establish a happy, prosperous and united Irish-Ireland. Something like a millenium was promised as he came to power in 1932. Beyond all attractions of economic policy or organisation or leadership, the basic appeal of de Valera was that he might recover for his people the vision splendid of Irish nationalism. But it was a mirage or a confusion of mirages, though that did not become evident until much later. Fortunately, this gradual revelation was also a maturing process in which the expectation of redemption by a superman was cast aside as a childish delusion, leaving only the sobering reflection that salvation of the people lies with the people themselves. Henceforward, there might emerge as leaders brusque bosses, or genial avuncular pipe-smokers, or earnest barristers, or amiable dons or ambitious accountants but never again a Messiah, never again a Caesar. If Parnell in the romantic conception was the lost leader, de Valera in cold historical truth was the last one.

And yet that cannot be the last word. Perhaps it is not fair to expect that a political leader of great eminence, or even of genius, should necessarily transform society or make a profound impact on *all* walks of national life. If we lay down such exacting and comprehensive criteria, then Churchill, de Gaulle or Franklin D. Roosevelt would hardly qualify for the heroic pantheon. We can, however, apply some other tests to determine the requisite quality of greatness. National leaders of rare stature differ from workaday heads of government not in the degree or range of their political skills, but in the unique way in which they personify popular aspirations, vague, naive and contradictory though these may be. This is a role performed by only one person at a time, and by no person for long periods of time. And unlike the political boss of an unexceptional calibre, the true national leader somehow lends his name and his personality to the period in which he flourishes. A century hence, historians will still discuss the age of de Valera, the era of O'Connell and the Parnellite decade: lesser men do not give their names to an age.

O'Connell, Parnell and de Valera all pass the test referred to. All three had tangible achievements: all three disapponted expectations. Fundamentally, however, historians would argue that all three achieved a sense of national self-respect for their people. Bread-and-butter issues aside, when a small nation has been placed by the facts of geography and history in uncomfortable proximity to a great power, the people of that small nation, scarred by such a history, crave not only material progress, not only political sovereignty but a psychological independence as well, so that their dignity and self-respect can be asserted against the superiority, contempt and disdain of the great power. In his time, particularly in the 1930s and 1940s — and pre-eminently in the celebrated reply to Churchill, de Valera made this unmistakable assertion of independence and dignity on behalf of his people. In the homely image beloved by the Irish poets when speaking of O'Connell, de Valera 'was keeping goal for us', *ag coimeád cúil dúinn*. In that service to Ireland lay his greatest achievement.

NOTES

1. My own assessment at that time attempted to strike a judicious balance: John A. Murphy, 'Eamon de Valera: the Politician', *Ireland Today* (Bulletin of the Department of Foreign Affairs), **872**, 26 September 1975, 6-9.

2. See *Sunday Independent*, 29 August 1982 for de Valera's 1963 reflections on the subject.

3. 'The Historical Perspective and the Early Years' in *Fifty Years of Fianna Fáil*, *Irish Times* anniversary supplement, 19 May 1976.

4. The most recent and comprehensive account of the return of the Treaty ports is in a major study of Irish neutrality, published while this book was in the press: Robert

Fisk, *In Time of War: Ireland, Ulster and the price of neutrality, 1939-45* (London: 1983), ch. 1.

5. Joseph T. Carroll, *Ireland in the War Years 1939-45* (Newton Abbot and New York: 1975), ch. 10; T. Ryle Dwyer, *Irish Neutrality and the U.S.A.* (Dublin: 1977), ch. 12.

6. E. de Valera, *Peace and War: Speeches by Mr de Valera on International Affairs* (Dublin: 1944), 59: NLI P 1295.

7. See the Earl of Longford and Thomas P. O'Neill, *Eamon de Valera* (Dublin: 1970), 353.

8. *Dáil Éireann,* Parliamentary Debates, lxxi, 38, 27 April 1938.

9. Longford and O'Neill, (1970), 353.

10. Dwyer, (1977), 51.

11. Gray to Welles, 23 June 1940, Roosevelt papers: cited in John Bowman, *De Valera and the Ulster Question* (Oxford: 1982), 234. For the 'unity offer', see also Fisk, (1983), ch. 6.

12. D.E., lxxvii, 592, 29 September 1939.

13. M. Moynihan (ed.), *Speeches and statements by Eamon de Valera, 1917-73* (Dublin: 1980), 454.

14. E. Larkin, 'Church, State and Nation in Modern Ireland', *The American Historical Review,* **80**, 5, (1975). The relevant pages are 1273 to 1276.

15. See Bishop Patrick Foley's (Kildare and Leighlin) description of de Valera, in letter to Mgr. Ml. O'Riordan, quoted in Larkin, op. cit., 1272.

16. Longford and O'Neill, (1970), 220.

17. For a not untypical example of clerical hostility, see Fr P. Tracy's letter to *Cork Examiner*, 14 September 1927. It implies that de Valera was involved in Michael Collins's death, and it concludes thus: 'This is the gentleman who since that date has to his credit all the long list of outrages perpetrated by his followers. He has never expressed the slightest regret for his career of infamy. Moreover, he has crowned it all by teaching his followers to trample on the sacred character of an oath. Now this is the hero to whom so many men claiming to be honourable are trying to entrust the supreme control over the lives and property of the Irish people. Are honour and virtue, and the whole of God's law, an empty formula?'

18. See, e.g., *Irish Press*, 16 February 1932 for report of election speech in Dublin by de Valera: '. . . the majority of the people of Ireland are Catholic, and we believe in Catholic principles. And as the majority are Catholics, it is right and natural that the principles to be applied by us will be principles consisent with Catholicity'. See also John Whyte, *Church and State in Modern Ireland, 1923-70* (1st Ed., Dublin: 1971), 40 ff.

19. Although see party advertisement in *Irish Press*, 16 February 1932 which spoke of 'governing in accordance with the principles enunciated in the encyclical of Pius XI on the social order'.

20. Tom Garvin, *The Evolution of Irish Nationalist Politics* (Dublin: 1981), 155.

21. See Whyte, (1971), 48.

22. *John Bull's Other Island* (Constable Edition, London: 1926), Preface, xx.

23. See the debate on the incident in D.E., xxxix, 418-552, 17 June 1931.

24. D.E., cxxv, 804, 12 April 1951.

25. Evelyn Bolster, *The Knights of St Columbanus* (Dublin: 1979), 72.

26. D.E., clxiii, 731, 4 July 1957.

27. Tomás P. Ó Néill agus Pádraig Ó Fiannachta, *De Valera, II* (Baile Átha Cliath: 1970), 335.

28. D.E., lxvii, 1890, 4 June 1937.

29. See Brendan Walsh, 'Economic Growth and Development', in J.J. Lee (ed.), *Ireland 1945-70*, (Dublin: 1979), 28.

30. Quoted Longford and O'Neill, (1970), 334.

31. D.E., xli, 906-07, 29 April 1932.

32. *Ireland in the Twentieth Century* (Dublin: 1975), 141.

33. M. Moynihan (ed.), (1980), 466ff.

34. Murphy, (1975), 141.

35. *The Hundred Best Sayings of Eamon de Valera* (Dublin, Cork: 1924): NLI P2027.

Eamon de Valera,
Charisma and Political Development

J.P. O'Carroll

Introduction

In a previous paper, I examined the charisma of Eamon de Valera and described its general characteristics and some of its implications for his style of politics and government.[1] In this paper, I want to focus more on the *sources of his authority, on his mode of validating it* and on their implications for political development. I am doing this because the essence of charisma lies in what the leader does to assert his authority and in the criteria he uses to validate it to himself and to his followers. If the essence of charisma is the leader's influencing of his followers and their willingness to be further influenced by him i.e., *the relationship* between a leader and his followers, we must examine this aspect of the phenomenon in detail in order to see its possible consequences for political development. A basic assumption of this paper is that the Treaty provided only an institutional skeleton on which the flesh of the political system would have to grow. The fostering of this growth was the primary task of the political leadership in the early years of independence. Success in this task lay in managing both the formal structures and the indigenous political cultures in a way which maximised their compatability and which thus harnessed hitherto latent energies of the people in the pursuit of their hopes and aspirations.[2]

The focus of the study does not imply a denial of the formal legal sources of much of de Valera's power but, rather, my interest in his charisma arises from the fact that it contributed an extra increment of power which was crucial to the success of his political career. The source of such success was precisely the *political* origin of Weber's interest in the phenomenon.[3]

My argument is that de Valera greatly enhanced the legitimacy of his authority by a process of culture management which owed its success to its ability to confirm to his followers his view of the 'superiority and integrity' of his values over those of his opponents. The study is based on an examination of speeches and statements of de Valera and also on a review of certain features of his foreign policy and international relations. In particular I focus on his use of myth and symbols and their power to appeal to, and, in some cases, to compel, his followers to accept and go along with him in his restoration of emotional nationalism as a currency of national politics.

The consequences of his charisma are seen in its influence on the nature of political discourse, on the style of politics and political organisation and on the priorities and progress of political development i.e., the mobilisation of political bias was given precedent over the more material goals of general economic development.

A further assumption is that while in normal circumstances political leaders are largely constrained by the political system, some leaders may, in times of crisis and change, find opportunity to influence the course of events to an extent considerably beyond the normal. In such times, some of the existing institutions may be seen to be no longer a binding force, and leaders with appropriate skills may be able to fill the vacuum thus created. The fact that they do so by bringing about a *bricolage* of cultural elements which succeeds in winning the support and confidence of a majority of the people, in no way diminishes their contribution.

The use of the concept 'charisma' implies not a surrender to its ideological blandishments[4] but a recognition of charisma's crucial contribution *at a particular stage* in our political development, i.e., when any other paths more acceptable to a sizeable minority would have been less likely to lead to an adequate revitalisation of our faltering political development of the late 1920s. Most of Europe, from Portugal to Turkey, followed the same path at that time. In our case, we reaped most of the benefits while avoiding the worst of the disadvantages because of de Valera's high ethical standards and because he largely accepted the institutional framework we inherited from pre-independence days.[5]

This paper is in three parts. The essential character of the politics of early independence and its relationship to the rise of charismatic leadership is first examined. In the second and major portion of the study, the sources of de Valera's charisma and the strategies he used to validate it are examined. In the final part we look largely at some immediate and long-term consequences of de Valera's leadership style for political development.

Nationalist hopes and political uncertainty: the necessary but not
sufficient conditions for the rise of charismatic leadership

In an uncertain world, there is something wonderfully compelling about people who are sure. In this section we will focus on the element of *uncertainty*; in the next on that of sureness. The rise of charismatic leadership has often been associated with crisis and transition arising from some fundamental change in society. The breakdown of traditional authority under colonial rule or the breakdown of the legal-rational colonial rule under the challenge of nationalism have both often been followed by the rise of charismatic movements. Two important by-products of the success of nationalist movements militate against any post-colonial government's quickly gaining a full measure of legitimacy. First, independence gives rise to very high hopes among all sections of the population. Each group hopes to achieve an immense improvement in its own situation. The growing realisation that the new government may have the giving of favours such as jobs and contracts, and the spread of universal suffrage may increase the level of hope. No government can satisfy all the demands of all the various social groups. The pressure on governments created by such open-ended hopes can be intense and it inevitably leads to a faltering in the growth of legitimacy. Second, since the very success of a nationalist movement in obtaining power depends on discrediting its colonial legal-rational predecessor, it cannot in a complete volte-face easily establish itself as a credible legal-rational system. These two by-products of the success of nationalist movements create powerful centrifugal tendencies in all states which have just achieved independence. The result is that in the post-colonial situation traditional authority often cannot be revived and legal-rational authority is under a cloud. These are the basis of the only *certainties* the people know of, and the *uncertainty* of such periods arises largely from the fact they are no longer fully credible.

The combination of high hopes and uncertainties is characteristic of early independence and leads to the 'stress' that Weber sees as the usual climate for the rise of charismatic leadership. In these circumstances legitimacy accrues to the leader who appears to offer a promise of fulfilling the high hopes of an electorate i.e., of restoring certainty to life, but now life *on an immensely improved level*. Thus, a new political game, *with a new object and new rules*, different from anything experienced under colonial rule or during the national struggle has to be evolved very quickly. The demands of the public are greater, more diverse and more strident and the authority of the elites is weaker. In these circumstances, an extraordinary source of authority must be created and for this the normal processes of democracy are usually inadequate.

When we examine the early history of the Cumann na nGaedheal government we find no such instability. In fact it quickly cleared up most outstanding details of the treaty settlement, ended the civil war and entered into orthodox relations, diplomatic, political and economic, with its neighbours. At home, comparatively few changes resulted from independence. Kennedy cites three main reasons for this failure to pursue 'what seemed to have been the accepted nationalist approach to economic development'. First, the pressing need to re-establish stability after the civil war made drastic innovations less desirable; (2) unwillingness to erode the good will of the British, who had just helped them to restore stability, by imposing tariffs and (3) the presence in the party of the more conservative elements of the country such as owners of large farms and members of the profession who had most to lose if tariffs were imposed.[6] Very quickly an air of business as usual, only under different management, was restored. However, the deterioration in the world's economic system led to economic problems. An emphasis on law and order and an accumulation of unpopular legislation soon eroded the government's initial popularity. By the end of the twenties these unpopular measures and an inevitable growing sense of disappointment among many groups such as small farmers and cottiers and eventually the middle classes, whose position now began to deteriorate rather than improve, created an air of questioning and uncertainty. Also, the failure of the ruling elite, because of a certain fastidiousness, to initiate any programmes which might even appear to offer a promise of fulfilling the hopes brought about by independence, combined with the above mentioned problems to undermine not alone the political suport but *also the legitimacy of the regime*. With two thirds of the electorate new to voting and eager to use their prerogatives it was imperative to create a power base from new coalitions. The party used neither ideological (nationalist) nor material (welfare) means to win for itself a solid social base in the fluid and exacting conditions of post-colonial politics.

In sum, the Cumann na nGaedheal government failed to create *new certainties* in a period of great expectation. No government in such circumstances can fulfil the expectations of all of the diverse groups who feel that, with independence, their day has come. But it will not survive unless it appears to try, and to try by means which appear credible and appropriate to a new era. Uncertainty is the result of failure to be seen to take action appropriate to the hopes of the times.

The Gestation and Growth of the Charismatic Relationship

Charismatic authority is validated through the perception of followers. In this section we attempt to show how de Valera influenced his followers' perception of his message and of himself. While the historical conditions of the time provided the necessary pre-conditions for the rise of charismatic authority, we have to look to the message of the leader to see how it provided the sufficient conditions for its gestation and growth. Charisma is a relationship which is built and maintained through reciprocal interaction between a leader and his followers. This is done in such a way that his authority is legitimated by an act of faith in the leadership.

The message not only involves an articulation of grievances but also poses an alternative world fundamentally different from that defined by his opponents. Mundane differences are raised to the level of an apparent clash of cultures. For example, while many of the public could not appreciate the importance of the difference between the Treaty document and de Valera's Document No. Two, de Valera saw them as being worlds apart. Also the deepest values are mobilised to support the charismatic. Finally, charisma is built up by a process which is particularly suited to the dilemma of the times. It restores certainty by a process of cultural bricolage which harnesses the uncertainties of the times to the absolute and sacred values of the past. In this way a leader, sure of his message and of his mission, restores certainty, making hallowed the present and the future through association with the past.

In this part of the paper we examine de Valera's presentation of himself and his message and evaluate the techniques he used to bring about acceptance i.e., how he fostered the growth of the relationship with his followers. We show how he used myth and symbols in his speeches and statements to reinforce his point of view by stirring basic values. We then examine his foreign policy activities and statements and show how he turned his handling of international relations into a vehicle for bolstering domestic support.

A complete and proper examination of this process would involve an examination of the process of statement of principles and ideas by de Valera and the growth of acceptance of these statements by various segments of the public at large and by the leaders who gathered round him. This paper will merely examine the nature of his message and indicate why it was particularly powerful and effective. Likewise the growth of the relationship between de Valera and his followers is adjudged only by reference to the growth or decline of the vote for his party. Obviously, much more evidence is needed to make a firm statement about the effect of the message, but we must start with a study of de Valera's sense of mission and then examine the nature of his message.

De Valera saw himself as a man with a mission to change 'fundamentally' the world of his following. This implies that (1) he believed in the absolute and fundamental correctness of his mission, (2) he was convinced that he was the one above all others to carry out the mission and (3) that he knew that the mission was what most people 'really' wanted.

The following are but a few examples from his statements of such beliefs.

On leaving America in 1920, he said, 'I came to you on a holy mission, a mission of Freedom'[7] and in the Treaty debate of 6 January 1921, we note the use of the first personal pronoun fifty times in two pages. This is the speech in which the famous statement occurs:

and whenever I wanted to know what the Irish people wanted I had only to examine my own heart and it told me straight off . . . .   (pp 92-4).

Other speeches offer numerous instances of his view of himself as a man with a mission, a mission to speak for even those who did not realise what their real aspirations were or who were unable to express them.

> . . . every man in Clare wanted to see Ireland a nation. They went out in 1916 because they knew *it was in the bottom of the heart of every Irishman, no matter what was on the surface* — there was only one desire, only one thing to satisfy every Irishman and that was free and absolute independence.   (pp 1-6). (The emphases here and throughout are mine).

In similar vein, his own views on the need for a leader (President Wilson) to express 'the feeling that was in the hearts of the plain people', is indicative of his views of the relationship between a leader and his following.

> To get a League of Nations founded required something more than the feeling that was in the hearts of the plain people. *That feeling was, he firmly believed, in three fourths of the world, but the people in whose hearts it was were unable to express it.*   (p. 27).

The above is a classic pattern of charismatic behaviour and it reflects all the essentials of the following passage from D.H. Lawrence, i.e., that only the few are granted the gift of power and that it is their duty to speak for the inarticulate masses who in turn are duty bound to follow them.

> Now we begin to understand the old motto. Noblesse Oblige. Noblesse means having the gift of power, the natural or sacred power. And having such power obliges a man to act with fearlessness and generosity, responsible for his acts to God. A noble is one who may be known before al' men.
> Some men must be noble, or life is an ash-heap. There is natural nobility, given by God or the Unknown, and far beyond common sense. And towards natural nobility we must live. The simple man, whose best self, his noble self, is nearly all the time puzzled, dumb, and helpless, has still the power to recognize the man in whom the noble self is powerful and articulate. To this man he must pledge himself.[8]

De Valera did note that the people were not always right — that principles were what mattered most — he felt he knew better than they what they wanted, e.g.:

> A war-weary people will take things that are not in accordance with their aspirations.   (p. 87).

What in his opinion was the final arbiter?:

> But in forcing acceptance of the "Treaty", majority rule runs counter to the fundamental rights of the nation and so clashed with a matter of natural right and justice.   (p. 137).

Here we come to some clues as to de Valera's own idea of what is basic and fundamental to life and its dynamics. Elsewhere I have characterised the nature of the message as being viewed as 'sole, eternal, certain, absolute, extraordinary and almost religious in character'. The following quotations support this view and remind one of the aphorism of Péguy that 'Everything begins with mysticism and ends with politics'. Speaking at Bodenstown on 21 June 1925 de Valera said:

> With regard, then, to our ultimate objective we can rest content with it. We know that it is *fixed* and *certain* — like the cause of freedom, *eternal*. It has its roots in the *God-given nature of man*.

> . . . What brought the Irish *people* round to conscious acceptance of Tone's principles? *Natural forces* and the proved failure of other methods. So too, the failure of the methods which are today taking away from our side a large section of the people *whose natural* place is with us, will cause these people to return again and never revert to their former attitude.

> For our part, we are content to rest for the moment if it must be so, simply faithful.   (pp 118-121).

The use of the words 'fixed', 'certain', 'eternal' and 'nature' in relation to his objective imply a strongly teleological outlook and a world view structured in terms of its relevance for the attainment of those objectives. This outlook, together with the almost Cartesian logic he brought to his arguments, made him a very formidable opponent.

He commended those who fought against the treaty and validated their actions by the statement 'the best in the soul of man tells us they were right'. (p. 96).

The nature of the dogma was reflected in the rhetoric. The Treaty Debate of 6 January 1922 rings with the words 'absolute', 'fundamental creed' — 'I believe', 'credo', 'untruth', 'absolute lie', 'heart and feeling of the nation', and 'the hearts and souls and aspirations of the Irish people'. (p. 92). In many speeches the language suggests Britain — 'The English', as the very necessary devil. In a reference to Wolfe Tone he refers to Britain as '*the never failing source of all Ireland's political evils* . . .'. (p. 119).

I think we have ample evidence of a number of important requirements for any would-be charismatic; (1) a belief that he himself has a mission; (2) that his mission is sacred and absolutely right; and (3) that he knows what people really want at a deep level of consciousness. We have also derived some insights into the type of criteria de Valera offered for the validity of his views — a mixture of sacred and secular.

However, these dimensions of the leader, while necessary prerequisites, are not sufficient for an understanding of charisma. They do not offer a reason why the message would be accepted. This has to be sought in the basic themes of the message and in the form and mode of delivery.

The basic themes of the message were: 'the Republic', 'unity', 'sovereignty', 'the language', 'Irish culture', and 'economic self-sufficiency'. They represented a mixture of ideas which Republicans had persistently put forward and also they reflected current grievances of an economic nature. As such, they would not have been sufficient to generate a charismatic following. But by the use of setting, myth, allegory, metaphor and simile de Valera transformed these various themes into what was perceived by many to be a completely new and powerful message of tremendous emotional impact. The creation of such a completely 'new' message from well-known themes is referred to as the process of bricolage[9] and it is the essential distinctive skill of the charismatic. It involves the creation of a new source of power. De Valera's most powerful technique was his use of myth since myth in particular has the ability to stir basic values and harness them in the service of the problems of transition i.e., in the restoration of assurance in times of uncertainty. *This use of myth is the essence of charismatic legitimation.* By the use of myth de Valera induced his followers to see *and value* the political world as he did himself.

The main characteristic of myth is that it is a story which usually involves an archetypal figure of exemplary character and fundamental significance. The values expressed in the story are so basic that each generation returns to the myth again and again and reinterprets it in the light of the issues and problems of the times. This faculty of uniting the uncertain present with the sacred, stable and heroic past renders myth a powerful tool for influencing perception. Myth is, in fact, a body of doctrine which validates behaviour and prescribes values. Not all myths however are to be found in the form of coherent narratives. Major and critical episodes in the life of a society can, in time, take on the form of myth and powerfully channel and restrict political initiatives for future generations. For Americans the frontier, the New Deal, The Great Society, for the French the Revolution and the 'vast enterprises' of the Gaullist era such as the 'force de frappe' all assumed a mythical character.[10]

The most effective strategy of de Valera's speeches and statements, and one which lies at the very core of their appeal, is their use of myth. A positive approach to the arguments and their rationale would mislead completely in an assessment of the source of their impact. This source lies not in their logic but in their ability to stir emotions and to 'draw together human energies outside and beyond the rational'.

Most are shot through with allusion to history and many specific myths appear regularly, none more so than that of 'the nation that stood alone' — 'the race that never ceased to strive' — 'The 300-700 years of despoliation'. On 17 March 1920 he used the phrase — 'We the children of a race that never ceased to strive'. (p. 35). The same myth was used in the famous reply to Churchill on 16 May 1945.

> Mr Churchill is proud of Britain's stand alone, after France had fallen and before America entered the war.
>   Could he not find in his heart the generosity to acknowledge that there is a small nation that stood alone, not for one year or two, but for several hundred years against aggression: that endured spoliations, famines, massacres in endless succession; that was clubbed many times into insensibility, but that each time, on returning consciousness, took up the fight anew; a small nation that could never be got to accept defeat and has never surrendered her soul? (p. 476).

Only slightly less frequently used were his references to the 'men of 1916' who in fact had become mythologised so quickly that one of his earliest speeches — that at the by-election in East Clare in 1917 contains a classic example of his use of myth. In this speech which was reported in the *Saturday Post and Clare Champion* he identified his policy with

> the policy for which the men of 1916 fought and died (cheers)! if they did not elect him on the principle of nationality for which men fought during Easter Week, the men of Clare would be showing that they repudiated the Irish heroes (never); they would show they would prefer to be English slaves to Irish free men (never, never).   (pp 1-6).

Even George Berkeley on the bicentennial of his death found himself called on to put his stamp of affirmation on Fianna Fáil's economic policies in another classic example of the use of myth to anoint the policies of the present with the sacrality of the past.

> Just over two hundred years ago there lived in Cloyne a wonderfully cultured, enlightened and kindly gentleman, who rose high above the prejudices of his class and loved his country and its people. This great kindly man, who was one of the foremost thinkers of his time, posed several questions about Ireland's economic development to which we in Fianna Fáil, since we first came into office in 1932, have endeavoured to provide the concrete answers. ... Bishop Berkeley asked questions such as these
>
> "Whether there be any other nation possessed of so much good land, and so many able hands to work it, which yet is beholden for bread to foreign countries?
>   Whether a fertile land, and the industry of its inhabitants, would not prove inexhaustible funds of real wealth, be the counters for conveying and recording thereof what you will, paper, gold, or silver?
>   Whether the industry of our people employed in foreign lands, while our own are left uncultivated, be not a great loss to the country?

Whether it be not wonderful that, with such pastures, and so many black cattle, we do not find ourselves in cheese?"·

When Fianna Fáil was founded just over a quarter of a century ago, we asked these same questions and believed that Berkeley's expected answers were still the true answers. We asked:

"Why, in this agricultural country, millions of pounds had to be spent in the purchase of foreign flour, whilst our own wheat-fields were untilled and our mills idle?

Why foreign feeding stuffs for cattle, costing millions of pounds, should be imported when they could be substituted by Irish oats and barley?

Why foreign bacon should be brought in when we could raise the pigs and manufacture that bacon ourselves?

Why we should be importing sugar when we had land to grow the beet and could build factories to manufacture it into sugar?

Why we should be importing cheese when we had the cows, and the milk, and could learn to manufacture it ourselves?

Why we should import boots and clothing when we could ourselve make them?

Why we should import pottery and earthenware when they also could be produced here?"

We asked these questions in Fianna Fáil as we had done in Sinn Féin, and, when Fianna Fáil came into office in 1932, we set about giving the answers in concrete form; . . . .   (pp 565-566).

The speech ends with the assertion that George Berkeley had been justified and no doubt many hearers felt that so also was Fianna Fáil.

At this stage we must look at some of the actual functions of myth in a society. We find in the speeches examples of the two main types of function served by myth. In the first case, myth as a historical reconstruction serves as a *charter* for behaviour by 'generally binding the volatile present to the traditionally and divinely structured regularity of the past'[11] It emphasises the continuity of society and its organisational features, it ransacks the past for historical precedent to sanction the present and it provides *emotional support* for attitudes and beliefs. We usually find this function served by speeches and statements which use myth to justify some action already taken or about to be taken in which we have succeeded or hope to succeed. A belief in a noble past urges us in the present to strain toward that nobility. The above three examples are of this type.

But myth can be of another type — it is generally used *to reconcile a public to inevitable truths*. The speech at Bodenstown on 21 June 1925 is a good example of this type. The civil war had been lost and fortunes of the Republicans were at their lowest ebb. He advised them that they should be 'content to rest for the moment, if it must be, simply faithful'. But the speech begins with an assurance to the audience that:

By your presence here today you proclaim your undiminished attachments to the ideals of Tone, and your unaltered devotion to the cause for which he gave his life.   (p. 121).

He thus associated the audience with the heroic past in order to mediate the contradictions of the course they were taking. They could thus feel they were not being false to their beliefs and principles. By re-affirming their ideals the inconsistency was resolved to a considerable extent.

Of course other mythical elements contributed to de Valera's power of communication. A political calendar evolved with fixed and moveable feasts which provided sacred occasions for important events. Many addresses were made on March 17th and at Easter, which was the anniversary of the 1916 Rising. The coincidence of the religious and political did not detract from the latter's effect. The founding of the Gaelic League, of the first Dáil and even the 1937 constitution were marked by full scale anniversaries or were the occasion of special political events. Heroes such as Parnell, Davis and Tone were all honoured by special celebration of their anniversaries. Bodenstown, Arbour Hill and Glasnevin were the sacred venues and even Rome and New York were the venue of addresses to Ireland. All of these mythical dimensions increased the effectiveness of communication and served the purpose of grounding the faithful in a world which imparted certainty, predictability, stability and security and moral coherence to their lives.

No description of the source of the strength of de Valera's appeal would be complete without reference to the powerful use he made of the Irish language in fostering a sense of Irish ethnicity and of peoplehood. Like many leaders at the time he had come initially to politics through his interest in the Irish language. The nationalist style was largely one of cultural nationalism and by his speeches and statements de Valera created anew, by a process of culture management, a movement largely based on emotional nationalism. The use of the Irish language on public occasions, even in token amounts, and the use of revived titles both greatly contributed to a sense of ethnicity and peoplehood. In a charismatic movement change comes from within the individual. The use of a language is a most powerful instrument of internalisation and of establishment of strong spontaneous links between the individuals and his 'ethnic' group.[12]

We have so far identified the implication of de Valera's presentation of himself and of his ability to assimilate, in his message, the political events of his time to the great events and people of the past. He acquired a *special reputation* by associating himself with the mystical bases of the nation. Those who expound the sacred mysteries are often credited with an understanding of them and, therefore, are seen to be the men whom, above all others, one should follow. This image of de Valera can be seen also in domains other than the political. The assertion that he was one of the few people apart from Einstein who 'really' understood the mysteries of the theory of relativity has similar implications. This apparent privileged access to the sacred mysteries implied to his followers the sanction of the sacred, provided justification for his views and enjoined confidence and trust. The effect of his message on his oppositon was that they were mesmerised into a degree ineffectuality.[13] In the case of both followers and opposition there was a suspension, to some degree, of rationality in favour of feeling and emotion. His use of myth, then, made him appear to be one with *the* basic political values. Together, these elements were a potent mixture — a carte blanche to structure basic relationships in society. They created the power needed to revitalise the faltering legitimacy of the regime and to re-energise the political system. One other element however, which in Ireland's case, operated in a uniquely powerful way remains to be examined i.e., the domestic impact of de Valera's foreign policy and of his pursuit of international relations.

In Ireland's case a number of factors created barriers to the growth and development of the political system. Unlike modern times there were very few structures between the level of state and that of the local community. Furthermore, given the largely petit-bourgeois nature of most communities it was particularly difficult to involve many in the idea of a structure beyond the limits of the parish. As Shils has noted 'the civil attachment, the moderate pluralist concern for the whole among other things is not the spirit of the primary group'.[14] Given the strong current of familism and the long tradition of communalism in Ireland, leadership at any time, (particularly prior to the Welfare State) had much to do to foster the civil attachment. Of course, the state had been recognised as a source of employment opportunities for members of families who could not be employed in the family farm or business but, otherwise, the family held aloof from the state. Most citizens could not comprehend it because of its abstract nature. This difficulty had to be solved before development could occur.

The main problem, however, which considerably exacerbated the problems of political development was that the status of the state itself was in question. Politics was primarily concerned with winning legitimacy for a particular view of what the constitutional status of the state should be. Both the civil war and de Valera's subsequent refusal to enter parliament had done much to hinder the growth of the political system. The result was considerable uncertainty. This uncertainty greatly undermined the confidence with which any citizen could invest his identity in the nation or state. This problem struck at the heart of the political system itself. It greatly contributed to the severity of the centrifugal forces and made Ireland's case almost unique.

Further difficulties arose from the geopolitical situation. Ireland's proximity to Britain and the disparities of power between them seemed to render unilateral action impossible. In these circumstances, particularly in view of the importance of the controversial nature of the status of the state, de Valera's choice of foreign affairs and his style of conducting international relations was crucial to his contribution to political development. They also contributed much more to development of a political community than in the case of other states in similar circumstances.

No aspects of the difference between de Valera's leadership and that of his predecessors illustrates better the reason for the failure of the one and the success of the other in building a political community than Cosgrave's choice of the finance as his personal portfolio and de Valera's of foreign affairs. The choice of economy and law and order represented a strategy of leading the nation by the *promise* of prosperity and material well-being. But such a policy encourages political divisions at all levels of decision-making. Economy is mundane and does not raise the hearts of men in the face of the hard tasks and sacrifices demanded of them. In line with the main themes of his dogma, 'the Republic', 'unity', 'sovereignty', de Valera's choice of foreign affairs had the advantage of automatically representing the 'nation' and its unity. As a basis for the creation of a symbolic universe which provides criteria for choice in a confusing environment, the *nation* has no equal. Foreign affairs is thus most important. When the idea of the nation is ideologised i.e., 'goes beyond the conception of "this is the way we do things" to a conception of "there is something unique, special and valuable about our way of doing things", it makes it possible to develop allegiance to and invest one's identity in a collectivity that goes beyond — in both space and time — one's primary group and face to face contacts'.[15] De Valera did not invent Irish nationalism but he re-created it and his choice of the foreign affairs portfolio signifies the role he played in the process of further ideologisation. In this section, we examine how his conduct of foreign affairs set up a symbolic universe which gave coherence and certainty to the lives of his followers. *This was precisely the task before any leader at that stage of political development.* It has also associated him and the institutions which he developed firmly with state. It raised party differences to the level of matters of fundamental value and the outcome was that for a very long time the currency of political discourse was really the constitutional dimension of independence and hence the legitimacy of each party's view of what the structures should be. The consequences of this outcome for political development is examined in the final section.

Foreign affairs in the case of Ireland differed from most other countries in that its first major dilemma was the constitutional dimension of independence.[16] As Keatinge has pointed out, as time went by, Cumann na nGael's claim that the Treaty gave freedom to achieve freedom seemed to the man in the street difficult to prove. Furthermore, his perception was not helped by the government's failure through inability or fastidiousness to make capital out of the real progress which was made. Statements like 'The Optional Clause has been signed *without reservation*' fostered certainty neither at an intellectual nor emotional level. The Treaty itself was ambiguous in regard to Anglo-Irish relations and the view of the position of a dominion in the Commonwealth was uncertain and rapidly changing.

Finally, the Cosgrave government's conduct of diplomacy at Commonwealth level, tainted it with the stigma of association with a discredited Home rule politics and their view that any changes must be by mutual agreement further limited their appeal. Even the British cabinet sub-committee[17] set up to examine the Irish situation, as Keatinge has noted, 'floundered in a sea of uncertainties'. In contrast, de Valera's insistence on nothing less than autarky, his unilaterism, his promise to remove all the symbols of British rule were clear-cut and simple and found many echoes in past nationalist isolationist rhetoric. By 1937 the new constitution removed 'the major question mark over Irish independence'. Again, uncertainty was replaced by certainty.

In the domain of foreign affairs no issue illustrates so many of the aspects of de Valera's leadership and its consequence as neutrality does and no episode unified the nation at home and abroad so much as what came to be known as 'de Valera's reply to Churchill'. The neutrality issue demonstrates his insistence on absolute independence, his ability to make a gesture which rendered concrete for his followers that which they could not comprehend in the abstract, his will to stand alone (at the international level) for something he believed deeply in and his ability to enhance his reputation by imparting a sense of security to people. One outcome of this episode was that he quickly became known to many as 'the man who gave Churchill his answer'.

But it also represented his ability to capitalise on a surge of public feeling, his mastery of symbolic manipulation — echoing the theme, 'the nation that stood alone' and it demonstrated his ability to create a myth — the myth of Irish neutrality. This myth created difficulties for politics in the long-term because within a short time neutrality 'was tending to become, in the popular imagination, a doctrine which was presumptious to question'.[18] At the time, however, the successful pursuit of neutrality provided irrefutable confirmation of our 'absolute' independence.

Foreign policy then, for any leader is a domain which can be used, in times of division and uncertainty at home, to bring about a measure of unification. In representing the nation as a whole it diverts attention from divisions in society. It also, through its symbolism, makes the citizen seem '*spontaneously* as well as necessarily involved'. Furthermore, it draws the citizen's attention to what he has in common with other members of society and provides a unifying symbol to which the diversity of the nation can be related. In Ireland's case, the pursuit of foreign policy by de Valera had a much more powerful domestic impact because, until 1948, it dealt to a great extent with the issue of the constitutional status of the state itself. In representing Ireland abroad to Britain, the Commonwealth, the United States of America, the League of Nations and the Vatican he was performing a role which superseded mere party politics. He was presenting the national self abroad and, inevitably, greatly assisting in the building of the national identity. A further consequence, of course, was that he himself became seen, both abroad and at home, as the personification of the new state. This added greatly to his effectiveness in domestic politics. He also bolstered the national identity by his efforts to convince the Irish people that, although Ireland was small and poor in material resources, it nevertheless had an important moral role to play in the world. His appointment as President of the Council of the League of Nations in 1932 and of its Assembly in 1938 no doubt confirmed these views. His pursuit of foreign affairs also pioneered in creating a social space in the international arena for one of the first small post-colonial states. The impression of 'unorthodoxy' which his foreign policy created abroad rendered his attempts to create a social space all the more effective. Moreover, in the domestic arena these policies were often seen to be even more apposite and very much in tune with the feelings and aspirations of many people e.g., the policy of neutrality and, earlier, the unilateral moves to dismantle the treaty. De Valera's choice of foreign affairs as a portfolio and his activity in the domain were therefore most potent in asserting his status as a national leader rather than as merely a leader of a party. His successes in that arena fostered the growth of a stronger and more coherent identity. But, most important, his pursuit of foreign policy increased immeasurably the legitimacy of the institutions he created.

Charisma and Political Development

Political development involves two distinct goals which may at certain times conflict. Conflict is particularly likely in the early post-colonial stage between the goal of building a political community and that of achieving a state strong enough to follow the path of modernisation. The Cumann na nGael government appeared to restore stability quickly and got on with the second goal, i.e. gradual modernisation, but they possibly underestimated the degree of popular support and allegiance they could depend on, particularly among the two-thirds of the electorate which were new to participation in elections. Few steps were taken to build these into a political community. Neither did they set out on a vigorous programme of modernisation which would have gone some way toward fulfilling the hopes of those who looked to independence for a great improvement in their lives.

Their policy of making very few changes continued after the onset of the depression even when demands for change had greatly increased. Fanning's study of the Department of Finance[19] shows clearly that the politicians followed the bureaucratic momentum in economic affairs, domestically and internationally. Bureaucracy is the kernel of legal-rational government and, while it is a most efficient mode of organisation in stable times, its momentum is such that it is not easily deflected. It is singularly unsuited to bringing about the types of changes needed in times of transition. In the Ireland of the late 1920s and early 1930s depression exacerbated the problems of transition. Despite the circumstances, Ireland was one of the last countries in Europe to change from a policy of free trade. Such a development policy was completely inadequate for solving the enormous problems of the circumstances either politically or economically.

In contrast, when de Valera came to power politicians took firm control of their departments and of many tasks which their predecessors had usually left to their civil servants. Political considerations were injected into what, under the previous administration, had largely been bureaucratic transactions between Dublin and Westminster. De Valera's overall emphasis on *the building of a political community to his liking,* overshadowed what in Cumann an nGael days had been their prime consideration, a gradual modernisation. In this sense de Valera's choice of foreign affairs as a personal portfolio and Cosgrave's choice of finance was indicative of the fundmental difference in their approach to political development. Cumann na nGael's emphasis on the economy reflected the words attributed to Nkrumah of Ghana 'seek you first the Kingdom of Affluence and all other things will be added unto you' and de Valera's policy reflected the alternative view that 'gross domestic pride can sometimes be more important than gross domestic product'.

De Valera's main influence however, was that his policy created a political community by restoring a single national goal, autarky, which mobilised support from a new coalition which proved to be stable. In this connection it must be pointed out that this strategy depends only on having a goal and does not require achievement of the goal. Criticism of de Valera for his failure to achieve the twin national aims of unity and restoration of language, therefore, misses the point.

The emphasis on the values of national pride enabled him to make almost automatic and instant emotional contact with a majority of his followers. This instant contact was engendered by myriad historical 'memories' fostered by the nationalist movement and organisations such as the Gaelic Athletic Association and the Gaelic League which contributed to a growing sense of peoplehood. It also evoked memories of 'the period when we were all united in the national struggle'. As a technique of mobilisation of bias it was much more powerful and appealing than an emphasis on peace, tranquility and law and order. Its strength and appropriateness to the situation, however, lay in the fact that it drew on much of what was beyond the rational. The irony of democracy is that if any of its preconditions are lacking a society cannot *by democratic means* restore democracy. Transition calls into question that tacit consensus on which democracy operates. The exercise of rational will and consent in the voting process cannot overcome the fracturing of the basic consensus.

By the re-introduction of emotional nationalism into the forefront of political life in the late nineteen twenties de Valera revitalised the development of the political community. He restored coherence and certainty to politics. He stirred the most basic values and mobilised them in favour of his definition of the situation and of his view of what the future should be. He thus created for himself the authority to refashion the forms and rules of the political game. This was his greatest contribution since by moulding both political culture and political structures he created the conditions necessary for effective political development. He thus ensured the survival of the political system. In doing so he performed a supreme national service. For no other Irish leader, then or since, can such claims be made.

NOTES

1. J.P. O'Carroll, 'Nation and State in the Republic of Ireland: The Role of de Valera in the Formation of the State', *States in Ireland: Power and Conflict. Proceedings of the Sociological Association of Ireland Conference.* (Dublin: 1980).

2. My use of the phrase 'hopes and aspirations' is taken, not from the vocabulary of de Valera, but from my conceptualisation of early independence as a period of high hopes and aspirations. Legitimacy in such circumstances is seen to accrue to the leader who is seen to offer the most credible promise of fulfilling such hopes. See E. Gellner, 'Democracy and Industrialisation', *European Journal of Sociology* **VIII**, (1967), 47-70.

3. Max Weber, 'Parliament and Government in a Reconstructed Germany', in Max Weber, *Economy and Society*, G. Roth and C. Wittich (Berkeley: 1978), (first published in 1921), 1381-1469. See also Rudolph Heberle, 'Charisma — its original meaning and application', *LSU (Louisiana State University) Journal of Sociology* 1.1 (1971), 144-156.

4. See B.P. Strydom, 'A Methodological and Ideology-critical Note on the Use of Concepts in the Socio-historical Sciences' in the appendix to this volume. His warning

about the dangers of the use of this concept is well taken. However, I believe that some modern sociology has over-reacted to the dangers of the concept and has, as a result, deprived itself of an important tool. I feel that judicious use of the concept is preferable to ignoring an important social phenomenon.

5. See John O'Connor, 'Article 50 of Bunreacht na hÉireann and the Unwritten English Constitution of Ireland' in this volume.

6. Kieran A. Kennedy, *Productivity and Industrial Growth: The Irish Experience* (Oxford: 1971), 28.

7. Maurice Moynihan (ed.), *Speeches and Statements by Eamon de Valera 1917-1973* (Dublin: 1980), 48. Note that the emphases in all of the quotations are mine. All references to de Valera quotations in the text are from Moynihan.

8. D.H. Lawrence, 'Epilogue' in *Movements in European History* (London: Original Edn., 1921). Published with the original 'Epilogue' first in 1971.

9. Henry Tudor, *Political Myth* (London: 1972), 52.

10. Philip Cerny, *The Politics of Grandeur* (London: 1980), 86.

11. G.S. Kirk, *Myth, its Meaning and Function in Ancient and Other Cultures* (Cambridge: 1970), 258.

12. F.S.L. Lyons, *Culture and Anarchy in Ireland 1890-1939* (Oxford: 1979), 43-45.

13. See Maryann Gialanella Valiulis ' "The Man They Could Never Forgive" ' in this volume.

14. E. Shils, 'Primordial, Sacred and Civil Ties: Some Particular Observations on the Relationship of Sociological Research and Theory', *British Journal of Sociology* 8, (1957), 130-145.

15. Herbert C. Kelman, 'Patterns of Personal Involvement in the National System: A Social Psychological Analysis of Political Legitimacy' in James N. Rosenau (ed.), *International Politics and Foreign Policy* (New York: 1969), 285.

16. Patrick Keatinge, *A Place Among the Nations* (Dublin: 1978), 61-80: especially p. 68.

17. David W. Harkness, 'Mr. de Valera's Dominion: Irish Relations with Britain and the Commonwealth 1932-1938', *Journal of Commonwealth Political Studies* VIII, 3 (1970).

18. Keatinge, (1978), 73.

19. R. Fanning, *The Irish Department of Finance 1922-58* (Dublin: 1978).

De Valera: Unique Dictator or Charismatic Chairman?

Brian Farrell

In twentieth century Irish politics de Valera was a phenomenon to rival, even outstrip, the nineteenth century giants, O'Connell and Parnell. Judged even by the crude measure of political longevity the record is impressive. First elected to the United Kingdom parliament in 1917 he was to serve continuously as a public representative for more than five decades until he ceased to be President of Ireland in 1973. He spent more than four decades as party leader, through two distinct phases of Sinn Féin and subsequently of Fianna Fáil. He became head of government for the first time in the original Dáil of 1919 and was to complete almost a quarter century of executive leadership as President of Dáil Éireann, President of the Executive Council and Taoiseach. With less than two decades to the end of the century it is safe to predict that no one will surpass this record.

But his very dominance makes a balanced judgment of that long career difficult. His reputation owes as much to the sometimes obsessive hatred of political opponents as to the extravagence of supporters. It has been acknowledged alike in the detached assessments of observers, native and foreign, in the measured terms of historians and in the analyses of political scientists. Many factors have contributed to make the image of 'the Chief' a fixed point of reference. His personal charisma was quickly appreciated: by the Volunteer prisoners in Dartmoor, by the electors of the re-organised Sinn Féin party. Those who thought he might be either cajoled or manipulated were soon disabused.[1] The ballad-makers sang 'We'll make de Valera king of Ireland', the people made him the symbol of Irish national resurgence and unity. In less than a decade he would be tumbled from that pre-eminence, become the most divisive politician of his generation and re-emerge as the leader of the party that would dominate Irish government and politics for the next half-century.

Fianna Fáil, under de Valera, presented itself as a cohesive national party, united at grass-roots, regimented in parliament and impeccably monolithic in government; there was neither dissent nor resignation. The party discipline appeared magical. It attracted new supporters seeking assurance and certainty, hypnotised opponents unable to compete, intrigued the uncommitted and the professional press. All tended to

35

explain the Fianna Fáil success in terms of 'the Chief'. In the troubled world of the 1930s as politics, in the great democracies as well as in totalitarian states, revolved around strong personalities, de Valera was seen as the unique dictator: a leader whose power, influence and authority were apparently only limited by his own commitment to constitutional and democratic principles.

But there is another dimension to de Valera's leadership that requires examination and demands recognition: the extent to which the Chief was dependent upon, was managed by, his supporters and lieutenants. This is not an exercise in reducing either the reputation or achievement of de Valera, still less an excursion into historical revisionism for its own sake. It is an effort to understand and appreciate the forces that helped shape the career, to penetrate the machinery that sustained the personal leadership, to balance the contribution of close associates to the creation of the de Valera myth.

Some of these considerations are illustrated in the very foundation of Fianna Fáil. In the aftermath of Civil War the republican Sinn Féin party entered a world of fantasy; abstentionism led to political decline.[2] As the party became weaker the vehemence of its internal debates became increasingly passionate. Energy that might have been concentrated on organisational efforts to win support was dissipated on internal arguments on points of principle. Yet de Valera persisted in his efforts to maintain the unity of this ramshackle, republican rump; he devoted himself to the task of balancing the conflicting aims of militant I.R.A., principled republicans unwilling to recognise the reality of Free State institutions and influence, and the more pragmatically minded members seeking a mechanism that could harness the party's undoubted potential strength for effective action. In the late months of 1925 and early months of 1926 it was not de Valera but Lemass who articulated the problems and choices facing Sinn Féin:

> One fact is beginning to emerge from out the confused mass of theory, praise and recrimination, hope and despair, that is hanging like a cloud over the national movement. Sinn Féin, for good or ill, is entering on another stage in its career . . . . there are some who would have us sit by the roadside and debate abstruse points about a *de jure* this and a *de facto* that, but the reality we want is away in the distance — and we cannot get there unless we move.[3]

That criticism was aimed at the Republican die-hards in Sinn Féin; its language also pointed at de Valera. With his customary caution, often pedantic manner and seemingly endless patience, the President of Sinn Féin had been skirting the dilemma facing his party. Now he was pushed to propose to the Ard-Fheis that once the admission oath of the 26-County and Six-County assemblies is removed, it becomes a question not of principle but of policy whether or not Republican representatives should attend these assemblies.

It was a narrow enough chink in the armour of principled Sinn Féin ideology, a formulation that might have won majority support. But Fr Flanagan proposed an amendment that it was incompatible with the fundamental principles of Sinn Féin 'to send representatives into any usurping legislature set up by English law in Ireland'. That narrowly carried the day. The second split within Sinn Féin, which de Valera had worked so long to avoid, was now unavoidable. He resigned the presidency which he had held since 1917.

He seems to have considered an even more acute abdication. According to the official biographers at this stage he was thinking again of relinquishing politics, returning to school-teaching and devoting his energies to the revival of Irish.[4] De Valera's own account to Michael McInerney was quite explicit:

> On that day in March 1926, I happened to be walking out of the Rathmines Town Hall with Sean Lemass. I had just resigned as president of Sinn Féin and I said to him, "Well, Sean, I have done my best, but I have been beaten. Now that is the end for me. I am leaving public life." Sean was shocked to hear me saying this, and he said: "But you are not going to leave us now Dev, at this stage. You cannot leave us like that. We have to go on now. We must form a new organisation along the policy lines you suggested at the Ard-Fheis. It is the only way forward." We discussed it further and at last I told him that I could not but agree with his logic and said I would do all the necessary things. But we were only a few people and we hadn't a penny between us.

Now, too much must not be made of an older man's recollection. The anecdote might be taken as illustrating an entirely human sense of dejection, a desire to be cajoled back into a pre-determined course of action. But over the next few weeks it is clear that de Valera allowed others to make the necessary moves to initiate the new party. It was Lemass who gathered the pro-de Valera members of the Sinn Féin Standing Committee for a formal break with the party and who then convened and managed the meeting at the old Sinn Féin headquarters at 23 Suffolk Street on Good Friday 1926 which decided to form a new party.

Of course it is unlikely that Fianna Fáil could have been launched without de Valera. Certainly it was he who insisted on the Irish title — and shrewdly made the point that it combined the advantage of underlining continuity with the earlier movement while defying accurate translation. Undoubtedly he exhibited his unrivalled skill in reducing the complex set of contemporary political circumstances to the single issue of the oath. But, from its inception, Fianna Fáil was a group enterprise. On his own de Valera could not have organised the detailed nation-wide structure stretching out into every parish. He accepted Lemass's insistence that the party's title should identify its character; it was Fianna Fáil, the Republican Party. At its inaugural meeting at the La Scala the party was presented not only with a political and cultural programme but with a set of social and economic aims that reflected more than one man's vision of Ireland. Over the next half-dozen years it was the men around de Valera more than the Chief himself who built the party into a powerful political machine combining strong local populism with a carefully structured national management. In the parliamentary arena, and not only during de Valera's absences from Ireland on fund-raising tours, it was the lieutenants who fashioned a credible alternative government team out of an Opposition front-bench. When victory first came in 1932 it was spear-headed, inspired and articulated by de Valera but it was the product of a group endeavour. When Fianna Fáil entered government it did so as a group and, as long as de Valera remained leader, that small set of men continued to work together as a team — no doubt committed to its leader but ready, in the closed council of Cabinet, to argue and disagree about the direction and pace of public policy.

The smallness and the durability of the leadership group within Fianna Fáil underlines the interdependence between de Valera and his lieutenants. Political opponents, intrigued by the party's extraordinary success and still hypnotised perhaps by their own experience of his charisma, tended to see Fianna Fáil as a one-man band and painted de Valera as a political pied piper leading his mesmerised followers to their own and the country's destruction. At the outset of the long debate on the nomination of members of the Government in 1943 de Valera deliberately refused to state exactly how the ministers would be allocated on the grounds that they would be put forward as a team. This provoked an Opposition outcry and repeated charges that, in the words of James Dillon,

> the first pre-requisite for membership of a government under Taoiseach de Valera is that you are a yes-man. In the heel of the hunt, whatever you say does not matter. What Taoiseach de Valera says is what you must do . . . . If an honourable man cannot see eye to eye he will go to his leader and get a sympathetic hearing, always assuming that you have a reasonable leader, but if you serve under Taoiseach de Valera, he will have his own way.

Even a cursory examination of the available official records of the early Fianna Fáil administrations reveals the inadequacy of this account. Under de Valera, then and later, Cabinet meetings were frequent and long. The party had come to power with an articulated programme. There was little need for debate on the main thrust of their purely constitutional political aims: they were committed to dismantling the Treaty settlement and substituting 'an Irish Constitution from top to bottom'.[6] For this de Valera was virtually exclusively in charge. But the implementation of other policy proposals was not so smooth. In particular there was considerable divergence of opinion on particular aspects of economic and social policy. Lemass's efforts to push through a radical, and not always considered, protectionism involved a substantial growth of state intervention in the economy. It encountered stiff opposition from ministers, and especially from Sean MacEntee in his long period as Minister for Finance, concerned to maintain a more orthodox approach to the relationship of government and business.[7] The party's commitment to a land policy that stressed further re-distribution soon came into conflict with efforts to promote agricultural efficiency. Far from being the driver of a complacent team of ministerial work-horses, de Valera often found himself the referee in vigorous and competitive fights between ministers and departments concerned, as in all governments, to secure maximum advantage for their own favoured schemes and policies.

Even when de Valera had clearly indicated his own commitment to a policy initiative it was possible to delay and divert decision. The long internal struggle to secure governmental approval for the introduction of children's allowances shows how powerful ministerial colleagues could and did use the administrative machine against the express wishes of de Valera.[8] In 1939 the topic was raised on a number of fronts. At the end of March on the estimate for the Department of Local Government and Public Health, James Dillon of Fine Gael suggested that family allowances should be paid to poor parents with large families. In April at a meeting of the Cottage Tenants and Rural Workers Association Senator Tunney of Labour proposed a subsidy for children on farms. Dillon's plan was taken up by the *Irish Standard* on 12 May. Two months later at a Cabinet meeting the Minister for Local Government undertook to examine the question of the institution of a system of family allowances.

There can be no doubt about de Valera's interest in this matter. He had long been concerned about Irish population decline, especially in rural areas and had enshrined in the Constitution his ambition

> that there may be established on the land in economic security as many families as in the circumstances may be possible (45.2.iii).

Sean MacEntee acknowledged this personal involvement when he forwarded a leader from *The Tablet* (12 August 1939) on 'Family and the Future' and asked

> that it might be brought to the personal attention of the Taoiseach. It deals with the population question in which the Taoiseach is intensely interested.

Other ministers were interested and the issue was soon joined. A memorandum from Frank Aiken in September on family allowances for agricultural workers and small farmers was followed a month later by a long memorandum from MacEntee which attacked the whole idea of state family allowances on a range of fronts. Some of the objections were practical: that this was an expensive redistributive scheme that would 'drive the unfit into matrimony' at the expense of the productive tax-payer. Others were theoretical: in essence that a Catholic country like Ireland should resist being dragged by way of family allowances along the road to the servile state.

It required a reminder from the Taoiseach's Department to prompt the promised memorandum from the Department of Local Government at the beginning of November. This was returned as technically deficient and subsequently resubmitted and considered by the Government at its meeting of 14 November 1939. Instead of pushing through an immediate discussion and decision de Valera opted for a compromise — a Cabinet Committee representing the differing ministerial viewpoints consisting of P.J. Ruttledge (Local Government), Lemass (Supplies), J. Ryan (Agriculture), F. Aiken (Defensive Measures) and T. O Deirg (Lands). In January, February, March and April 1940 the Taoiseach's Department wrote to Local Government to enquire what progress had been made. In April Lemass tried to circumvent the delays within the department by submitting a personal scheme allegedly representing the Committee's views.[9] This was too audacious for de Valera. He persisted with establish-ed procedures, sending reminders at fortnightly intervals. Their tone moved from the formal note 'to inquire whether examination of the mat-ter with a view to its submission to the Government has been completed' (14 May), to the firmer 'the Taoiseach desires that the examination of this matter should be expedited and that it should be submitted to the Government with appropriate observations at an early date' (3 June), to the explicit 'I am to point again that the Taoiseach desires that the matter should be regarded as one of considerable urgency' (12 June). the process of jogging administrative and ministerial elbows continued throughout the summer. It was only in September 1940 that a full submission was ready for the Government. Even then ministerial opponents continued to argue; MacEntee circulated four memoranda on the topic in September. There was further delay and ministerial disagreement about precise terms of reference when the project was referred to an inter-departmental committee of civil servants in October 1940. Once again de Valera's de-partment was forced to prod the civil servants into action; in September 1941 the secretary to the committee minuted that no report could be ex-pected before December. The delay was raised by way of parliamentary question in the Dáil in April 1942.[10] In July Seán T. O'Kelly was writing to de Valera that the final form of the report was not yet settled and 'it would be undesirable if anything were said which could be construed as giving official benediction even to the principle of family allowances'. Eventually in October 1942 the civil servants report was circulated. It was only then discussed by the Government, legislation introduced, and the scheme came finally into effect in 1944.

This case is quoted at some length to confirm the point that de Valera, even on policy issues in which he took a close personal interest, was far from being a dictatorial chief executive. The image of a Taoiseach who simply 'looked into his heart' and then acted without consulting his Cabinet colleagues may have fitted the prejudice of partisan opponents.[11] It was far from the truth. It misrepresented not only the character of de Valera and his relations with colleagues but the very nature of the office and role of Taoiseach. Certainly the Taoiseach is the single most powerful actor on the Irish political scene but he acts within a set of constraints — constitutional, legal, political, cultural — and ignores them at his peril. Any attempt to adopt a presidential, still less a dictatorial, pose is a recipe for failure. After all, even in the powerful elective monarchy of the United States, it is recognised that the essence of the chief executive's office lies not in command but in persuasion: the real power of the American president is the power to persuade.[12] The same is true of the Taoiseach. He must be sensitive to and on occasions prepared to accommodate the views of others. He cannot hope to have things his own way.

That is a lesson that de Valera seems to have known by instinct. Throughout his early career there are numerous examples of his willingness to recognise and accept the effective power of persuasive action. In 1915, he was prepared, however unwillingly, to join the I.R.B. in order to obtain fuller information about the proposed Easter Rising; in 1917 he deliberately recruited Eoin Mac Neill for his Clare bye-election campaign on the grounds that 'the clergy are with Mac Neill and they are a powerful force'.[13] It should not be forgotten that his selection as President of the newly organised and greatly expanded Sinn Féin in that year was based not only on his acceptability to the different strands of opinion within the organisation but also on a recognition of his capacity to formulate and manage compromise. There was an inherent duality in that Sinn Féin which might be crudely represented in terms of its uncompromisingly militant republican wing and its moderate parliamentary democratic wing; de Valera was chosen as the man most likely to harness them in tandem.[14] Over the next four years he managed to balance those disparate forces and symbolically maintained the facade of a single national united purpose. That unity could not, did not, survive the splits revealed in the Treaty debate.

The question of de Valera's responsibility for the nature of that division and the subsequent civil war is the subject of a different discussion. For more than fifty years it has been argued, often bitterly and passionately, in moral terms. For purposes of this paper it is enough to note it as the great single conspicuous example of the failure of his persuasive skills. That failure must have coloured his subsequent exercise of political leadership. He would never again throw his political charisma into the scale of competing forces. Instead he reverted to a cautious, patient, persuasive search for a middle ground between principle and reality; to an incrementalist pursuit of agreed policies; to a readiness to sacrifice pace to consensus. In the process he helped to lead the fragment of an ideological republican rump into an enduring centrist political movement that has secured close to majority support for half a century.

The price of that success was a style of leadership that accomplished less than it promised and less than it might have achieved. Perhaps the most obvious example of de Valera's failure to translate his own most cherished ambitions into effective practice was the continuing decline of spoken Irish. At the level of language teaching in schools and the formal minimal use of Irish in the state service a temporary advance was accomplished; the Gaeltacht, a political as well as cultural heartland for de Valera, declined. The 'unique dictator' stopped far short of husbanding the full resources of the state apparatus to achieve his chosen goal. In this case, it may be argued, it was the inertia of the society that frustrated effective action. On the other hand it might be suggested that a more forceful and determined leader would have applied a richer range of inducements and stringent penalties to secure the compliance and application that rhetoric and exhortation conspicuously failed to inspire.

On other occasions it was the obstruction, reluctance or inadequacy of senior colleagues that restrained action. But, again, if de Valera was acknowledged as chief, he acted throughout as chairman.[15] There was little turnover of ministerial talent; the original group of comrades, once recruited to office, were allowed to work through to old age or, at worst, edged gently out of office. In virtually all cases an alternative post and status was provided. Nothing was done in a hurry. All was managed with a delicacy that bordered on timidity. There were no outright sackings. None of that taste for butchery often held to be a necessary characteristic of modern British prime ministers. When de Valera ceased to be Taoiseach in 1959 there were still four members of his original nine-man Cabinet of 1932 in office.

There were few efforts to exercise discipline by moving ministers up and down the Cabinet hierarchy. Reshuffles seemed designed as much to obscure as to establish a pecking order. At the outbreak of war in September 1939, for instance, there was a major re-organisation in which only two ministers retained their portfolios (de Valera as Taoiseach and

Minister for Foreign Affairs and Ryan as Minister for Agriculture) but it is still impossible to decipher the full significance of the various changes made. De Valera was prepared to tolerate and able to manage a considerable degree of friction between his Cabinet colleagues. In time it could be argued this consumed an increasing proportion of his time and energy. He tended to become the adjudicator rather than the initiator of policy. Although some ministers of the time have insisted that in the 1950s 'Dev's was still the decisive voice' there is ample evidence to indicate that he was now too much incapacitated by age and blindness to be in full control. Noticeably, it is only in this period that the closed Cabinet circle of first generation Fianna Fáil leaders was opened up to allow in younger men. Even then, in 1951, the first younger minister appointed was the son and namesake of one of de Valera's closest early associates, Erskine Childers. When de Valera named his last government in 1957 the half-dozen newer men (Childers, Lynch, Blaney, Boland, Moran and Ormonde) were still outweighed by eight veteran founding-fathers (de Valera, Lemass, MacEntee, Ryan, Aiken, Traynor, Smith, Moylan).

That older group, men then associated with de Valera for more than three decades, represented a wide span of interests, opinions and priorities. Some could readily be labelled conservative in both social and economic terms. Others belong to at least a pragmatic-liberal group in Irish political development. They were not held together by a unique dictator but by a charismatic chairman who, in the words of an astute observer outside that magic circle, had a 'strong personality and plays on it'.[16] That personal authority was not typically exercised by domination but by persuasion. De Valera's style of chairmanship, in government and party alike, was provokingly patient with opposition, agonisingly tolerant of the irrelevant, overwhelmingly understanding of the stupid. He used exhaustion rather than coercion to secure maximum consent to, and preferably unanimity in, decision-making. If that style was in part imposed by political necessity, it also in part reflected aspects of de Valera's own personality. In 1943, confronting Opposition accusations that he had again selected a Cabinet of yes-men, he argued

> When we have discussed and differed and come to a conclusion in advance, as we do, it is very easy to suggest, because they are loyal — having accepted a decision — in putting it into effect that they are only "yes-men". Some of these men were in the National movement before I was. They are men of independent mind and character. It is shameful to suggest all the time that they are simply "yes-men". If the arguments that are put up are good enough to convince people, and if there is in a team loyalty enough, when a decision has been arrived at, to keep to it, is that a question of being "yes-men"? Is there any other way in which a Party or a group can work? Does not everyone know that we are all individual souls, that we have an individual outlook upon

things and that our opinions at any particular time depend on a whole variety of conditions?[17]

The questions might be extended. They might well include the question: just how much did de Valera achieve? Fortunately that is to be answered by another speaker at this centenary conference. Perhaps it is enough here to conclude with a final point: that de Valera's rhetoric requires extensive scrutiny and close reading before it can be used as a measure against which to assess the political career and achievements. Fortunately we can now draw on the unrivalled knowledge and experience of Dr Maurice Moynihan in using that rich vein of material.[18] In that richly textured context it becomes possible to re-read and re-interpret one of the most frequently-quoted and misunderstood of all the de Valera public statements, the wireless broadcast of St Patrick's Day 1943. It is a vision of an ideal Ireland

> The Ireland which we have dreamed of would be the home of a people who valued material wealth only as the basis of right living, of a people who were satisfied with frugal comfort and devoted their leisure to things of the spirit — a land whose countryside would be bright with cosy homesteads, whose fields and villages would be joyous with the sounds of industry, with the romping of sturdy children, the contests of athletic youths and the laughter of comely maidens, whose firesides would be forums for the wisdom of old age. It would, in a word, be the home of a people living the life that God desired that man should live.

But before accepting that 'frugal, good-living and Gaelic new Jerusalem' as even an idealised statement of public policy it should be put into context.[19] The speech was an exhortation on the fiftieth anniversary of the Gaelic League. It was overtly addressed to the Irish of the diaspora and must have evoked for many the happy images of a distant rural childhood frozen in the web of emigrant memories. It was also intended for a domestic audience that must have included many followers, concerned like some leaders of the party, with the growing divergence between the programme laid out in the La Scala address of 1926 and the real Ireland of the 1940s. For them, there was re-assurance in this vivid evocation by a man who personified their own inarticulate and sometimes contradictory day-dreams.

Yet it scarcely represented the real thrust of policy. It certainly did not reflect the preparations for post-war planning already being developed by a small Inner Cabinet under de Valera's chairmanship. Through the 1930s within the Fianna Fáil Cabinet a small set of largely urban-based ministers had shaped the priorities and allocated the resources of government. Pre-eminent in terms of vigour, effectiveness and influence was Sean Lemass. Now it was the same apparently unlikely combination of de Valera and Lemass that was attempting to think through the appropriate responses to the needs of post-war Ireland. It is enough here to make the point that those embryonic schemes bore little relation to the dream-world conjured up in the St Patrick's Day address. But mention of the de Valera-Lemass relationship — and it was a key relationship through more than a key quarter-century of Irish politics — is a further reminder of the theme of this paper. Viewed from outside, these two men, so different in interests, inclinations, temperament and style were a contradictory pair; yet this was a political marriage that endured disappointments and frustrations and strains. It could not have survived without a considerable degree of conciliation, compromise and concession on both sides. If there were no other evidence available, Lemass's association through a life-time in government would be eloquent testimony to the inadequacy of regarding de Valera as any kind of dictator.

He was not that. Not even, perhaps, to be regarded as a charismatic chairman. But de Valera was a Taoiseach able to husband the support, harvest the loyalty and maintain the unity of a remarkable generation of senior political leaders. It was these trusted lieutenants as much as the man himself who determined the course of Irish politics in the age of de Valera.

NOTES

1. Cf. William O'Brien to Tim Healy, 2 May 1918 'de Valera is personally a charming as well as an honest man but he is too good for this rough world of old Parliamentary hands and will no doubt subside into a meek instrument of Dillon's'. N.L.I. Ms. 8556/19 quoted in B. Farrell, *Chairman or Chief? the role of Taoiseach in Irish Government* (Dublin: 1971).

2. See P. Pyne 'The Third Sinn Fein Party: 1923-1926', *Economic and Social Review*, I, 1-2, 1969-1970.

3. Quotation from 'The Need for Sinn Fein: a fighting policy', *An Phoblacht*, 22 January 1926. This is the fifth in a series of six articles by Lemass. For discussion see B. Farrell, *Sean Lemass: a political biography* (forthcoming), chapter I.

4. Earl of Longford and Thomas P. O'Neill, *Eamon de Valera* (Dublin: 1970), 40; Tomás P. Ó Néill agus Pádraig Ó Fiannachta, *De Valera*, II, (Ath Cliath: 1970), 181. The quotation below is from M. McInerney, 'The Name and the Game', *Irish Times* supplement on Fianna Fáil, 19 May 1978. In an earlier published version McInerney quotes de Valera as saying 'it looks as if that is the end for me, Sean. I'm chucking politics altogether' *Eamon de Valera* (Dublin: 1976), 55.

5. For a typical example of this 'one-man band' accusation see the long debate on the nomination of members of the Government, 1-2 July, 1943 in DE, vol. 91, cols. 45-223. De Valera's refusal below is at columns 45ff and the Dillon quotation at col. 80.

6. From a speech at Ennis, Co. Clare in *Irish Press*, 1 July 1935.

7. On policy disagreements see R. Fanning, *The Irish Department of Finance 1922-58* (Dublin: 1978). In particular, see chapter 6 and Farrell, *Lemass*, chapters 3 and 4.

8. The following account of the childrens' allowance controversy is based on Cabinet and Government minutes and files S.11265 A/B, S.12117 A/B in the State Paper Office, Dublin. The references below include: Dillon speech in DE, vol. 76, col. 406, 30 March 1939; Tunney speech reported in *Irish Press*, 17 April 1939; government meeting in GC 2/83, 11 July 1939.

9. Lemass memorandum in S. 11265 B. It is quoted in Farrell, *Lemass*, Chapter 4. MacEntee memoranda in same file. Government decision to refer issue to an interdepartmental committee in GC 2/207, 4 October 1940.

10. Norton's parliamentary question on 15 April 1942 was given an uninformative reply. O'Kelly's letter of 11 July in S. 11265 B.

11. De Valera towards the end of the Treaty debate had asserted 'whenever I wanted to know what the Irish people wanted I had only to examine my own heart and it told me straight off what the Irish people wanted', Dail Debates 1921-22 (Treaty debate), p. 274, 6 January 1922. Subsequently the phrase was repeatedly used by opponents to imply an attachment to arrogant authoritarianism. Cf. e.g. in the course of the debate on the new Constitution John Marcus O'Sullivan, DE, vol. 67, cols. 215-6, 12 May 1937.

12. On the power to persuade see R. Neustadt, *Presidential Power: the politics of leadership*, (New York: 1962).

13. The quotation is from R. Brennan, *Allegiance* (Dublin: 1950), 152. For previous reference to I.R.B. membership see Ó Néill agus Ó Fiannachta, I, 43-4.

14. On the reorganisation of Sinn Féin 1917 and nomination of de Valera see B. Farrell *The Founding of Dail Eireann: parliament and nation-building* (Dublin: 1971), chapter 2.

15. For further discussion of de Valera and his Cabinet relations see Farrell, *Chairman or Chief*, chapter 3. On the 1939 reshuffle see DE Vol. 77, Adjournment Debate, 27-29 September 1940, cols. 259-606 and discussion in Farrell, *Lemass*, chapter 4.

16. S. MacBride to J. McGarrity, 19 October 1933 in NLI Ms. 17,456, McGarrity papers.

17. DE, vol. 91, cols. 218-9. 2 July 1943.

18. M. Moynihan ed. *Speeches and Statements by Eamon de Valera 1917-1973* (Dublin: 1980). The full text of the broadcast is on pp 466ff.

19. Quotation from John A. Murphy, *Ireland in the Twentieth Century*, (Dublin: 1975), 141. Cf. Tim Pat Coogan, *Ireland since the Rising* (London: 1966), 71-2. Also T. Garvin, 'The Destiny of the Soldiers: tradition and modernity in the politics of de Valera's Ireland', *Political Studies*, **XXVI**,3, (1978), 346ff.

The Primacy of Form:
A 'Folk Ideology' in de Valera's Politics

Gearóid Ó Crualaoich

Introduction

Folklore is mentioned only once in six hundred pages of Maurice Moynihan's recent edition of speeches and statements by Eamon de Valera.[1] It occurs in the course of Mr de Valera's Senate speech on the Institute for Advanced Studies Bill in May 1940. In justification of the Bill's intentions in regard to Celtic Studies he explained that work of a similar nature had already been undertaken by, for instance, the Manuscripts Commission. He then said: 'We have also had to deal with the body of folklore which, it was obvious, we should set about collecting as quickly as possible while it was still in a fairly pure form'. In a footnote to the text of the speech Maurice Moynihan sets down that the Irish Folklore Commission was established by de Valera's Government in 1935 to undertake the preservation, study etc., of all aspects of Irish folk tradition. De Valera's relationship to that folk tradition and his stated concern for its preservation in pure form is, I suggest, an element in recent Irish history that deserves consideration.

De Valera and Folklore Studies

Speaking in April 1926 of the aims of the party he proposed to found de Valera had restated his conviction that there lay in the heart of every Irishman a native, undying desire to see his country not only politically free but truly Irish as well. Perhaps the clearest, and certainly the best known statement of de Valera's vision of what that truly Irish country would actually be like is the passage in the famous radio broadcast of St Patrick's Day 1943 with its references to cosy homesteads, joyous fields and villages and fireside forums for the wisdom of serene old age. It should be remembered, I think, that de Valera presented this picture of Irish society explicitly as the formulation of a dream, a dream claimed by him for Fianna Fáil and, in retrospect, for the Volunteers of a decade previously. He acknowledged that its origin lay with Davis and the Young Irelanders in their attempts to devise a modern, national programme for the regeneration materially and spiritually of a historic nation and he saw in the ideals of the Gaelic League a continuation of the philosophy of Davis. Now the Gaelic League was very concerned with

47

folklore and folk tradition and Douglas Hyde, who in his latter-day role as President, is spoken of by one of de Valera's biographers as the 'embodiment of Ireland's spiritual emancipation',[2] was pre-eminent in promoting its collection and study. As Professor of Modern Irish in U.C.D. Hyde had, in the early 1920s, played a very large role in the inspiration and academic formation of the man who was to personify much of the story of folklore studies in Ireland in the twentieth century. That man was James Hamilton Delargy, the founding father of the Folklore of Ireland Society whose planning and establishment was taking place in precisely the same period at which Fianna Fáil was founded.[3] In the first number of the Society's journal, *Béaloideas*, published in June 1927, Delargy, its editor, spoke of preserving for the nation and transmitting to its future generations an authentic record of the folklore of the Irish people. He also referred to 'nonsensical rubbish which passes for Irish folklore both in Ireland and outside' at the then present day.[4] Delargy too had *his* dream, *his* vision connecting his life's vocation to Ireland and the Irish people. T.K. Whitaker has recently quoted for us — from a short autobiographical piece of Delargy's — a description of the latter's return to Dublin from Scandinavia in 1928 and his feelings as the mail-boat neared the coast:

> I went right out to the bow and I saw the Irish hills . . . and I said "the tradition of Ireland is behind those hills and we've got to rescue it before it's trampled into the dirt" . . ., because it was a jewel of great price and one had to see that it was given a refuge and an appreciation by the Irish people.[5]

This vocation was one of which de Valera would obviously approve and his government was later, in 1935, to provide an annual grant of more than £3,000 to the Folklore Commisison of which Delargy was to be Honorary Director from its inception until the year when de Valera also finally relinquished public office — 1973. During that time, and especially up to the end of the 50s the Folklore Commission amassed a huge corpus of traditional lore along with a very considerable body of ethnographic description of the material culture and social organization of those whom we might term the plain people of Ireland, those same plain people whose political aspirations and expectations de Valera and his party claimed best to respresent and on whose behalf Fianna Fáil sought to wield power. It is my contention that the image of himself and of his party that de Valera offered to the Irish people in general took into account the 'folk' proclivities of a large proportion of the Irish electorate.

De Valera and a National Mythology

Oliver MacDonagh has spoken of an ideological frigidity in Irish politics and Irish political thinking from 1870 on and suggests likely explanations.[6] I am suggesting here that a possible corollary of such a phenomenon is that it became possible over sixty years for the Gaelic League and the Volunteers and de Valera to build a national ideology on an essentially static conception of a 'truly Irish' way of life, a static conception that derives from both the eighteenth century Romantic roots of Davis's vision and also older and perennial, native, Gaelic roots involving the personification of Irish sovereignty in a mother-figure who must be delivered from bondage and rejuvenated by the selfless sacrifices of her children, the 'scattered children of Éire', 'our sweet, sad mother' as de Valera himself put it in 1920.[7] Such a 'truly Irish' way of life, in essence both noble and loyal, was envisaged as morally superior to the way of life of the modern, cosmopolitan, commercial world and it was to the prior claim of this superior life-style on all Irish people that de Valera continually drew the attentions of the Irish electorate and their parliamentary representatives. Now much of the Irish electorate in the period of the twentieth century prior to the Second World War was still relatively free of the grosser effects of the transformation of social and political sensibilities that accompanies — and, in this instance, did later accompany — more or less total exposure to forces of modernisation in technology, economy, social organization and education, and it was where some version of a traditional or pre-modern mentality still survived that de Valera and Fianna Fáil attracted the greatest measure of a fairly unreflecting allegiance. In a countryside where versions of the Barbarossa legend — of the sleeping giant who is destined one day to liberate his people — were still being collected in 1940s and 50s,[8] de Valera wore easily the proferred mantle of Chief. The messianic character of an aspect of de Valera's public image has been generally, I think, acknowledged.[9] It is as anti-Christ however, rather than as a version of the *Christus* that he is by some remembered. The full impact of the legend that he was born with the mark of the Cross on his back is, I feel, more properly ambiguous.

Denis Gwynn has written that 'de Valera's command of public confidence owed little to popular appeal but rested upon his long record of austere integrity and patriotism and his sagacity as a political leader'.[10] This seems to me to underestimate the folk proclivities of very many communities of the plain people of Ireland from whom de Valera sought and received support as a type of uncrowned king who, in the words of Oliver MacDonagh 'alone among modern Irishmen . . . had reached the rank of O'Connell, Parnell and — if the anti-kings be counted also, Carson'.[11] If, in the aftermath of civil war, the Irish people had turned away from the idea of romantic nationalism and had set their faces to the matter-of-fact task of building a free state, a sufficient number of them were, from 1932 on, willing to entrust the continuing political and socio-economic development of that state to a man who, while his vision of a free and truly Irish society was based on a stereotype deriving ultimately from an antiquarianism that even in the 1920s was outmoded, could still represent, in the contemporary world, a continuation of ancient cultural identity.

If it is true that to many of his countrymen and women, supporters and opponents alike, de Valera was a folk hero or anti-hero, it does not follow that he himself projected himself as such in the national and political arena. Just as the Cromwell or Swift or O'Connell of folklore are to be distinguished sharply from the historical persons, whose names these stereotypes bear, so too the flesh and blood de Valera can remain entirely separate from whatever version of himself could be built up from the archives of that same Folklore Commission which his government supported financially. It is not to de Valera the folk-hero that we need look to find a folk-connection. It is in the thought and action of de Valera the man, the actual, historical, political leader, that we can find operating a model of the Irish people — or at least of a majority of them — that is to a certain extent based on notions of the 'folk'. That model has, it appears to me, very interesting relationships both to a European perception of the life and culture of so-called folk societies that is essentially nineteenth century in character and also to a twentieth century perception of peasant society that finds its characteristic expression in the writings of anthropologists such as Robert Redfield and George Foster.[12] Both perceptions ignore 'class' issues and it is, I believe, significant that a political model of Irish society congruent with them should find such favour among the twentieth century Irish electorate.

Idealization of Peasantry

The characteristically nineteenth century strand of de Valera's social thinking derived in large part from the philosophies of cultural nationalism developed in Germany and England under the influence of the romantic reaction to eighteenth century notions of social organization. It was itself characterized as a way of thinking by an idealization of 'the peasant' — an idealization commonly encountered in the approach to traditional society in the European countryside of many amateur scholars and social observers throughout the nineteenth century. Such idealization tends to lift 'the peasant' and traditional society in general out of history, regarding them both as changeless, as somehow not subject to the process of continuous transformation that is the actual lot of all societies in the real socio-economic world. Another aspect of such idealization, has, historically, been to regard traditional society as far less 'tainted' by industrialism, by technological development and by the commercialized relationships that go with a fully monetized economy, than has actually been the case. Despite the fact that the Irish people as a whole were in the 1920s very far indeed from being simple-minded and naive as regards transactions of an economic nature in the modern world, de Valera still chooses in July 1928 to lecture the Dáil, and the Irish electorate, on the subject of economic policy in the following terms:

> We . . . had to make the sort of choice that might be open, for instance, to a servant in a big mansion. If the servant was displeased with the kicks of the young master and wanted to have his freedom . . . He had to give up the idea of having around him the cushions and all the rest that a servant in a mansion might have, and the various things that might come to him from the table of the lord.[13]

Is this the imagery of the medieval manor-house or the Kiltartan countryside? Some may, perhaps, suggest that it is the imagery of Bruree, since he goes on:

> If a man makes up his mind to go out into a cottage, he must remember that he cannot have in the cottage the luxuries around him which he had when he was bearing the kicks of the master . . . [but] has to make up his mind to put up with the frugal fare of the cottage.

Whatever the source of such imagery one is struck by its artificiality in relation to the life-experience of the overwhelming majority of the people to whom his remarks are ultimately addressed. The tone of the passage contrasts in the starkest manner with the hard-headedness in regard to matters economic of the first of the classic Gaeltacht autobiographies,[14] which was to be published in the following year.

And yet the historians tell us that it was due at least in part to its economic policies that Fianna Fáil came to power in the 1932 General Election. The message of economic self-sufficiency — no matter how awkwardly or ahistorically illustrated — had, it seems, its own inherent attractions for a majority of the electorate. But that message in itself, however or by whom illustrated, seems to me to be peculiarly suited to a time and place where the idea prevails that a hitherto exploited and depressed peasantry is at last in the position of being able itself to appoint the individuals who will form its government. Surely, it is implied, self-sufficiency will be the lot of a people whose thrift and self-restraint had previously been cruelly traded on by a hated ascendancy, but who are now largely in control of their own destinies and who live in a society where class differences are officially non-existent. This establishment view of rural Ireland in the 1930s has, it seems to me, elements that bear some comparison with aspects of the perceptions of peasant society developed in anthropology at that period and I feel that such a comparison is relevant to my theme even though it is doubtful if de Valera himself or any members of his government were in the 1930s and 40s very conversant with the theories of 'peasant society' then being advanced by certain transatlantic scholars.[15]

There has always been a sense of controversy in Ireland surrounding the terms 'peasant' and 'peasantry' in their application to the Irish rural population. Some people have regarded them as unpleasant and hostile labels imposed for our humiliation by scholars having that ulterior motive. The title of Kenneth Connell's book, *Irish Peasant Society*[16] is still regarded by some as being consciously provocative. There are obviously good grounds for caution in the use of general appellations of the type 'peasant' and it is true that the peculiar circumstances of Irish political and socio-economic history demand that certain specific qualifications be borne in mind when the term is used in the Irish context. This however is a matter of degree, and qualifications of a similar nature must equally apply in the case of every individual community to which the term is applied. Some of the main qualifications that are urged in the Irish case are that the alleged 'peasantry' includes large elements of a depressed aristrocracy (thus maintaining everyone's chances of being, in reality, descended from high kings); that a literate tradition of poetry and learning survives among the people at large, if only in a vestigial way (there is the tradition of Greek and Latin-quoting farm labourers); and that, unlike — so it is alleged — the case of Central European or Central American populations, the memory of past glory and of another order of social organization perpetually fuels a desire to throw off the demeaning yoke of foreign oppression and to resume a very different life style from that prevalent in the countryside in recent centuries. Two of de Valera's statements have direct relevance to this issue. In the course of his address at the opening of the Athlone Broadcasting Station in 1933 he spoke at some length of Ireland's history and of her contributions to European culture. In regard to the tradition of Irish learning he points out that it was never wholly lost — 'even during the darkest period of the English occupation'. 'The "hedge schools", taught by wandering scholars, frustrated in a measure the design to reduce the people to illiteracy . . .' 'Some of the finest poems . . . were written . . . by men who spent their lives in poverty, dependent on the hospitality of an impoverished and outcast peasantry'.[17] Here we have the term 'peasantry' itself applied in a more or less straightforward way. Five years later in 1938, however, we get clear evidence of the line of thinking already referred to which sees the Irish peasant as really a type of aristocrat-in-disguise. In his speech at the inauguration of Douglas Hyde as first President of Ireland de Valera addressed the new office-holder as follows:

In you we greet the successor of our rightful princes and, in your accession to office, we hail the closing of the breach that has existed since the undoing of our nation at Kinsale.[18]

Such rhetorical denial of true 'peasant' status to Irish rural society is something that seems to me to go hand in hand with a tacit acquiesence in the use of a largely 'peasant' model for thinking about and managing social and economic development in the years of de Valera's ascendency. And such a model was not wildly inappropriate to the facts of the case as they were then officially perceived. The general changeover from tenant-farming to peasant proprietorship had had little effect on the nature of rural society or the structures of agriculture. With the safety valve of emigration, the kind of rural life-styles that are so graphically depicted in the pages of Arensberg and Kimball[19] could suggest themselves as the typical life-styles of a population living to a pattern that was unbroken from time immemorial, while a new metropolitan elite could, since the revolution, maintain a seemingly benign form of the old structural ascendency over the 'liberated' countryside.[20] Here was indeed a source of that 'truly Irish' order of things that was so important a part of the national dream. Cleared of its Big Houses — in reality or by selective vision — the hinterland of the essentially pre-industrial Irish market towns was at once the source of economic self-sufficiency, in all but a few instances where imported frugal luxuries were not to be decried, and also the heartland of moral and social values bearing testimony to the spirituality and selflessness of the Irish people.

Stereotyping in 'Peasant' Model

In a sense this vision of the Irish countryside fits well enough with the notions of peasant society being developed by such as Redfield, and Foster;[21] These ideas — largely the product of fieldwork, in Mexico and elsewhere — had led within anthropology to 'peasant society' being proposed as an exact term for an autonomous, stable category of social organization rather than as a loose description of an intermediate stage in some inevitable social progression from hunting-gathering to urban living. For Redfield any list of the central elements of peasant society would include the following: being definitely rural but relating to market towns; forming a segment of a larger regional population that itself contained urban centres; lacking the isolation, political autonomy and self-sufficiency of tribal society; retaining old identity, integration and attachment to soil and cults.[22] Now, as is well known, the theory of peasant society has developed almost out of recognition since Redfield published his classic study of Tepoztlán in 1930 and his concept of 'peasantry' — that I see as matching the model implicit in de Valera's social and economic theory fifty years ago — is today to be regarded as inadequate conceptually and methodologically. One of the chief objections to it is that it lifts the society it purports to describe out of the actual, historical social and economic complexities of the real world and substitutes mechanistic abstractions for the endlessly dynamic and contingent ramifications of individual and group choice in the actual circumstances of every community at every specific time. A similar observation can surely be made also in regard to the vision of the life of the Irish people that de Valera promoted from the day he came to power. They — the Irish people — were to be largely untroubled by developments within any historical process. Their tranquil, Christian lives were to be an example to a world far gone on the paths of unprincipled and materialist excess. The bed-rock of the Irish way of life that was to contrast so much with the way of the world outside our shores was of course the age-old certainty of our cultural identity and cultural values. The very first speech of de Valera the parliamentary democrat, delivered on his arrival in Ennis in June 1917 to contest the East Clare bye-election had given warning of this *leitmotif* of de Valera's social and political thought: the necessity to see behind changing appearances to the timeless realities that are the really worthy objects of human endeavour. Speaking of free and absolute independence for Ireland, he said of the men of 1916 that 'they went out . . . because they knew it was in the bottom of the heart of every Irishman, no matter what was on the surface.'[23] This choice of the continuity of identity and value as something superior in significance to any developments on the social and economic plane continues throughout de Valera's political career in terms of his radical pursuit of and emphasis on Irish sovereignty and independence primarily at a constitutional and symbolic level. The social and economic conservatism that accompanied this constitutional radicalism cannot, of course, in any sense be attributed entirely to a single individual. Large historical and structural factors inhibited any extreme, revolutionary aftermath to the establishment of the Irish Free State. Nevertheless, I contend that the conception of a folk or peasant-type society that seems to me to lie at the heart of de Valera's and Fianna Fáil's political philosophy from 1932 to 1959 made it easier for both leader and party to get on with the 'real' job of manifesting and reinforcing Irish sovereignty while leaving Irish society relatively unaltered. But it cannot be forgotten that support for this political philosophy was given again and again by the electorate who demonstrate, in their loyalty to the Chief in the face of dire social and economic necessity, the need for all of us to look beyond economic welfare alone in order to see the political meaning of individuals and their actions. Throughout a period of economic hardship and military threat a large proportion of the Irish electorate responded positively to de Valera's constant emphasizing of the sovereignty of the people, their superior qualities, their noble history, their glorious cultural heritage, the rightness of their national cause. This response is, to my way of thinking, evidence of the continuing political efficacy in de Valera's day of a mentality deriving not from the consciousness of 'class', in any modern sense, but rather from the consciousness of collectivities whose focus is primarily neither political nor economic.

Stereotyping of Folk Traditions

In his celebrated reply to Winston Churchill de Valera reached what I think of as the highest point of his career as a veritable personification of national identity. In this broadcast he speaks not only for the Irish people but for *Éire* herself, thanking on her behalf the Gaels who had not failed her: '*Níor chlis sibh orm, a Ghaela*'.[24] One cannot avoid feeling the pressure of mythology here and sense the looming of mythological personnages.

The *Cailleach Bhéara*, shaper and guardian of the landscape itself and goddess of sovereignty, comes to mind. She has inhabited Gaelic consciousness from pre-historic times and her legend was still in de Valera's day being recounted to the full-time collectors of the Folklore Commission. The temptation to see a mythological correspondence between de Valera and the *Cailleach Bhéara* cannot however be easily indulged, and not simply because of gender difficulties. A major aspect of the *Cailleach* tradition is her fertility and her general lasciviousness, and these qualities would surely not appear to any conspicuous degree in de Valera's public image. That public image in fact, in its austerity, aloofness, respectability, sombre and dignified good sense fits very badly with the tone and quality of much of the genuine folklore and traditions of the very people whose sovereignty and cultural identity de Valera took it upon himself to personify. The gaiety, the earthiness, the humanity of the Irish folk imagination sits uneasily with the stereotype of Irish folk tradition that emerges from an examination of the pronouncements on the subject by the founder-leader of Fianna Fáil and the role he chose to adopt under its inspiration. There is a correspondence in this regard between the ideas of de Valera and those of Pope Pius XII who has been quoted as follows[25] on the subject of folklore:

> Folklore takes on its true meaning in correcting the errors of a society which ignores its healthiest and most fertile traditions. It strives to make it maintain a living continuity with the past, not a continuity imposed by outside forces, but one resulting from the profound feelings of generations, which have found in folklore the expression of their special aspirations, their beliefs, desires and sorrows, their glorious memories of the past and their hope for the

future . . . In Christian countries when the faith is strong, religious faith and the people's lives form a unity comparable to the unity of body and soul. Where such unity is still preserved, folklore is not merely a curious survival from the past ages; it is a manifestation of present-day life, which recognises its debt to the past and attempts to maintain itself and adapt itself intelligently to new situations. It preserves the people from cultural laziness which is a sign of the degeneration of the social organism.

These sentiments could well, it seems to me, have been those of de Valera himself, as, on occasion, indeed, his own pronouncements seemed appropriate to a Supreme Pontiff. In the Athlone broadcast to which reference has already been made, the following passage occurs:

The Irish genius has always stressed spiritual and intellectual rather than material values. That is the characteristic that fits the Irish people in a special manner for the task, now a vital one, of helping to save western civilisation. The great material progress of recent times, coming in a world where false philosophies already reigned, has distorted men's sense of proportion; the material has usurped the sovereignty that is the right of the spiritual. Everywhere today the consequences of this perversion of the natural order are to be seen. Spirit and mind have ceased to rule. The riches which the world sought, and to which it sacrificed all else, have become a curse by their very abundance.

Such statements offer little evidence of any great degree of enthusiasm for the fruits of economic development. They also lack any relish for the mundane involvement in the matter of sustaining life on the material and corporeal level that must be the primary and sustained task of the ordinary bearers of even the most magnificent of cultural traditions.

One may wonder as to the quivalent degree of fit between Ulster Unionist folk tradition and the mind and manner of Carson who in many respects stands in relation to that tradition as de Valera does to the Southern Nationalist one. It is interesting to note their co-occurrence as folk characters in the repertoire of a border community in Fermanagh where the two traditions co-exist. In his recent study of the folklore and history of the small Ulster community of Ballymenone, Henry Glassie gives the following two verses joining de Valera and Carson in a common frame:

> Sir Edward Carson had a cat
> it sat upon the fender;
> And every time he fed the cat,
> it cried out, No Surrender!

> De Valera had a cat,
>   he fed it on a plate;
> And every time he hit the cat,
>   it shouted, Up Free State!

Glassie's own commentary is as follows:

> The men make a mirrored pair. So do their cats who repeat party slogans when fed and symbolize the people who humbly and loyally surrender their human will to ideology.[26]

A folk proclivity as an element in the popular reaction to political leadership by a great public figure who touches on values commonly regarded as eternally indispensable by the plain people is not, it seems, to be regarded as the exclusive possession of the Southern Irish.

Summing Up:

Three separate aspects of the style and content of de Valera's leadership of both Fianna Fáil and Dublin governments during nearly three decades of power up to 1959 seem to be capable of being perceived together as a cluster of mutually reinforcing phenomena resistant to class consciousness and characteristic of a politics carried on at a definite remove from the pragmatic realities of the current moment. I hope that what I have been saying in this paper until now has made it clear both what these phenomena are and how they can be seen as being related in the way I propose. Listed together they comprise:

(a) de Valera's consciously indulged role as representative, at a symbolic level, of the sovereignty and cultural identity of the Irish people

(b) the stereotype underlying de Valera's and Fianna Fáil's vision of the nature and potential of Irish society

(c) an actual propensity in the popular imagination of the times to run in moulds deriving from a traditional universe of discourse rich in the materials of folk narrative

The combination of these led, it seems to me, to the establishment in most of Ireland of a style of politics in which the surface landscape of political decision-making and executive implementation was somehow of less moment than the formal way in which, beneath this landscape, the structure of political reality was reinforced.[27] Thus, in a sense, whatever *was* said and done out of the range of things that could possibly be said and done hardly mattered once the things that *were* said and done were the right things to *say* and *do*. And a majority of the Irish electorate quickly learned, from 1932 on, that it could depend entirely on de Valera and his party to say and do the *right* thing, whatever it actually was that, from day to day or budget to budget, they *actually* said and did.[28]

Today, three leaders later, a degree of structural rigidity
and a degree of abstraction from the realities of life as encountered and
experienced by people outside the party may appear to be still the lot of
Fianna Fáil in the aftermath of its charismatic founder. For many kinds
of reasons, saying and doing the right thing in today's politics means
something altogether different from what it meant prior to 1960. For
many better off and professional-class Catholics then of course, an
adherence to Catholic social principles was a fundamental criterion of
the 'rightness' in question. For many more, however, I feel, the issues of
sovereignty and identity were paramount. For most Irish people at that
time the leader of Fianna Fáil played the right note.[29] With the effective
passing of de Valera from the political scene after 1960 the clarity of the
signal faded.

Increasingly, in recent years, public debate and actual economic and
social development have opened up and called into question the foundations of political ground that was *terra firma* while de Valera ruled.
The Northern Question has not been the least of such issues, but any list
would include Health, Civil Liberty, Public Morality and the National
Aims in relation to topics as various as Language and the Ownership of
Wealth. The very heavy weather that Irish politicians at present make of
the business of deciding on and implementing constitutional and
legislative reform owes, I think, some part of its explanation to the continuing influence on the Irish political system of the ideology and practical style of the great figure who towered over it for so long. In particular
for the party he himself founded, difficulties persist in adapting the practise of politics to the circumstances of a world so different from that in
which de Valera's vision of our destinies seemed to so many to be of
universal significance.

NOTES

1. Maurice Moynihan (ed.), *Speeches and Statements by Eamon de Valera 1917-1973*
    (Dublin: 1980), 438.

2. Mary C. Bromage, *De Valera and the March of a Nation* (London: 1956), 266.

3. An interesting piece of evidence for de Valera's early closeness to those in Gaelic
    League circles who were most involved with folklore is provided by Ernest Blythe in
    the second volume of his memoirs (de Blaghd, 1970, pp 8, 9). Blythe met de Valera
    for the first time in 1914 in Dublin while he himself was in the course of a journey to
    Co. Kerry. De Valera was just then presenting himself as a candidate for a position
    in the Department of Mathematics at University College, Cork, and asked Blythe to
    take with him to Kerry a letter to An Seabhac (Pádraig Ó Siocfhradha) in which de
    Valera sought that Ó Siocfhradha should canvass on his behalf the Chairman of
    Kerry County Council, a member of the Governing Body of U.C.C. Ó Siocfhradha

was, of course, to be President of the Folklore of Ireland Society at its inception in 1927 and for many years afterwards. It is interesting also to record Blythe's impression of Ó Siocfhradha's dubiousness that the Chairman of the County Council could be induced to vote for the awarding of the position in question to an Irish speaker or, in Blythe's own term, a *Gaeilgeoir*.

4. Séamas Ó Duilearga (ed.), *Béaloideas*, 1(1927), 5.

5. T.K. Whitaker, 'James Hamilton Delargy, 1899-1980'. *Folk Life*, 20, (1982), 101-106.

6. Oliver MacDonagh, *Ireland: The Union and its Aftermath* (London: 1977), 158-160.

7. Moynihan (ed.), 35.

8. Daithi Ó hÓgáin, 'An É an tAm Fós É', *Béaloideas*, 42-44 (1976), 213ff.

9. For a very full account of messianism in Irish tradition see Breandán Ó Buachalla, 'An Mheisiasacht agus an Aisling' in Pádraig de Brún, Seán Ó Coileáin and Pádraig Ó Riain (eds.), *Folia Gadelica: Essays Presented to Professor R.A. Breatnach*, (Cork: 1983).

10. Denis R. Gwynn, 'De Valera, Eamon' in *Encyclopaedia Britannica*, 15th ed., Macropaedia, 5, 624.

11. MacDonagh, (1977), 113.

12. The use of the term 'folk society' in anthropology has to be distinguished from what folklore scholars might mean by the term. For anthropologists 'folk-society' had come to mean 'peasant-society' by the mid 1950s. Various implications and applications of the use of these terms in the social sciences are pursued in Potter *et al.* after a fashion that adheres fairly closely to the basic positions of Redfield and Foster. See Jack M. Potter, May N. Diaz and George M. Foster, *Peasant Society: A Reader* (Boston: 1967).

13. Moynihan (ed.), 154.

14. Tomás Ó Criomhthain, *An tOileánach* (Baile Átha Cliath: 1929).

15. In relation to folk models it should be noted that there is, in anthropology, a more technical sense of the term than is intended in my use of it in relation to de Valera's thinking on the nature and potential of Irish rural society. In that technical sense 'folk-model' means a model deriving from the native, practitioner point of view rather than the point of view of the outside observer. It is as descriptions of social reality based on the perceptions of participants that Redfield originally presented his Yucatan studies. Lévi-Strauss similarly distinguishes the 'statistical model' of the analyst of social structure from the 'mechanical model' of the participant. See Claude Lévi-Strauss, 'Social Structure' in Sol Tax (ed.), *Anthropology Today: Selections* (Chicago: 1962), 325. It could perhaps be argued that the model of Irish rural society dominating Fianna Fáil planning of the political economy during the years of de Valera's ascendancy was, by virtue of falling between these two stools, necessarily a poor instrument. Tom Garvin, 'Theory, Culture and Fianna Fáil: a Review' in Kelly, O'Dowd and Wickham (eds.), *Power, Conflict and Inequality* (Dublin: 1982), 177, points out that parallels between Fianna Fáil ideology and the arguments of functionalist anthropologists can suggest an 'organic' relationship between society and political formations that contrasts with the 'manipulative' relationship suggested, in the case of Fianna Fáil itself, by Peter Mair, 'The Autonomy of the Political: The Development of the Irish Party System'. *Comparative Politics*, 11, (1979), 445-465.

16. Kenneth Connell, *Irish Peasant Society* (Oxford: 1968).

17. Moynihan (ed.), 232.

18. Moynihan (ed.), 354.

19. Conrad Arensberg, *The Irish Countryman* (New York: 1937); Conrad Arensberg and Solon T. Kimball, *Family and Community in Ireland* (Cambridge Mass: 1940).

20. While the term 'Peasants' does occur in the index to Arensberg and Kimball's work, the full entry there against it reads: 'See "Farmers".'

21. George M. Foster, 'What is Folk Culture?', *American Anthropologist*, 55, (1953), 159-173;
George M. Foster, 'Peasant Society and the Image of the Limited Good', *American Anthropologist*, 67 (1965), 293-315;
Robert Redfield, *Tepoztlán: A Mexican Village. A Study of Folk Life* (Chicago: 1930);
Robert Redfield, 'The Folk Society', *The American Journal of Sociology*, 52, (1947), 293-308;
Robert Redfield, *Peasant Society and Culture: An Anthropological Approach to Civilisation* (Chicago: 1956).

22. A.L. Kroeber, *Anthropology* (New York: 1948), 284.

23. Moynihan (ed.), 1.

24. Moynihan (ed.), 471.

25. Seán Ó Súilleabháin, 'Irish Oral Tradition' in Brian Ó Cuív (ed.), *A View of the Irish Language* (Dublin: 1969), 56.

26. Henry Glassie, *Passing the Time: Folklore and History of an Ulster Community* (Dublin: 1982), 297.

27. It is, presumably, at least partly for its efficacy as reinforcement of this kind that folklore is taken as seriously as it is in most Eastern bloc countries. As Vitányi makes clear, there is, in Hungary at least, much cultural policy directed towards the preservation of authentic folk art — not in museums but as a catalyst among the youth of contemporary society who seek outlets for their own creativity. Folklore, with its content of humanism, its anonymous universality and its creativity is, in this light, to be regarded as existing in its own right as an aspect of contemporary urban culture that yields, in the view of the Hungarian establishment at least, an autonomus reinforcement for the value of collectivization. See Ivan Vitányi, 'The Function of Folklore in Modern Society', Typescript of contribution to the UNESCO Seminar on the 'Impact of Industrially Developed Societies on Traditional Culture and Popular Arts' held at The Institute for Culture, Budapest, 11-13 December 1978.

28. The continued existence of this style of thinking about political problems is provided by very recent press reports (*Irish Times*, 27 September, 1982, p. 1) of a Government minister having berated the leader of the opposition for allegedly withdrawing, in relation to a certain subject of current debate, from 'his solemn undertaking to support an amendment to the Constitution'. The Minister is quoted as having said that this alleged withdrawal not only indicated 'a tacit acceptance to provide a legislative framework which would allow legalised abortion in certain circumstances' but '*worse still*', (my italics) 'it indicates that the party has no feeling for the traditional values of the Irish people and is more concerned with being "fashionable" '.

29. This is true of the Irish living in Ireland. The degree to which de Valera had ever spoken for the Irish diaspora after 1922 is problematic. Whatever of the transient plausibility of the 'peasant' model at home there was surely an ever-increasing gap between the de Valera/Fianna Fáil vision of a free, Catholic and Gaelic-speaking Ireland — especially as regards the nature and quality of its social relationships — and the life experience of the vast majority of the overseas Irish. For the overseas Irish it is perhaps also the case that both de Valera's penchant for playing a mythological role and their own folk proclivities were of considerably less significance, and there was, of course, no genetic imperviousness to class consciousness on the part of 'the Irish race'. At home, however, Irish society and its intellectual and political leaders were still, in de Valera's day, prone to be resistant to the class realities of social structure in ways that certain very famous social thinkers have regarded as a deplorable form of mystification.

De Valera and Sovereignty: a Note on the Pedigree of a Political Idea

M.A.G. Ó Tuathaigh

The relationship between the 'national' and the 'social' question has been one of the most fertile sources of controversy in modern Irish history, and, indeed, in recent Irish historiography. The precise terms in which this relationship has been formulated have shown considerable variation. For example, one formulation centres on the competing claims (and prospects) of 'class' and 'community' as the key determinants of political and social cleavage in modern Ireland. The most direct formulation of the relationship, however, and the one with which we are mainly concerned here, is that which seeks to establish the connection between the constitutional status of Ireland and its economic and social well-being.

While in recent years this debate has, for obvious reasons, centred largely on the crisis in northern Ireland, this concentration has not been total by any means. The belated publication in 1977 of a version in English of Erhard Rumpf's *Nationalism and Socialism in Twentieth-century Ireland;* David Fitzpatrick's work on the geography of Irish nationalism, and more recent analyses of Irish nationalism by Tom Garvin and D.G. Boyce; these and other studies have been concerned, inter alia, with the relationship between the social and the national question.[1] But the most pointed discussion of this precise problem — at a theoretical as well as an empirical level — has emanated from a broadly Marxist group of historians and political scientists whose primary concern is the crisis in Northern Ireland.[2] The debate is, of course, much older than the crisis in Northern Ireland. In fact, the point of this short essay is to suggest that at the beginning of the twentieth century, in the period leading up to the establishment of the Irish Free State, there was something approaching a consensus among Irish nationalist leaders regarding the connection between constitutional status and economic conditions. We will try, with specific reference to de Valera, to indicate the historical pedigree of this consensus of ideas on the creative possibilities of political sovereignty. Finally, we will try to identify the point at which this consensus began to be undermined in the period of de Valera's political ascendancy.

From the eighteenth century, at least, Irish nationalist rhetoric, in both the Anglo-Irish and the Gaelic mode, had developed certain basic ideas about this connection between constitutional and economic conditions. Stated baldly, the central proposition was that only a self-governing Ireland — that is, one with an autonomous legislature — could effectively see to the economic progress and social harmony of the country. On the economic dimension, the contribution of the colonial nationalist writers is reasonably well-documented, particularly by Louis Cullen.[3] From Swift and Molyneaux to the remaining patriots in Grattan's parliament, the idea that legislative independence was a prerequisite for Irish economic progress was refined and restated again and again. In particular, the eighteenth century saw several concentrated bursts of polemical writing, linking economic problems to constitutional and political controversies. Thus, as Cullen has demonstrated, the 1720s and 1770s were both decades of economic crisis in Ireland, and in both decades there was a lively polemical literature and 'economic analysis' couched in predominantly political and constitutional terms.[4] In 1779 the clasic text appeared with Hely Hutchinson's *The Commercial Restraints of Ireland*, a work of considerable influence, not least on later generations of historians.

Less well-known, perhaps, than the colonial nationalist writings, is the Gaelic contribution to the nationalist consensus on the connection between constitutional and economic circumstances. This is not surprising: the Gaelic sources are accessible to fewer historians, and furthermore, are more problematic as sources, being part of a large corpus of popular literature, mostly in verse. It will not be possible here to do more than advert briefly to one important aspect of this Gaelic dimension.

Since the early seventeenth century one particular stream of Gaelic literature — the best known version of which is the '*aisling*' or dream-poem — spoke of cultural revolution coming as a result of military liberation and drastic political change in Ireland.[5] Again and again in these *aisling* poems the version of change/revolution — often couched in messianic or millennial terms — follows a standard sequence: a liberator will arrive, conquer the usurpers, and then put into effect a 'cultural revolution', the two constant elements of which were, firstly, the restoration of Gaelic learning in general and the poets in particular to a position of special favour, and, secondly, the suppression of protestantism and the restoration of catholicism to its 'former' position of glory, before persecution and the penal laws were used against it. Now, because military defeat and political subjugation had been accompanied during the conquest by religious discrimination, cultural displacement (the Gaelic language and institutions being eclipsed by the English) and economic confiscation (i.e. land), the pivotal sense of grievance which lies at the

heart of the Irish nationalist consciousness since the seventeenth century
has always contained a mixture (always uneasy, often incongruous,
sometimes lethal) of religious, political, economic and linguistic
elements. Accordingly, the revolutionary prophecy of the Irish *aisling*
poems tended to be complex and comprehensive.[6] This literary formula
— the revolutionary prophecy — survived the language change from
Irish to English from the late eighteenth century through the nineteenth;
except that the prophecy itself became increasingly sectarian in genuine
popular literature (e.g. street ballads and garlands etc.). In many of these
ballads 'Luther's and Calvin's breed' were threatened with extirpation,
but now without any saving grace of the hope of a revival in learning or
poetry.[7] We are not concerned here with the vexed question of whether
or not (and, if so, how far) this kind of popular prophecy literature
represented *real*, that is to say rational, political expectations.[8] What is
important, however, is the fact that a rather simple version of political
cause and cultural effect pervaded parts of Irish popular literature in both
languages by the late eighteenth and early nineteenth century.

What we would suggest, therefore, is that already by the end of the
eighteenth century there was available in Irish nationalist rhetoric —
albeit from very different sources — a version of political independence
as a key determinant (for some a guarantor) of economic prosperity and
social and cultural contentment. [It might also be added here that Orange
oppositon to the Act of Union is a further, if less obvious, manifestation
of this central idea.]

At any rate, nothing that occurred in Ireland under the Union undermined this basic proposition — the 'link' thesis — in the mainstream of
Irish nationalist thinking. Indeed the fact that in the aftermath of the
Union the contrast between an increasingly industrialized and expan-
sionist Britain and a relatively retarded (at least industrially) Ireland
became wider, served to focus nationalist propaganda on *the Union itself*
as the main source of this economic retardation, the main explanation for
the depressing contrast between the economic fortunes of the two
islands. The great famine, with its horrific mortality and the emigration
which accompanied and followed it, added a powerful emotional charge
to the nationalist case. This social catastrophe, so the argument went,
could never have happened had there been in existence an Irish parliament, responsive to the needs of Ireland and its people. [This, of course,
was the most moderate version of the nationalist charge of British
culpability for the famine; the most extreme version was Mitchel's
charge of genocide] .

The two main nationalist movements for legislative independence —
albeit of a limited nature — in nineteenth century Ireland shared some
basic assumptions on the economic and social implications of

constitutional demands. For example, Daniel O'Connell, though no analyst of economic problems, made the commercial and financial clauses of the Union a major propaganda issue during the Repeal campaign. Moreover, even during the period 1835-41 when he was in general support of the Whig ministers, O'Connell continued to insist that no Westminster-centred government, however well-disposed towards Ireland, could effect the same degree of economic progress and social contentment in Ireland as could a native Irish parliament.[9] The Home Rule case in the 1880s had an even sharper edge of economic grievance to its constitutional demands. This was due to the economic crisis of the late 1870s and early 1880s, which produced a fresh crop of polemical writings linking the constitutional status with the economic condition of Ireland. In 1881 Hely Hutchinson was quoted at length in Edmund Blackburne's pamphlet *Causes of the decadence of the industries of Ireland*. In 1882 and again in 1888 Hely Hutchinson's own work was reprinted twice. The nationalist case was further fuelled by the appearance in 1896 of the Report of the special Commission on Financial Relations, which (though based on questionable assumptions) seemed to bear out nationalist claims that Ireland had been overtaxed under the Union.[10]

It should be stated at this point that this link thesis within Irish nationalist orthodoxy, which we have been describing, was not without its doubting Thomases. The young, conservative, Fintan Lalor, for example, took some time to accept the necessity for political change as a precondition for economic improvement.[11]

More significantly, the internal debate and division in the Fenian ranks on the advisability of Fenian involvement in the 'land war' (so recently discussed by Bew and Moody), on the grounds that a 'satisfactory' solution of the land question might create a sufficient level of social harmony to undermine support for political autonomy for Ireland, is evidence of further doubts about aspects of the link thesis.[12] These were prepared to concede that, while Home Rule might not be killed by kindness, the demand for it might well be anaesthetized by comforts.[13]

The most important, and from the de Valera perspective the most relevant, formulation of the link argument at the end of the last century was, of course, the Sinn Féin programme of Arthur Griffith. Griffith's particular refinement of the argument was his assertion that national sovereignty was unimaginable without economic sovereignty, and that the most effective and appropriate form of economic sovereignty was self-sufficiency. An Ireland enjoying a large measure of political autonomy should be an economically self-sufficient Ireland. In this sense, Griffith was suggesting the precise economic policy through which an Irish state could create the promised land.[14]

Turning briefly to the notion of cultural independence, and its relationship with political independence, it has to be said that with the exception of Thomas Davis the cultural implications of 'national independence' attracted comparatively little attention from nationalist politicians and publicists up to the end of the nineteenth century.[15] The one major exception to this generalization is the issue of religious affiliation, and the religious dimension of cultural identity. In this area the evidence firmly indicates that Church leaders, and particularly the Catholic bishops, were very conscious of the implications of political autonomy for religious life and for more general cultural modes within a future Irish state.[16] In the secular domain there was a revival of the debate on 'cultural sovereignty' at the end of the nineteenth century, with D.P. Moran's Irish-Ireland propaganda, the founding of the Gaelic Athletic Association, the founding of the Gaelic League, and the Irish Literary Revival associated with Yeats, Lady Gregory and others.[17] The issues and views which divided these groups were, in many ways, as numerous and as substantial as those which they had in common. But they all, in their different ways, questioned or rejected the view that *political* independence should be the sole, over-riding concern of those interested in an independent national life for Ireland. This was not, of course, a rejection of the dynamic possibilities of political sovereignty; merely a warning that 'national independence' meant rather more than a local parliament in College Green. For nationalists, including many Home Rulers, active in the political or revolutionary movements of the period 1880-1912, the issue was one of priorities. Political independence was the precondition for intellectual renewal; or, as Justin McCarthy announced in 1890, once the political issue was resolved 'the minds of Irish men and women will begin to settle down, and the lecture halls, the studies and the studios will be opened again'.[18] Hyde's attempt to reject the link thesis, by insisting that the language revival movement remain apolitical, was ultimately defeated in 1915 (despite the prestige and affection which Hyde enjoyed within the Gaelic League), when in the historic Ard-Fheis of that year Pearse and the political activists persuaded the League to declare itself in favour of a 'free Ireland'.[19] Cultural independence could not be apolitical. For the politically conscious the achievement of political independence was the precondition for any more comprehensive 'national independence'. Even the revolutionary socialist, Connolly, through his participation in the 1916 rising, accepted the orthodox nationalist order of business; the connection with Britain would have to be broken as a first step in any fundamental national and social revolution in Ireland.

De Valera and those like him who had 'been to school' at the Gaelic League, and had become sharply politicized during 1910-1916, emerged under the banner of reconstructed Sinn Féin in 1917-18 as the power-brokers of the emerging Irish State. They all shared a strong belief in the creative possibilities of political sovereignty. De Valera's views in this regard were fairly conventional. There is no evidence that he had read particularly widely, or that there was any original streak in his thinking on the subject of national independence. He believed, in the first instance, that Ireland needed to be politically 'free' before economic and social problems could be handled in earnest, and, secondly, that economic progress and social harmony were the proper ends of the exercize of political sovereignty.[20] Many years later (in 1966) he summarized the dominant view of the Sinn Féin leaders of 1918:

> Political independence alone was not the ultimate goal. It was to be, rather, the enabling condition for the gradual building up of a community in which an ever-increasing number of its members, relieved from the level of exacting economic demands, would be free to devote themselves more and more to the cultivation of the things of the mind and spirit and, so, able to have the happiness of a full life. Our nation could then become again, as it was for centuries in the past, a great intellectual and missionary centre from which would go forth the satisfying truths of Divine Revelation, as well as the fruits of the ripest secular knowledge.[21]

Apart from the pervasive religiosity of tone, these views were not uniquely de Valera's; they were shared by many of the Sinn Féin élite who came to political prominence and power during 1917-21. Even the Irish Labour Party, through its voluntary withdrawal from the 1918 general election in order to allow the electorate to decide on the 'national' (i.e. constitutional) question, acknowledged the dominant nationalist orthodoxy on the primacy of constitutional status in determining other aspects of national life.[22]

In Dáil Éireann, from its earliest days, Sinn Féin deputies voiced their hopes and expectations of an independent Irish State. Here is an example from the Dáil debates of 21 January 1919:

> Tá ár dtír agus ár muintir le fada fé dhaorsmacht agus fé cheangal ár namhad. Táimídne inniu ag briseadh na gceangal agus ag cur na smachta ar neamhnidh, ach tá rian na gceangal agus na hannsmachta uirthi. Siad an obair agus an tráchtáil mór-chuislí na tíre. Insna cuislibh sin a théann fuil na tíre, an fhuil sin a thugann beatha agus sláinte dá corp agus spionadh dá h-anam. Táid siad san i leith na brúite agus na briste againn de bharr na h-annsmachta. Níl an rith ceart sa bhfuil agus dá bharr san tá atanna gránna ann anseo agus ansiúd ar chorp na tíre, sna cathracha, sna bailtí agus fén dtuaith féin. Comhartha dhúinne na hatanna san ar ghalar a raghaidh i méid agus a dhéanfaidh, b'fhéidir, ár dtír do mharú mara leighistear é. Má tá uainn ár dtír a mhaireachtaint agus a bheith beo i dteannta í d'fhuascailt caithfimíd í a shlánú. Deinimís é go cruinn agus go h-ealaíonta. Tuigimís go cruinn sa ghnó san cad is í ár dtír — an Éire seo a bhíonn mar thaidhreamh agus mar

thairgnearacht ag an uile dhuine dá clainn ó thús a óige. Tuigimís gurb í an tír seo í, álainn mar a dhein Dia í, saibhir le saothar a muintire, geal lena ngáire, aoibhinn lena meidhir, naofa lena gcreideamh agus a ndea-mhéin. Tuigimís gurb í an mhuintir seo againn ag maireachtaint go meidhreach agus go síochánta i measg an tsaibhris a bhronn Dia orthu agus á oibriú chun a gcothaithe é.[23]

Vintage de Valera, one might say; early intimations of the famous 1943 *aisling* of comely maidens and athletic youths. Quite so, except that the speaker was Richard Mulcahy. Again, on 10 April 1919, Eoin Mac Néill informed the Dáil as follows:

Tuigimíd an droch-staid ina bhfuil Éire; tá sí bochtaithe, brúite; tá gach aon ní goidte uainn le fada ag an namhaid agus an lá atá inniu ann tá an namhaid i bhfad níos measa nár mar bhí sé ariamh . . . . Caithfimíd troid ina aghaidh sin, caithfear saoirse do bheith i slí bheatha na ndaoine, chomh maith le saoirse sa stát; caithfeam saoirse do bheith againn chun ár n-earraí féin do chur thar lear . . . .[24]

This version, that Ireland had been beggared economically and culturally because of her political subjugation and that she would prosper under a native government, was the dominant view among political leaders on both sides of the Treaty debate in 1921-2. De Valera repeatedly returned to this theme of political independence being the 'enabling condition' for national reconstruction. Here, for example, is what he told the inaugural meeting of Fianna Fáil at the La Scala Theatre, Dublin, on 16 May 1926:

I think I am right also in believing that independence — political freedom — is regarded by most of you, as it is regarded by me, simply as a means to a greater end and purpose beyond it. The purpose beyond is the right use of our freedom, and that use must surely include making provision so that every man and woman in the country shall have the opportunity of living the fullest lives that God intended them to live.[25]

Six years later, during Fianna Fáil's first year in office, he re-affirmed this intention:

. . . I am sure that we are expressing the view of everyone here when I say that this organisation [Fianna Fáil] from its start pledged itself not merely to try to secure independence politically in this country, but to try and secure its economic dependence also.[26]

Of course, such statements must be understood in the immediate political context in which they were made, and with an eye to the immediate political purposes which they were meant to serve. But the frequency and consistency of these kind of statements, taken in conjunction with de

Valera's fairly conventional views on national independence, justify our taking them at face value.

With the establishment of the Free State in 1922 the nationalists who formed the Cumann na nGaedheal government now had an opportunity to test the validity of these assumptions regarding the creative possibilities of political sovereignty — even if there were limitations on that sovereignty. The early Cumann na nGaedheal governments did indeed attempt to construct a version of cultural autonomy — as it had been formulated during the preceding generation — by their policy for the revival of the Irish language as the vernacular of the people. On the economic front, the Cumann na nGaedheal ministers were not full-blooded Sinn Féiners; that is to say they did not pursue a policy of economic self-sufficiency. They adopted a modified Free Trade policy, with, for example, no curbs on the free flow of capital or labour. The basic patterns of Irish economic and social life were not drastically altered by the experience of native government during its first decade.

De Valera's criticism of the Free State ministers for their failure to bring about major economic and cultural change in the twenties was part of his general charge of apostasy against Cumann na nGaedheal: as they had tragically compromised political sovereignty (in supporting the Treaty) so also had they inevitably blighted those desirable economic and social consequences which *full* political sovereignty would produce. For their part, Cumann na nGaedheal spokesmen did not renounce their faith in the importance of constitutional status in determining economic and social progress; but the actual responsibilities of government, the influence of the civil service, and economic conditions in the outside world, all combined to set limits to what the government felt could be done.[27] More and more, ministers began to use the language of 'realism' and 'practical considerations' (of geography and economic logic) to explain the limited nature of the changes being sought by government policy. De Valera denounced this kind of language as being nothing more than a device to explain away lack of courage and enterprise in confronting such crucial problems as rural depopulation, industrial retardation, emigration and unemployment. Speaking in the Dáil in July 1928 he denounced the Cumann na nGaedheal government for introducing into the country 'the spirit of cynicism . . . . It is that cynicism, that callous sort of effort, which is withering up everything — you can see it here in the Dáil. Sneers follow any attempt to build up a really constructive way. When any suggestion in that direction is mentioned, you get the withering sarcasm of the people who call themselves realists. The fact is that they are only narrow materialists, and they are not good materialists at that. Fundamentally they are only so-called realists.'[28]

Well, in 1932 Fianna Fáil and de Valera were in power; the opportunity was now at hand to banish sneers, narrow materialism and so-called realism, and to let idealistic 'construction' have its head. In a world economy sunk in depression (with Protection being resorted to by all trading States), [Fianna Fáil pursued a policy of full-blooded protectionism, intensified by a tariff 'war' with Britain over the withholding of the land annuities, throughout most of the nineteen-thirties. The drive for cultural autonomy was intensified, through new schemes and fresh exhortations for the Irish language revival.]

[The constitutional changes which culminated in the 1937 Constitution effectively gave 'full' political sovereignty to the twenty-six county State.] And yet social and economic miracles did not happen, at least not in the way in which de Valera had seemed to imagine or to expect that they would. In cultural terms progress on the language revival policy was disappointingly limited. Indeed, the most salient manifestation of cultural autonomy as a consequence of political autonomy was the extent to which the dominant Catholic ethos of the majority population in the new Irish state was given concrete expression in legislation and in the Constitution.

In economic and social life, industrialization did indeed take place during the thirties, and social welfare initiatives (including improved housing) testified to the compassionate energy of the government. But the great leap forward did not materialize. Emigration and rural depopulation were not halted. The link with sterling was maintained. The free flow of capital and labour between Ireland and Britain was not interfered with. Full-blooded protectionism (the classic economic Sinn Féinism) was being strongly diluted by the late thirties. Between the Coal-Cattle pact of 1936 and the Anglo-Irish agreement of 1938 Ireland's trade pattern was returning to 'normal'; that is to say the economy of the Irish state was being re-integrated into the larger trading economy of the neighbouring state. In short, by the late thirties, as de Valera's and Fianna Fáil's radical reforming energies seemed already close to exhaustion, there might seem to have been ample evidence for a revaluation of the 'link' thesis. Did political sovereignty produce or guarantee economic progress and social contentment? Or, more specifically, did political sovereignty enable a government to achieve certain specific economic and social targets to which it was committed and which enjoyed popular support?

Of course, these questions had frequently been raised by individuals and by minority groups (of the right and left) since the foundation of the Free State. By the late thirties it was inevitable that they would be asked, both of and within Fianna Fáil. Lemass's misgivings on aspects of the protectionist policy and the founding of Clann na Talmhan in 1938 represented, in very different ways, early signs of doubt on the socio-economic consequences of Fianna Fáil's exercise of political sovereign-ty.[29] In this context it is certainly arguable that the war came at an oppor-tune moment for the political fortunes of de Valera. Assuming the mantle of national leader in a time of national emergency greatly increased de Valera's political stock, and muffled or postponed criticism of his 'record' on social and economic progress during the thirties. But in the post-war years doubts and dissension began to re-emerge. Economic crises and social dislocation in the fifties were accompanied by unusual instability in party politics. In particular, the rise of Clann na Poblachta — drawing substantial support from Fianna Fáil defectors — raised basic questions on the *raison d'être* of a sovereign Irish state. But the point of Clann na Poblachta's criticism of the growing conservatism of Fianna Fáil was its claim that de Valera's party was failing (or had failed) to do the necessary social and economic tasks which were the proper end of the exercise of political sovereignty.[30] In short, up to the fifties it was for failing to realize expectations relating to the exercise of political sovereignty rather than for the assumptions on which these expectations were based that Fianna Fáil was mainly criticised.

The question inevitably arises, did de Valera himself ever come to question either his assumptions or his achievements? The evidence here is unsatisfactory. On the one hand there are a few tantalisingly brief com-ments which give some indication of second thoughts. For example, in November 1951, de Valera, replying in the Dáil to a suggestion regarding the use of external assets, warned against seeking simplistic remedies to complex questions, and concluded, somewhat resignedly:

> It is only necessary to think that out, not merely to talk in phrases and to ac-cept them as formulae, to see that things expressed in phrases like that are funamentally untrue. There are certain things you can do and things you can-not do. The truth is that, in the long run, the amount you can do is not very much. I have been a long time studying these matters.[31]

On the other hand, however, in all major public speeches up to his retirement from active politics in 1959, de Valera gave little evidence of any serious misgivings on the way in which political sovereignty within the twenty-six county state had been exercised since 1937.[32]

It was only with de Valera's departure from active politics, and his suc-cession by Sean Lemass, that a new rhetoric of economic and social endeavour began to dominate the vocabulary of political debate in Ireland.[33] [Lemass's economic strategy of the sixties had enormous im-plications for the concept of sovereignty in Ireland — foreign investment and international trade, with their implications for foreign policy; developments in mass communications and their consequences for cultural patterns within Ireland.] These implications, which lie outside the scope of this paper, have only recently begun to attract serious, scholarly attention and discussion. The context within which this re-appraisal will continue in the immediate future is likely to be shaped to a considerable extent by the impact of the conflict in Northern Ireland on Irish society as a whole, and in particular on the versions of the concept of sovereignty which are in circulation within that society.

NOTES

1. E. Rumpf and A.C. Hepburn, *Nationalism and Socialism in twentieth-century Ireland* (Liverpool: 1977); David Fitzpatrick, *Politics and Irish life, 1913-21* (Dublin: 1977); Fitzpatrick, 'The geography of Irish nationalism 1910-21, in *Past and Present,* **78** (1978), 112-44; D.G. Boyce, *Nationalism in Ireland* (London and Dublin: 1982); Tom Garvin, *The Evolution of Irish Nationalist politics* (Dublin: 1982).

2. Austen Morgan and Bob Purdie (eds.), *Ireland: Divided Nation, Divided Class* (London: 1980) contains articles (and references to other works) by many of the participants in this debate.

3. See the essays by Cullen (and works cited therein) in L.M. Cullen (ed.), *The formation of the Irish Economy* (Cork: 1969).

4. Cullen (ed.), (1969), 116-120.

5. A recent analysis of some of this material is Breandán Ó Buachalla's study of the aisling in P. de Brún, S. Ó Coileáin and P. Ó Riain (eds.), *Folia Gadelica* (Cork: 1983), 72-87

6. The writer hopes to explore this theme at greater length in another place.

7. See, for example, G.D. Zimmermann, *Irish Political Street Ballads and Rebel Songs* (Geneva: 1966).

8. See Ó Buachalla, article cited above. Also the introductory chapter to Seán Ó Faoláin's *King of the Beggars* (Dublin: 1970 edition).

9. A. MacIntyre, *The Liberator: Daniel O'Connell and the Irish Party, 1830-1847* (London: 1965).

10. Cullen (ed.), (1969), 120.

11. See, for example, T.P. O'Neill, 'James Fintan Lalor', in J.W. Boyle (ed.), *Leaders and Workers* (Cork: n.d.).

12. Paul Bew, *Land and the National Question in Ireland 1858-82* (Dublin: 1978); T.W. Moody, *Davitt and Irish Revolution 1846-82* (Oxford: 1981).

13. On similar misgivings among Home Rulers see F.S.L. Lyons, *John Dillon: A biography* (London: 1968).

14. For Griffith, see R.P. Davis, *Arthur Griffith and Non-Violent Sinn Fein* (Dublin: 1974).

15. This is notwithstanding the links between some Fenians and the cultivation of the Irish language.

16. Emmet Larkin, *The Roman Catholic Church and the Creation of the Modern Irish State, 1878-86* (Philadelphia and Dublin: 1975).

17. For a recent somewhat over-schematized account of social and cultural movements in this period see F.S.L. Lyons, *Culture and Anarchy in Ireland, 1890-1939* (Oxford: 1979).

18. Cited in Boyce, (1982), 232.

19. Seán Ó Tuama (editor), *The Gaelic League Idea* (Cork: 1972), 31-40.

20. For a survey of the recent literature on the background to the establishment of the Free State see this writer's 'Ireland: 1800-1921', in Joseph Lee (ed.), *Irish Historiography 1970-79* (Cork: 1981), 94-97.

21. Maurice Moynihan (ed.), *Speeches and Statements by Eamon de Valera 1917-1973* (Dublin and New York: 1980), 606.

22. Arthur Mitchell, *Labour in Irish Politics 1890-1930* (Dublin: 1974), 78-170; B. Farrell, *The Founding of Dáil Éireann* (Dublin: 1971).

23. *Dáil Éireann, Miontuairisc an Chéad Dála*, 21 January 1919, 23-4.

24. *ibid.*, 10 April 1919, 53.

25. Moynihan, (ed.), 140.

26. Moynihan, (ed.), 227.

27. For the influence of the civil service see Ronan Fanning, *The Irish Department of Finance 1922-58* (Dublin: 1976). For an insight into the 'official mind' of Cumann na nGaedheal see James Meenan, *George O'Brien: A Biographical Memoir* (Dublin: 1980).

28. Moynihan (ed.), 159.

29. On Lemass see J.J. Lee, 'Sean Lemass', in J.J. Lee (ed.), *Ireland 1945-70* (Dublin: 1979). Also Lee's unpublished paper, *Economic strategy in the 1930s* delivered at University College, Galway, in April 1982.

30. There is as yet no full scale study of Clann na Poblachta. But see the perceptive comments in Rumpf and Hepburn, (1977), 146, 1523, 185, 217, 219, 233. Also, Michael Gallagher, *Electoral Support for Irish Political Parties 1927-73* (London: 1976).

31. Moynihan (ed.), 556.

32. See, for example, Moynihan (ed.), 570, (May 1954).

33. See Frank Litton (ed.), *Unequal Achievement: The Irish Experience 1957-1982* (Dublin: 1982).

Eamon de Valera and
the Partition Question

T. Ryle Dwyer

Prior to the establishment of Dáil Éireann Eamon de Valera seemed to have some rather definite views on the Ulster question. His message to the Unionists was that they should abandon their allegiance to Britain, or 'we will kick you out'.[1] While speaking in County Down in early 1918 he actually described the Unonists as a 'rock on the road' to Irish freedom before adding rather ominously, 'we must, if necessary, blast it out of our path'.[2]

There was no indication he had changed his thinking before going to the United States on his eighteen month tour in 1919, but he showed a distinct softening of attitude upon his return. By then, of course, the Government of Ireland Act of 1920, which was more popularly known as the Partition Act, had already become law. The Sinn Féin regime in Dublin had refused to recognise the partition resulting from the act, yet de Valera revealed a willingness to accept a form of partition.

'There is plenty of room in Ireland for partition, real partition, and plenty of it', he explained to a correspondent of the Manchester *Guardian* in February 1921. De Valera went on to suggest that the whole island be parcelled up into administrative units which could be associated in a confederation like Switzerland: 'If Belfast — or for that matter, all Carsonia as a unit — were a Swiss Canton like Berne, Geneva, or Zurich, it would have more control over its own affairs, economic, social, and political, than it is given by the Westminster Partition Act. The real objection to that Act — prescinding from the question of its moral and political validity — is that it does not give Belfast and Ulster enough local liberty and power. In an Irish confederation they ought to get far more.'[3]

Even though he had obviously given some consideration to the various forms of government, he proceeded in terms which suggested he really did not understand the difference between federal and confederate forms of government, seeing that he used the two terms interchangeably. In 'this federal system, whether dominion or republic', he explained immediately after referring to the Swiss model, there could be a bicameral federal parliament consisting of a national council elected in accordance with population, and a council of counties consisting of two deputies per county. 'This Federal Assembly would deal only with such questions as concern Ireland as a whole (railways, customs, foreign relations, etc.), but owing to the autonomy of the counties would raise only a small Federal revenue — that of Switzerland is only about three millions. Moreover, the people of Ireland, and not this federal assembly would be sovereign.'[4] He proposed that eight counties, or 30,000 voters, could insist on any act being submitted to a direct vote of the people for ratification, and that about 50,000 people should be able to demand a referendum on proposals which, if accepted, would become law without ever passing through the parliament.

That de Valera ever suggested a federation or confederation seemed to indicate a recognition that Northern Protestants had genuine fears of Irish unity. Yet there was little evidence he really appreciated the intensity of their feelings, because the outlined provisions for referenda would obviously undermine the sectional rights supposedly being protected in the federal or confederate system. As a result the proposal would not afford the minority any real guarantee against discrimination.

De Valera, as President of the Irish Republic, revealed a rather shallow perception of the depth of the Ulster problem, which he seemed to think could be resolved by a combination of economic incentives and economic pressure. For example, he advocated seeking favourable trade terms from the Soviet Union 'so as to use them as a lever to bring portions of the North — "Ulster" — to the side of the Republic'.[5] At the same time he made it clear he was ready to support — and even intensify — a boycott of goods produced in Belfast in an attempt to force the Six Counties to agree to Irish unity. This, of course, probably only intensified the fears of Northerners by providing concrete proof of the kinds of discriminatory pressure the southern majority could exert. His stance on the boycott issue seemed to typify a superficial view of Unionist intransigence as something which would crumble under economic pressure from the rest of the island.

'When the elections come', de Valera predicted in March 1921, 'they will prove that industrial Ulster is not so blind to its own interests as to court being severed from its great market in the agricultural areas in the rest of the island. The boycott of Belfast goods which is now operating is but the opening stage of what will become a complete and absolute exclusion of Belfast goods in the Partition Act is put into effect.'[6]

Once partition was effectively established with the King's opening of the Stormont Parliament in June 1921, the British launched their peace initiative which eventually led to the signing of the Anglo-Irish Treaty some months later. At first Prime Minister Lloyd George hoped to set up a tripartite conference between representatives from Britain, Northern Ireland, and the Twenty-six Counties, but de Valera refused to partake in such talks because he was afraid Britain would exploit the differences between the Irish factions to blame the inevitable failure of the conference on them. Nevertheless he went over to London for some private meetings with Lloyd George in July 1921 to explore the grounds for a conference. In the midst of these discussions the British formally offered to confer a limited form of dominion status on the Twenty-six Counties while insisting that Northern Ireland's status could not be changed without her own consent.

In his formal reply on 10 August 1921 de Valera wrote that his government would agree to 'a certain treaty of free association with the British Commonwealth group . . . had we an assurance that the entry of the nation as a whole in such an association would secure it the allegiance of the present dissenting minority, to meet whose sentiments alone this step could be contemplated'. He added that if the British would stand aside, the Irish factions would settle partition between themselves peacefully. 'We agree with you', he wrote, ' "that no common action can be secured by force".'

This was a highly significant assurance in the light of views expressed earlier by de Valera. Back in 1918 he had concluded that Britain had undermined the Irish Convention by assuring Ulster Unionists that they could not be coerced. They then exploited the assurance to insist on having their own way. Thus when the nationalists balked, the Convention inevitably ended in failure. 'It was evident to us', de Valera wrote at the time, 'that with the "coercion-of-Ulster is unthinkable" guarantee, the Unionists would solidly maintain their original position.'[7] Consequently when he gave the British a similar assurance himself in August 1921, he must have realised that any overall settlement might have to include partition.

De Valera actually told a private session of the Dáil a fortnight later that, if Britain would recognise the Irish Republic, he 'would be in favour of giving each county power to vote itself out of the Republic if it so wished'.[8] The only alternative would be to coerce the Unionists, and he warned his colleagues that if they tried such coercion, they would be making the same mistake with the majority in Northern Ireland that the British had made with the rest of the island.

In the ensuing negotiations Britain basically met de Valera's demand that she stand aside and allow the Irish factions to settle partition amicably between themselves. The British delegation signed the Anglo-Irish Treaty with representatives of the Dáil on behalf of the whole thirty-two counties of Ireland without even consulting the representatives of Northern Ireland. As such the Treaty was a British betrayal of Northern Unionists, but the latter's interests were protected by a provision which would allow them to withdraw from the new Irish state within one month. In that event, however, the Treaty stipulated a

Boundary Commission would be set to redraw the border 'in accordance with the wishes of the inhabitants, so far as may be compatible with economic and geographic conditions'.

Although de Valera was bitterly critical of the Treaty, he basically supported its provisions regarding Northern Ireland. This became evident when he presented a private session of the Dail with Document No. 2, which was his own proposed alternative to the Treaty. The Ulster clauses in this alternative were prefaced with the declaration that 'without recognising the right of any part of Ireland to be excluded from the supreme authority of the national Parliament and Government' the Dáil would nevertheless accept the Treaty's partition clauses 'in sincere regard for internal peace, and in the desire to bring no force or coercion to bear upon any substantial part of the province of Ulster'. The relevant clauses of the Treaty were then included in Document No. 2 practically verbatim.

'We don't recognise the right of any part of Ireland to secede, still for the sake of so and so we are willing to accept it', he told the Dáil on the first day of the Treaty debate.[9] 'The difficulty is not the Ulster question. As far as we are concerned this is a fight between Ireland and England. I want to eliminate the Ulster question out of it.'[10] He was therefore ready to agree to the Treaty's provisions concerning Northern Ireland even though he found them objectionable from the standpoint that they provided 'an explicit recognition of the right on the part of Irishmen to secede from Ireland'.[11]

'We will take the same things as agreed on there', de Valera explained, 'Let us not start to fight with Ulster. Let us accept that, but put in a declaratory phrase which will safeguard our right.'[12] In short, he was ready to accept Northern Ireland's secession but was anxious to give the public impression that he was not formally acknowledging what he was in fact accepting.

During the public debate in the Dáil, de Valera never even alluded to the partition question. And when he released Document No. 2 to the press he omitted the six clauses relating to the Ulster problem and replaced them with an addendum stipulating that the Six Counties would be granted 'privileges and safeguards not less substantial than those provided for' in the Treaty. The partition question really played no part in his objections to the Treaty. Indeed, in the midst of the civil war he acknowledged, in effect, that there would be a better chance of ending partition while the Treaty was operative than if it were replaced by Document No. 2. Even though he planned to act as if his alternative were the Treaty, he nevertheless acknowledged, for instance, that 'whilst the Free State were in supposed existence would be the best time to secure the unity of the country'.[13]

Having virtually ignored the partition question during the Treaty debate, de Valera began to raise the issue with increasing emphasis following the civil war. He contended the Irish people really did not understand that they had been deceived by the promise of a revision of the border in line with the Boundary Commission, but he publicly predicted they would soon realise what had happened once 'the boundary clause has been waived, or some new ignominious bargain has been struck to evade it'.[14] Behind closed doors he was even more specific. On 7 August 1924 he told Republican colleagues 'the clause about the Boundary Commission was a ridiculous clause. It was meant to fool and could be used at any time to get out of anything on the grounds that the taking away of portion of the Six Counties might be uneconomical.'[15] This was indeed what actually happened little over a year later.

In the interim de Valera continued to denounce partition in general terms in his public addresses. Speaking in Ennis on 15 August 1924, for instance, he emphasised there would be no question 'of any possible assent by us to the dismemberment of our country. You cannot have a sovereign Ireland if you have an Ireland cut in two.'[16] In Dundalk the following week he explained he was refusing to sit in Leinster House because it was a partition parliament, which was obviously a disingenuous explanation, seeing that he had already declared privately that if the Treaty-oath were removed, the question of entering the Free State Dáil 'would be a matter purely of tactics and expediency'.[17] Nevertheless he acted publicly as if he were abstaining on the principle that taking his seat would amount to a formal recognition of partition.

When Northern elections were called for the autumn of 1924 de Valera announced that Sinn Féin would put forward candidates so the people in the area could demonstrate 'their detestation' of partition. He even defended the seat he had won himself in south Down in May 1921, but when he went to speak in Newry he was arrested, served with an exclusion order, and put back over the border. The following day he ignored the order and crossed the border to speak in Derry, but he was again arrested, taken to Belfast, and sentenced to a month in Crumlin Road Jail after he had refused to recognise the court.

The publicity generated by his actions helped to create the mistaken impression that the partition issue had been a major consideration in his opposition to the Treaty. Indeed this impression would eventually become quite widespread. He therefore benefited politically from the backlash that followed after the Boundary Commission decided against transferring the contiguous nationalist areas of the Six Counties on the grounds that to do so would render Northern Ireland an uneconomical unit and would thus violate the provision of the Treaty stipulating that transfers should be in line with economic and geographic considerations.

The decision seemed a travesty of justice. The Six Counties had not originally been chosen as a historic region, but simply as the largest area in which the Unionists would have a safe majority. This was done with blatant disregard for the fact that two of those counties actually had nationalist majorities, as had most of the areas that were contiguous to the Twenty-six Counties. In fact, the nationalists formed a relatively greater minority in the partitioned area than the Unionists were in the island as a whole. Hence if the British really believed the Unionists had a right to partition by virtue of their numbers, then the nationalists in the Six Counties had an even greater right to withdraw from Northern Ireland.

De Valera was therefore bitterly critical that nationalist areas were being abandoned to Orange domination. 'To my mind, he declared, 'to abandon these communities for any consideration whatever is not merely an act of unpardonable injustice but a national disgrace'.[18]

With Sinn Féin still refusing to sit in the Free State Dáil, de Valera and his colleagues could only denounce the agreement scrapping the Boundary Commission. Some members wanted to take their seats in an attempt to prevent ratification of the agreement, but a majority decided against the move. There soon developed a split within Sinn Féin over the issue of sitting in Leinster House. This led to de Valera's resignation from the party and the founding of Fianna Fáil.

At the inaugural meeting of Fianna Fáil on 26 May 1926 he explained his aim was to sever the Free State's constitutional ties with Britain 'one by one until the full internal sovereignty of the Twenty-six Counties was established beyond question'. Then, he said, 'the position would be reached in which the solution of the problems of successfully bringing in the North could be confidently undertaken'.[19]

In his broadcast following the Fianna Fáil election success of 1932 it was significant that de Valera only referred to partition after first dealing with unemployment, the oath, and land annuities.[20] For the next few years he tended to play down the partition question while he concentrated on other matters. He told the Dáil on 1 March 1933, for instance, that 'the only policy' which was practical for ending partition was to secure for 'the people in this part of Ireland such conditions as will make the people in the other part of Ireland wish to belong to this part'. He reiterated the same theme the following November at the Fianna Fáil Ard Fheis. Partition could not be ended by force, he said. 'The only way it can be solved,' he added, 'is by having a livelihood for our people down here which will be the envy of the people in the North and make them see that their future lies with their own people and not with strangers'.[21]

Having unilaterally dismantled as much of the 1921 Treaty as he could by late 1937, de Valera initiated negotiations with the British on the remaining differences between the two countries. He went to London in January 1938 for formal talks, which were to drag on intermittently for the next three months. During the discussions he stressed the importance of ending partition. If the British would help bring about Irish unity, he convinced tham he would satisfy their security needs by providing them with any facilities they might need in wartime.

But Neville Chamberlain, the British Prime Minister, contended his hands were tied. He admitted partition was an anachronism but added he could do nothing about it because the British public would not stand for coercing the majority in Northern Ireland. Consequently he suggested Dublin should try to win over the Northern majority gradually by extending the hand of co-operation across the border.

The British, who were anxious for better Anglo-Irish relations, were prepared to abandon their Treaty rights to Irish facilities and also to drop their claim for the controversial land annuities. But in return Chamberlain initially insisted the Twenty-six Counties should give preferential treatment to imports from Northern Ireland. This de Valera resolutely refused to do. The talks might actually have collapsed on this issue had the British not backed down following the intervention of President Franklin D. Roosevelt, who let it be known that he believed an Anglo-Irish agreement would open the way for closer Anglo-American relations.

In explaining the benefits of the Anglo-Irish agreements, which were formally concluded in April 1938, de Valera declared that all the outstanding issues between Britain and Ireland had been settled with the exception of partition. 'The whole Irish race can now concentrate on that one', he added.[22]

The question of national minorities soon took on a major international significance when Hitler demanded that the Sudetenland of Czechoslovakia with its large German population be handed over to Germany. De Valera, who had years earlier criticized the cynical manner in which the treaties drawn up following the First World War had divided up territory without regard to the wishes of the inhabitants, viewed the Sudeten crisis as a logical consequence of the earlier mistakes. He was convinced there was justice in Hitler's claim to the Sudetenland, which he equated with his own claim to Northern Ireland. While in London on his way to Geneva, where he would shortly be elected President of the Assembly of the League of Nations, de Valera told Sir Thomas Inskip, the British Attorney General, that the Dublin government had its 'own Sudetens in Northern Ireland' and he sometimes considered 'the possibility of going over the boundary and pegging out the territory, just as Hitler was doing'.[23]

Under the circumstances it was not surprising the Irish leader vociferously supported the appeasement of Hitler on the Sudeten question. On the evening after the ill-fated Munich Agreement was signed, de Valera addressed the Assembly of the League of Nations in his capacity as its President. He emphasised that the organization should tackle the unresolved issues which were leading to repeated international crises. In particular, he said that an attempt should be made to settle the problems of national minorities. 'We have seen the danger we run by leaving these problems unresolved', he said.[24]

On his way home de Valera called on Chamberlain in London and pleaded with him to end partition on the lines of the Munich settlement. But Chamberlain again replied his hands were tied.

Believing the Prime Minister's unwillingness to act boldly on the partition issue was prompted by a lack of popular support in Britain, de Valera set out to whip up the necessary public approval. On 13 October 1938 he gave a widely publicised interview to a correspondent of the London *Evening Standard* in which he held out the possibility of concluding an alliance with Britain in return for the ending of partition. Of course, this had been his approach during the Anglo-Irish talks earlier in the year, but this time he talked about it publicly. It was possible, he said, 'to visualise a critical situation arising in the future in which a united free Ireland would be willing to co-operate with Britain to resist a common attack'. If the British would only convert the Unionists in Northern Ireland to the idea of Irish unity on fair terms, then the Irish people would feel they had something worth fighting for. But if partition still existed at the outbreak of another war, he warned that co-operation would then be impossible because of opinion in Ireland. 'No Irish leader will ever be able to get the Irish people to co-operate with great Britain while partition remains', he explained. 'I wouldn't attempt it myself, for I know I should fail.'[25]

Emphasising that he wanted to see Irish unity brought about early enough so it would be securely established before the outbreak of another major war, the Taoiseach reiterated his willingness to compromise with the Northern majority. 'Keep your local parliament with its local power if you wish', was his message to them. 'The Government of Éire asks for only two things of you. There must be adequate safeguards that the ordinary rights of the nationalist minority in your area shall not be denied them, as at present, and that the powers at present reserved to the English Parliament shall be transferred to the all-Ireland Parliament.'[26]

At the Fianna Fáil Ard Fheis a few weeks later de Valera announced he was asking the American Association for Recogniton of the Irish Republic and two ethnic Irish-American newspapers, the New York *Irish World* and San Francisco *Leader*, to help 'in making known to the American public the nature of partition and the wrong done by it to the

Irish nation'.[27] John Cudahy, the American Minister in Dublin, had no doubt de Valera was embarking on an overall plan to marshall Irish-Americans as a force to exert pressure for Irish unity.

The Taoiseach told Cudahy the Munich settlement was an indication that orderly international negotiations were — if not dead — at least in moribund abeyence, so he wanted Ireland to put her own house in order. In effect, he was staking his claim for the nationalist areas of the Six counties, just as Hitler had done with the Sudetenland. De Valera proposed, for example, that a plebiscite should 'be conducted by voting units in rural and urban districts which alone would reveal the sentiments of Northern Ireland as a whole'.[28]

Speaking in the Seanad on 7 February 1939 he said he would use force to secure Irish unity, if he thought it would be successful. 'I am not a pacifist by any means', the Taoiseach explained, 'I would, if I could see a way of doing it effectively, rescue the people of Tyrone and Fermanagh, south Down, south Armagh, and Derry City from the coercion which they are suffering at the present time, because I believe that, if there is to be no coercion that ought to apply all round'. He added there was 'not the slightest doubt about it that if there were not British military forces in those areas, those people would move to come in with us, and we would certainly take them.'

During the speech de Valera explained that he had not asked the British to coerce the Six Counties, because he believed members of the British government would like to see Irish unity but felt unable to do anything about it because the majority in Northern Ireland obviously wanted partition, with the result that the British people would not tolerate efforts to compel the North to sever her ties with Britain. His policy, therefore, was simply 'to instruct the British people'. He was not asking them 'to do anything in the way of coercing those in the North-East who do not want to come in with us but to cease actively encouraging that section to keep out'. He had no apologies for using propaganda because, he said, if force were to be ruled out, then it was necessary to use propaganda 'to appeal to common sense and to good will'.[29]

'We have tried to inform our people', he added, 'not merely here, but our own people throughout the world wherever they might be, wherever they might have a voice, and wherever they could bring their influence to bear'. The real bar to unity was the favour the British were bestowing on Northern Ireland which, he contended, had the affect of preventing the working of 'the ordinary natural laws' that would bring the two Irish communities together. 'What is the use in our holding out attractions to them if, when we offer something, twice as much is offered by the people who are competing'.[30]

De Valera certainly had a good case in calling for the transfer of the contiguous nationalist areas. There was no valid moral justification for compelling those areas to remain within Northern Ireland. Observing that the boundary ought to be revised, one senator asked if the Taoiseach had ever requested the British to transfer the contiguous nationalist areas.

'I have not', de Valera replied, 'because I think the time has come when we ought to do the thing properly. That would only be a half-measure.'[31] In other words he was looking for the whole of the Six Counties or nothing and was apparently making an issue of the possible transfer of nationalist areas only for propaganda purposes.

He had already declared on numerous occasions that he was ruling out the use of force because it would not be effective while the majority in Northern Ireland wanted partition, but he proceeded to make no real effort to win over the Northern majority. In fact, Seán Ó Faoláin contended in a 1939 biography of de Valera that the Dublin government had been effectively promoting partition 'by refusing to demonstrate a practical spirit of tolerance and broad-mindedness'.[32]

Before Fianna Fáil came to power in 1932 there was discrimination in the Twenty-six Counties against Protestant values in such matters as divorce, birth control, and censorship. De Valera himself had actually become involved in a celebrated incident in 1931 when, as Leader of the Opposition, he supported people in County Mayo who were demanding the removal of a librarian on the grounds that she was a Protestant. Believing that the post could be considered as being of an educational nature, de Valera contended that the people of Mayo, who were overwhelmingly Roman Catholic, were 'justified in insisting upon a Catholic librarian'. He then went on to declare that when it came to serving Catholic communities in medical or educational matters, Catholic applicants should be preferred over Protestants. 'If I had a vote on a local body', he said, 'and if there were two qualified people who had to deal with a Catholic community, and if one was a Catholic and the other a Protestant, I would unhesitatingly vote for the Catholic'.[33] If that statement were taken to its logical conclusion, it would have meant the effective barring of Protestants from many positions in the Twenty-six Counties.

After gaining power de Valera and his colleagues often made the mistake of implying that 'the only true Irishmen were Catholics', but in fairness to him, it should be noted that he 'did not act on the doctrines which he had propounded in the Mayo library debate'.[34] In fact, he was instrumental in having the founder of the Gaelic League, Douglas Hyde, who happened to be a Protestant, selected as the first President under the 1937 constitution.

Even though Fianna Fáil had not instituted the discrimination against

Protestant values, de Valera's government did intensify that discrimination by extending a ban on the advertising of contraceptives to their sale and importation. In addition, divorce — hitherto illegal — was made unconstitutional in the new constitution of 1937, which not only closely reflected Roman Catholic social teaching but also acknowledged 'the special position of the Roman Catholic Church as the guardian of the Faith professed by the great majority of citizens'. Censorship reached virtual draconian proportions with many Irish writers of international distinction being banned, sometimes on ludicrous grounds. There was also institutionalised discrimination within the civil service and education system in favour of those able to use the Gaelic language — for which Northern Unionists had little affection.

De Valera actually declared publicly that he would prefer the restoration of Gaelic as the everyday language of the people to the ending of partition. 'If I were told tomorrow. "You can have a united Ireland if you give up the idea of restoring the national language to be the spoken language of the people",' he said, 'I would, for myself, say no'.[35] On another occasion he explained that if he 'had to make a choice between political freedom without the language, and the language without political freedom', he would choose the latter.[36] Faced with this kind of reasoning, Northern Unionists could hardly be blamed for thinking de Valera might favour taking away their freedom within a united Ireland, if they refused to use the language. Moreover the economic nationalism he was espousing could have had little appeal for Northerners whose more industrialised economy was dependent on export markets which could not be filled by the Twenty-six Counties.

'No Northerner', Seán Ó Faoláin wrote, 'can possibly like such features of Southern life, as at present constituted, as its pervasive clerical control; its censorship; its Gaelic revival; [or] its isolationist economic policy'.[37] De Valera obviously understood the implications of at least some of those features but showed no readiness to do anything about them. In fact, he indicated that there was no room for further compromise on the 1937 constitution, which he said was designed, 'as far as possible', to reconcile the conflicting aspirations between the two parts of the island. Consequently he was showing little inclination to adopt policies which would at least alleviate the legitimate fears of the Northern majority and thereby make the process of reconciliation that little bit easier.

Having thus ruled out both further conciliatory gestures and the use of force, how did de Valera propose to solve the problem?

When referring to the question of minorities in general back in 1934 he had explained that the best solution would be to transfer the minority to its ancestral home, if possible. When applied to the Irish situation, he was not thinking of transferring the nationalists from the Six Counties, but Unionists in the area to Britain. He subsequently suggested, for example, that if the Northern majority continued to refuse the offer of local autonomy in return for the transfer of powers vested in Westminster to a central Irish parliament, then there should be a solution on the lines of a provision in the Treaty of Lausanne (1923), in accordance with which Greece and Turkey exchanged certain populations. The Taoiseach believed that if no other solution were agreed upon, then the problem could be solved by transferring Scottish-Irish Protestants from Northern Ireland to Britain and replacing them with a similar number of Roman Catholics of Irish extraction from Britain.[38]

His propaganda campaign was to get 'the Irish people all over the world using whatever influence they have to try to bring partition to an end'.[39] In March 1939 he went to the Vatican for the coronation of Pope Pius XII and used the occasion to deliver a St Patrick's Day address over radio from Rome to people at home and 'especially', according to his departmental secretary, to people of Irish birth or descent in the United States. Describing partition as 'an open wound', de Valera appealed 'to all who may hear me, and especially the millions of our race scattered throughout the world — to all who glory in the name of Ireland — to join us in a great united movement to bring it to an end'.[40]

He had already made plans for a six week coast-to-coast tour of the United States in May. At the time he was convinced there would be another major war the following autumn, which seemed to strengthen his chances for unity because the British were so anxious for Anglo-American co-operation that there was a possibility of persuading them to abandon Northern Ireland in the hope of at least neutralising the traditional anglophobia of Irish-Americans. The trip was postponed at the virtual eleventh hour and then rearranged for September 1939, but it had to be cancelled with the outbreak of war in Europe.

From de Valera's standpoint the postponement and subsequent cancellation were most inopportune. He was at the height of his international prestige in 1939 and would have had a most impressive platform from which to appeal to Americans, especially Irish-Americans. As the New York-born son of American emigrants, he would have been returning not only as Taoiseach of Ireland but also as President of the Assembly of the League of Nations. He felt that the outbreak of the war had undermined a golden opportunity of ending partition. 'He used to tell me during the war', one of his authorised biographers recalled, 'that if only it had been postponed for a while there would have been a chance of bringing about a united Ireland'.[41]

In the following months, however, de Valera was to show that he was even more determined to keep Ireland out of the conflict than to end partition. This became apparent in June 1940 when he declined a formal British offer to accept 'the principle of a United Ireland' on condition the Dublin government agreed to enter 'the war on side of the United Kingdom and her allies forthwith'.[42]

Whether the British would have implemented this plan over the objections of Northern Unionists is open to question, but this really is of no concern to this study because de Valera was so opposed to the offer that the British concluded he would reject it even if its implementation were fully guaranteed. He emphasised that the only solution was for Northern Ireland to withdraw from the war and then agree to unity so that the new united Irish parliament could consider declaring war on the Axis powers. Although he did not rule out the possibility of such a declaration being adopted, he candidly predicted it would probably be defeated even if he supported it himself.[43]

Nothing ever came of this British offer, nor did de Valera show any interest when the British made further overtures in 1941 and 1942. Yet he repeatedly contended that because of the partition grievance the Irish people would not tolerate the country joining in the Allied war effort. He protested so much about this partition grievance that David Gray, the United States Minister, concluded the Taoiseach was going to try to enlist the support of Americans for the ending of partition as part of the overall international peace settlement in the postwar period. Viewing this as a threat to postwar Anglo-American co-operation, Gray persuaded both Roosevelt and Churchill to discredit de Valera by depicting him as unsympathetic to the Allied cause. This was accomplished by getting the Taoiseach to refuse an American request for the immediate expulsion of German and Japanese representatives, who were depicted as an espionage threat to the lives of American soldiers preparing for the Allied invasion of Europe in 1944. The American press reacted somewhat hysterically to the refusal by characterising de Valera as a Nazi sympathizer.

With the refusal still fresh in the minds of the American people at the end of the war, he had to wait for more propitious circumstances to launch his postponed anti-partition campaign. Meanwhile, his government ran into such serious difficulties as inclement weather, an energy crisis, and the rise of Clann na Poblachta — which posed the first constitutional threat to Fianna Fáil's republican support. All seemed to conspire against his government. Thus when he began to revive his anti-partition efforts in 1947, his move looked suspiciously like an effort to shore up Fianna Fáil's republican support and at the same time take the minds of the electorate off their economic woes.

'Twenty-six of our counties are a republic', de Valera declared in October 1947, and if the Irish people continued to support Fianna Fáil, it would have 'a better chance of securing the whole of Ireland as a republic than any other party'.[44] But Clann na Poblachta's impressive growth continued. It won two Dáil by-elections the following month, and these successes were compared with the Sinn Féin by-election victories of 1917. There were even predictions that at the next general election the new party would emulate the Sinn Féin showing of 1918. In an obvious move to deny Clann na Poblachta enough time to organise itself properly, de Valera called a surprise general election for February 1948, even though the existing Dáil, with its safe Fianna Fáil majority, had still some fifteen months to run.

During the election campaign he stated he was ready to take up his anti-partition efforts where they were interrupted by the war. He announced he would appeal for international help and that he would go to the United States to drum up support. 'I promise', he told a rally in Sligo, 'that the pressure of public opinion of the Irish race, not in Ireland only, but throughout the world, will be concentrated on this question'. He added that he intended to enlist the support of 'public opinion not only of those who have Irish blood in their veins, but of their fellow citizens — men and women — of other races'.[45]

Fianna Fáil easily won enough seats to remain the largest party in the Dáil, but it lost its majority, and John A. Costello of Fine Gael was elected Taoiseach at the head of a coalition government. In spite of that set back de Valera went ahead with his plans to visit the United States, where he remained for four weeks touring the country from coast-to-coast. He then made a six week visit to Australia and stopped off in New Zealand on his way home. Throughout his travels he emphasised the partition grievance, which he contended was largely responsible for the Irish decision to remain neutral during the Second World War.

On returning to Dublin in time for the Fianna Fáil Ard Fheis in June 1948 he announced he had made arrangements for anti-partition campaigns in the United States, Australia and New Zealand. 'We have a splendid case', he told the Ard Fheis. 'Partition is on a rotten foundation and it will totter and end. All we want to do is to make up our mind to make the proper assault.'[46]

Since being forced into opposition the Fianna Fáil leader's attitude on the partition question had been showing distinct signs of hardening. Some people suggested this was simply because he had been relieved of the responsibility of office and could speak out with blatant disregard for the international consequences. They asked why he had not spoken in such a manner while in office.

'The reason is', de Valera responded, 'that we have been doing things in regular order'. His approach, he said, had been 'strictly in accordance with the plan and programme announced by Fianna Fáil at its inaugural meeting nearly thirty-three years ago. We then set before us the securing of full independence for this part of Ireland as the first step on which we would concentrate, so that this being achieved, the problem of partition might be isolated for the combined and coverging attack of all who loved Ireland or were concerned with the broad right of a nation to be free.'[47]

Not to be outdone on the partition issue, the coalition government called an all-party conference in January 1949. De Valera attended and played a major role in the ensuing campaign by fulfilling several speaking engagements in English cities, where he again sought to exploit the anomalies of partition for propaganda purposes. Speaking in Newcastle on 13 February 1949, for instance, he contended that Counties Femanagh and Tyrone should be handed over to the Twenty-six Counties. 'We demand', he said, 'that these counties where there is an overwhelming majority against partition should be given back to us in all fairness and justice'. Nevertheless he added that this 'would not solve the partition problem, because our ancient homeland would be severed and mutilated'.[48] In short, he would not be satisfied with the transfer of just those two counties. Indeed he probably did not want those two counties or the other contiguous nationalist areas transferred at all because there would then be so little support for Irish unity in what would remain of Northern Ireland that the ending of partition would become even more difficult.

Notwithstanding his Newcastle remarks, de Valera made no further calls for the transfer of the nationalist areas following his return to power in 1951. He admitted he could think of no policy which would have any chance of success 'within a reasonable time'. He ruled out the use of force and added that there was no likelihood of being able 'to cajole them either'.[49] He just advocated that the Irish people should be ready to seize on any opportunity of securing Irish unity in the future. It was obvious he wanted the nationalists in Northern Ireland to be ready to help. As things stood, he explained, 'about one-third of the people in that area are our supporters and want to have the unity of the country. What you really have to win over is, therefore, the difference between one-third and one-half, that is, one-sixth'.[50]

During his remaining years in active politics de Valera continued to play down the partition question. 'The one policy' that had any chance of success, he declared, was 'a policy of trying to establish decent relations between Britain and the Six Counties and ourselves'.[51] Yet he made no real moves to improve those relations. He was unwilling, for example, to eliminate the discrimination in favour of Roman Catholic and nationalist values in the Twenty-six Counties. Of course, he believed that compromising would be a futile gesture.

'Is there anyone foolish enough to think that if we are going to sacrifice our aspirations that they are going to give up their cry of not an inch?' de Valera asked in the Dáil. 'For every step we moved towards them, you know perfectly well they would regard it as a sign that we would move another, and they would not be satisfied, in my opinion, unless we went back and accepted the old United Kingdom, a common parliament for the two countries.'[52]

He was probably right. Eliminating the discrimination against Protestant and unionist values would likely have had no more impact on the unionist desire for retaining the British connection than eliminating discrimination against Roman Catholics in the North would have undermined the opposition to partition in the rest of the island. Yet it would have removed a legitimate cause of unionist anxiety and Dublin could, if it wished, have had a stronger base from which to enlist international support for pressurising Britain to hand over the contiguous nationalist areas and insist on the elimination of discrimination against Roman Catholics in what would remain of Northern Ireland.

De Valera, of course, seemed more interested in exploiting the propaganda value of the injustices being suffered by the nationalists in the Six counties than in securing the redress of the actual grievances. He was obviously quite content to have the contiguous nationalist areas remain within Northern Ireland in the hope that the people there would help bring about Irish unity. He apparently believed, for example, that the Roman Catholics, with their higher birth-rate, would eventually become the majority population in Northern Ireland. Then, he contended, they 'would, at a propitious time, call for a plebiscite to end partition'.[53] Thus he seemed prepared to wait for that day, even if it meant adopting his own variant of the unionist policy of 'not an inch'. As a result he must take some of the responsibility for the political stagnation in the Six Counties. When he retired from active politics in 1959 the unionist majority in Northern Ireland were as entrenched as ever in their opposition to Irish unity. As a result one can only conclude that if de Valera really did want to win them over, as he so often stated, then his efforts were a dismal failure.

NOTES

1. Speech in Cootehill, 2/9/17, *Gaelic American*, 31/10/17.

2. Mary C. Bromage, *De Valera and the March of a Nation*, (Dublin: 1956), 73; Maurice Moynihan (ed.), *Speeches and Statements by Eamon de Valera 1917-1973* (Dublin: 1980), 62.

3. *Manchester Guardian* quoted in *Gaelic American*, 26/2/21.

4. *ibid.*

5. de Valera, memo., n.d., Michael Collins Papers (Private Source).

6. I.O. (pseudonym of C.J.C. Street), *Ireland in 1921*, (London: 1921), 59.

7. de Valera to Patrick McCartan, 7/2/18, John Devoy Papers, NLI.

8. Dáil Éireann, *Private Sessions*, 29.

9. *ibid.*, 137.

10. *ibid.*, 153.

11. *ibid.*

12. *ibid.*

13. de Valera to Joseph McGarrity, 10/9/22, McGarrity Papers, NLI.

14. *Eire*, 7/7/23.

15. Comhairle na dTeachtai, 'Minutes', 7/8/24, q. in Anthony Gaughan, *Austin Stack* (Dublin: 1977), 321-2.

16. Moynihan (ed.), 115.

17. de Valera to Mary MacSwiney, 7/8/23, q. in Thomas O'Neill, 'In Search of a Path: Irish Republicanism 1922-1927, *Historical Studies*, X, (1976), 157.

18. Moynihan (ed.), 123.

19. *ibid.*, 135.

20. de Valera, speech, 4/3/32, *Recent Speeches and Broadcasts*, (Dublin: 1933),9-14.

21. Moynihan (ed.), 257.

22. *ibid.*, 350.

23. Deirdre MacMahon, 'Malcolm MacDonald and Anglo-Irish Relations', UCD thesis, 209.

24. de Valera, *Peace and War*, (Dublin: 1944), 76-80.

25. Moynihan (ed.), 361.

26. *ibid.*, 360.

27. *Irish Press*, 4/12/39.

28. John Cudahy, despatch No. 159, 20/10/38, U.S. Diplomatic Papers, National Archives, Washington, D.C.

29. Moynihan (ed.), 366-76.

30. *ibid.*

31. Seanad Éireann, *Debates*, 39:1539.

32. Sean Ó Faolain, *De Valera* (London: 1939), 156.

33. DE, 39:517-8.

34. J. Whyte, *Church and State in Modern Ireland 1923-70* (Dublin: 1971), 47-48.

35. Moynihan (ed.), 375.

36. Ó Faolain, (1939).

37. *ibid.*, 156.

38. de Valera, *Peace and war*, 27-31; T. Ryle Dwyer, *Irish Neutrality and the USA, 1939-47* (Dublin: 1977), 15; *Irish Press*, 13/12/39.

39. Moynihan (ed.), 371.

40. *ibid.*, 379.

41. Lord Longford quoted in *Irish Independent*, 17/9/82.

42. Longford and Thomas P. O'Neill, *Eamon de Valera* (Dublin: 1970), 366.

43. Dwyer, 179-99.

44. *Irish Press*, 27/10/47.

45. *ibid.*, 29/1/48.

46. *ibid.*, 23/6/48.

47. *ibid.*, 9/8/48.

48. *ibid.*, 14/2/49.

49. Moynihan (ed.), 543.

50. *ibid.*

51. *Irish Press*, 1/3/54.

52. Kevin Boland, *Up Dev* (Dublin: 1977), 144.

53. John Bowman, *De Valera and the Ulster Question 1917-1973* (London: 1982), 313.

'The Man They Could Never Forgive' The View of the Opposition: Eamon de Valera and the Civil War

Maryann Gialanella Valiulis

In 1932, at the Eucharistic Congress in Dublin, W.T. Cosgrave, one of the leaders of Fine Gael, adamantly refused to attend the official reception at the same time as Eamon de Valera, the leader of the government.[1]

In 1948, a coalition comprising an odd assortment of political parties — ranging from middle-class conservatvies to radical Republicans — joined together to oust Fianna Fáil from power. Richard Mulcahy, then leader of Fine Gael, the dominant party of the Coalition, willingly stepped down and yielded his place as Taoiseach to John A. Costello, a distinguished lawyer who was acceptable to all members of the Coalition. In fact, Mulcahy, himself a controversial figure because of the executions of the Civil War, actively worked to persuade Costello to accept the leadership of the Coalition, to harmonize all the varied elements in the government. To insure the Coalition's accession to power, Mulcahy sacrificed personal ambition and accepted the relatively minor role of Minister for Education.[2]

Why was Cosgrave so unwilling to observe even polite formalities with Eamon de Valera? Why was Mulcahy willing to sacrifice political power? And why was Fine Gael willing to enter into a coalition with republicans, the very people with whom they had fought a civil war, simply to take the reins of power from, and disrupt the hegemony of, Mr de Valera?

The answer to all these questions is the same: Eamon de Valera was the man they [Treatyites, Free Staters, Cumann na nGaedheal and Fine Gael leaders] believed to be primarily responsible for the Civil War. Although they acknowledged that there would have been some hostility to, some disturbance over, the acceptance of the Treaty, they felt that the Civil War became such a prolonged and devastating conflict only because de Valera, the recognized leader of the revolutionary movement, supported those who opted for rebellion. More importantly, they believed that de Valera's decision was based not on principle, but on personal ambition. To the Opposition, de Valera threw the country into a bitter and deadly conflict, destroyed the unity of the Irish nationalist movement, and jeopardized the nascent state — all for personal aggrandizement. Power, not principle, seemed to them to be the motivating force behind de Valera's actions. Other Republicans could be forgiven. They were men of principle, men who had been led astray, men who did not understand. Hence the coalition of 1948. But Eamon de Valera was different. He was the man the leaders of the Opposition could never forgive — and never trust again.

The Civil War period was a critical divide in Irish history, not simply because of the hostility, death and destruction it engendered at a formative stage in the nationalist movement, but also because it influenced the perception of the first generation of government leaders toward past events and the political decisions they were to make in subsequent years. Especially and primarily, the attitudes and beliefs of the first Free State government leaders toward Eamon de Valera were formed and frozen during this civil war period.

The events of 1922-1923, in fact, became both a perceptual prison and a perceptual prism for the men of the Irish Free State: a perceptual prison because the Civil War defined for them the parameters and limited their perception of all other events to within this frame of reference; a perceptual prism because the Civil War became the looking glass through which both the past and the future were viewed, were refracted, dictating a particular interpretation of the past and influencing future actions and reactions. The perceptual prison/prism of the Civil War hindered the emergence of an underlying political consensus which assumes that, despite political differences over policies, there is a basic, common adherence to a democratic value system and a common commitment to the accepted form of government. Because they believed that de Valera had caused the Civil War, betrayed them for personal aggrandisement, and sanctioned rebellion against the expressed will of the people, the Opposition leaders would never trust him as a political leader. They remained, therefore, extremely suspicious of both his motives and actions and doubted his commitment to democratic representative government.

In order to understand the virulent antagonism and the perceptual prison/prism framework, it is necessary therefore, to re-examine the Civil War period from the point of view of the Free State leaders. The events of the period are well-known: the negotiations with the British by Michael Collins and Arthur Griffith that resulted in the Treaty; the denunciation of the Treaty by de Valera and a section of the Cabinet; its ratification by Dáil Éireann in January of 1922; and the subsequent split over the Treaty that ended in armed rebellion by a section of the army and the drift into civil war.

The leaders of the Free State felt betrayed by de Valera's rejection of the Treaty. This sense of betrayal is a leitmotif running through the Civil War period. Men like Collins, Griffith and Mulcahy believed that they had given 'Dev' their unquestioned loyalty during the revolutionary period. 'Whatever de Valera does, I agree to that', Griffith was alleged to have remarked at the time of the German plot arrests.[3] Or as Mulcahy wrote: 'But there was no service that any of us were capable of rendering in our own way that we didn't pay him, both from a certain personal kind of feeling for him and for what he represented and was, as the head of our government and our national movement.'[4] De Valera answered such loyalty by betraying them, rejecting the Treaty publicly before even discussing it with Collins or Griffith, before even hearing their explanation. This public repudiation which Mulcahy described as 'an infamous performance . . . tantamount to his meeting Griffith at the boat at Dun Laoghaire and slapping him publicly across the face,'[5] particularly angered the Free State leaders, who believed that they had received a poor return for their allegiance to their chief.

Feeling that they had been betrayed and believing that de Valera had opposed the Treaty because of his desire for personal power led the Free Staters to a particular interpretation of his role and objectives in both the revolutionary and civil war period.

The Free State leaders believed that de Valera, given the time he spent in jail and in America, never became intimately involved with the post-1916 revolutionary struggle. Consequently, after he returned to Ireland in December of 1920, because the political and military scene had changed so radically, de Valera felt he was in danger of being politically eclipsed and becoming militarily irrelevant.

The Treatyites based their view on the fact that de Valera played little, if any, part during the initial stages of the Anglo-Irish War, in policy discussions on the conduct of the army.[6] The 1916 Rising, in which de Valera had participated, had been a grand heroic gesture, made by noble men for a noble cause. Now, however, the Volunteers were fighting a totally different kind of war — a guerilla war complete with ambushes, flying columns, and intelligence squads. De Valera was obviously uncomfortable with this new kind of warfare as evidenced by his 'ease off meeting' with the Dáil in January of 1921 when he advised that they go more slowly and by his comment to Mulcahy that

> You are going too fast. This odd shooting of a policeman here and there is having a very bad effect, from the propaganda point of view, on us in America. What we want is one good battle about once a month with about 500 men on each side.[7]

To men like Collins and Mulcahy, de Valera's reactions indicated that he was hopelessly out of touch with military reality and therefore did not appreciate the military implications of renewing the war with Britain if the treaty were rejected.

Moreover, the Free Staters wondered if personal rivalry and jealousy had not also influenced de Valera. By the time de Valera returned from America, Michael Collins had certainly become a rival to de Valera in terms of power, influence and notoriety. The Big Fellow had captured the imagination of the public and, given both his administrative and military skills, was at the heart of the Irish drive for independence. De Valera was thus faced with a political rival who, however loyal, was still a popular hero. This element of rivalry might help explain de Valera's suggestion that, in the heat of the Anglo-Irish War, Collins be sent to America, an idea Mulcahy described as possible only from 'a person living in fairyland' — out of touch with the political and military realities of the time.[8] Collins had a more earthy, and perhaps more realistic assessment of his Chief's motives as evidenced by his comment that 'the long whore won't get rid of me as easy as that'.[9] Certainly, personal rivalry as well as personal affection were among the many variables which determined attitudes toward the Treaty and hence to the Civil War. And to the anti-de Valera group, it was significant that although Collins successfully resisted going to America, he was sent, against his better judgment, to London to negotiate the Treaty, to compromise the Republic. De Valera, however, remained in Dublin.

As is obvious from any reading of the period, the delegates to London, conscious of the divisions within the Cabinet, knew they were going to have a difficult time with the Treaty. They believed, however, they could count on de Valera's support and his influence to bring the extremists into line. They thought de Valera had moved out of 'the strait jacket of republicanism' with his plan for External Association, embodying as it did both an oath of allegiance and links with the British Commonwealth. Although the negotiators and the supporters of the Treaty in general, were aware of the distinctions between the Treaty and External Association (Document No. 2), they could not believe that such nuances would make a qualitative difference to de Valera. Certainly to fight a civil war over what seemed to them to be mere quibbling differences smacked of sheer opportunism.

The Treatyites argued that de Valera had been willing to compromise with the British from the time of the preliminary negotiations with Lloyd George and that he had known compromises would have to be made in any settlement with England. Yet once the Treaty was signed, de Valera wrapped himself in the mantle of uncompromising Republicanism — External Association notwithstanding. Those in favor of the Treaty could make sense of de Valera's apparent about-face and continued opposition to the treaty only in terms of a personal power play. By casting his lot with the section of the army which rebelled against the Treaty, De Valera was able to place the burden of compromise and the stigma of the oath, of partition and inclusion within the Commonwealth on his opponents' shoulders. He was left free to criticize the Free State without having to provide viable, credible options. Collins, for example, was now forced to assure his comrades that he was as good a Republican as ever and that the Treaty was simply a stepping stone to the Republic. De Valera's objectives, according to Mulcahy, were to destroy 'the Treaty party leadership', particularly Collins and Griffith, and their achievement.[10] Mulcahy also thought that de Valera supported the rebels because, at least in the beginning, he did not believe that the Free State could rally the rank and file of the people to support them. In effect, de Valera misjudged both the appeal and the staying power of the Free State and the determination of the first government to establish its authority.

From de Valera's decision to reject the treaty and support armed rebellion against the expressed wishes of Dáil Éireann flowed, in the interpretation of the Treatyites, a host of evils. Its immediate consequence was a civil war which was more widespread and more destructive than the Free State leaders had anticipated. Both Collins and Mulcahy had initially hoped to neutralize some of the Volunteer divisions opposed to the Treaty by convincing them to refrain from actively engaging in armed rebellion and thus isolating those elements determined to fight the Free State. A key element in this plan was to convince Liam Lynch, a figure of tremendous influence not only in Cork but among the Volunteers generally, not to participate in the rebellion. They failed and Lynch became Chief of Staff of the Irregulars. Mulcahy specifically blamed de Valera for Lynch's decision to go actively anti-Treaty. Mulcahy wrote:

> . . . it is difficult to understand what either I or Collins left undone to hold him out of the fight and I think there could be no other influence that . . . could bring himself [Lynch] . . . into the fight except that of de Valera.[12]

Mulcahy believed the civil war would have been a much smaller, much more localized affair 'if the reaction of de Valera to the Treaty had been different or even if de Valera had stopped short of approving of the use of arms by the Irregulars . . .'[13]

De Valera was also accused of destroying the magnificent spirit of unity and togetherness which had previously characterized the I.R.A. by his deliberate distortions of the Treaty. Mulcahy, in particular, paints an almost idyllic, albeit not totally realistic, picture of the harmony and unity of purpose which existed prior to de Valera's endorsement of the anti-Treaty position. Mulcahy believed that the jaundiced picture that was circulated about the effects of the Treaty put the more susceptible members of the Volunteers in an untenable position, making armed rebellion against the Free State the only viable alternative:

They had heard from the highest possible level that the plenipotentiaries had, as it were, behind the backs of de Valera and other members of the Government, broken their word in London and had done something that they should not have done; ... they were told that in [the] future they would be the King's army ... and that while the British Army could go out now, it had every legal right to return where and whenever it pleased .... . The binding and immobilizing influence of the oath to the Republic was pressed home on them; and the inflexibility of any possible interpretation of that word [Republic] in practice, except in accordance with some brainwave of de Valera's or some aspect of de Valera's conscience, was pushed home. The eyes of their dead comrades were turned upon them, and the eyes of important people like Stack and Sean T. O'Kelly etc. who were ready to sacrifice their lives, either deliberately or in terms of a bet, against the idea of de Valera ever doing wrong.[14]

Given these pressures and distortions, it was no wonder that some volunteers went astray — or, more correctly, to men like Collins and Mulcahy, were deliberately led astray.

Another almost equally important consequence of de Valera's decision to reject the Treaty was the long-range effect of repudiating the will of the parliament of the people. To those who had chosen to accept the Treaty, to fight for majority rule, de Valera's decision 'struck a bad blow at our democratic dream',[15] hallowing and glorifying the gun as an acceptable alternative to democratic rule. In particular, Free State leaders, ignoring the strained relations between de Valera and Lynch, held de Valera responsible for the policy of assassination of Dáil deputies and the precedent which that set in regard to the use of violence against the state. Mulcahy felt that de Valera invented the Republic of November, 1922, not out of any particular devotion to the constitutional tradition, but as 'a moral justification for destroying, if necessary by assassination, the Parliament of 1923'.[16] Again de Valera was culpable, sanctioning an act of wanton destruction that struck at the heart of representative government not to establish an illusory Republic, but simply to destroy the Parliament of the Free State.[17]

The split in the nationalist movement caused by de Valera, the 'smothering in violence and turmoil the true voice of Irish nationalism',[18] made, to the Free Staters, the dream of the revolutionary movement of a free, united Gaelic Ireland almost an impossibility. Michael Hayes saw the consequences of de Valera's decision not to support the Treaty and the resultant Civil War as debilitating to the nationalist vision of Ireland. In a speech commemorating the Treaty, he said:

The sight of Irishmen fighting one another in Ireland brought comfort and solace to our enemies at home and abroad. It stiffened the Northern Unionist; it rent asunder the Irish language movement, and made the revival of Irish incalculably more difficult that it would have been in an atmosphere of constitutional progress and pooled intelligence on agreed topics.[19]

To the leaders of the first Free State government, the Civil War was a senseless tragedy that exacted an exhorbitant price in men, in ideals, in national spirit, a tragedy, however, that possibly could have been avoided if de Valera had not deserted them.

It is no wonder, then, that de Valera's decision to enter the Dáil in 1927, following Kevin O'Higgins' assassination (for which de Valera was not held responsible) both appeared to justify and strengthen the negative opinion held of him by the Free State leaders. The Treaty oath, worth a civil war in 1922, was somehow transformed into an empty formula. The government leaders could not understand why de Valera could accept in 1927 what he refused to accept in 1922, unless the question was one not of principle, but of power. It seemed to them that de Valera and his followers 'did what they might have done in 1922 without bloodshed, without destruction of property and without all the worst evils of Civil War'.[20] De Valera's entry into the Dáil, complete with his taking the oath of allegiance, confirmed everything that the Free State leaders had grown to believe about de Valera since 1922.

Cumann na nGaedheal leaders, even after de Valera's entry into the Dáil, remained skeptical of his conversion to parliamentary and constitutional opposition. In part, their apprehension was based on the fact that in 1927 neither de Valera nor members of his party expressly renounced the use of force or violence. Rather, Fianna Fáil referred to itself as a 'slightly constitutional party' and Cumann na nGaedheal leaders concluded that de Valera continued to believe that violence against the state in defence of the Republic was morally justified, but for the present was simply politically and practically inexpedient.[21]

Obviously Cumann na nGaedheal was suspicious of the aims and ambitions of the Fianna Fáil government. When de Valera assumed power in 1932, and 'opened the jails' for I.R.A. prisoners, Free State leaders wondered if there was to be a repetition of Civil War tactics. They vividly remembered the difficulty Collins and Griffith had in explaining the Treaty to the electorate because hostile elements of the I.R.A., not willing to allow free speech to 'traitors' disrupted meetings, blocked roads, and threatened speakers.[22] The parallels between 1922 and 1932, to them, were striking. Cosgrave and his party saw a distinct threat from the I.R.A. to their rights of freedom of speech, freedom of the press, and freedom of assembly. Cumann na nGaedheal leaders believed that de Valera could not be trusted to afford them sufficient protection to speak at public meetings and guarantee their right to function as a legitimate political opposition. Believing that, they turned to the Army Comrades Association and then to the Blueshirts for protection. In his speech to the

United Irish Party conference in 1934, Cosgrave alluded to this perceived threat against their basic political rights when he said that the present
Minister's 'policy of twelve years ago is now being put into practice once
more. It does not surprise me.'[23]

In essence, Fine Gael leaders concluded, at each successive change initiated by Fianna Fáil governments, that de Valera was out to destroy the
democratic framework of the state, enhance and enlarge his own power
and the position of his party, and eliminate all opposition. A brief glance
at the descriptions of de Valera used by leaders like Mulcahy will indicate
the strength of these feelings. De Valera is pictured as an 'all-controlling
shepherd with well-directed dogs';[24] a Taoiseach, who 'Nero-like is fid-
dling with the electoral system in an effort to insure the perpetuity of his
party';[25] a 'Fianna Fáil tiger' that 'tasted more and more blood', which
served only to 'increase its lust for power';[26] a leader whose nationalism is
'narrow, vindictive and dominated by Party spirit',[27] and who is
motivated by a 'determination to substitute for a representative Irish
Parliament a Parliament in which an Ascendancy Party will grip the
country through its grip on government and hold it for a long time';[28] an
Opposition leader who dangerously cried, ' "I hate this Government",'[29]
and attempts to 'malign and vilify the personalities of their opponents'.[30]

The leaders of Cumann na nGaedheal/Fine Gael realized, of course,
that each step that de Valera took to dismantle the Treaty, that each additional power that de Valera claimed for Ireland was the greatest proof
that those who accepted the Treaty were right, that it was a stepping
stone to a Republic, conferring on them the freedom to achieve freedom.
Yet they looked with dismay as de Valera, it seemed to them, unnecessarily violated the terms of the agreement of 1922. They found
themselves, in their implacable hostility to de Valera and their almost
visceral distrust of their former chief, castigated as the pro-British party,
foes of the Republic, thwarters of the goals of Irish nationalism. Consequently, they were unable to make political capital out of the fact they
were indeed right in 1922. De Valera may have spent the years between
1922 and 1932, first outside the boundaries of democratic government
and then outside the porticoes of power, but it was the founders of the
Free State government who were doomed to spend most of their subsequent years in the political wilderness — a fact which must have
strengthened their view of Eamon de Valera as a man they could never
forgive.

NOTES

1. *The Irish Times,* 6 September 1967.
2. Interview, Fr Fergus Barrett, 26 July 1981.

3. Richard Mulcahy Papers, (Archives Department, University College Dublin); Comments on P. Beaslai, *Michael Collins and the Making of a New Ireland* (Dublin: 1926), Vol. II, 159, hereinafter cited as Comments.

4. Comments, Vol. II, 74.

5. *Ibid.*, Vol. II, 190.

6. *Ibid.*, Vol. II, 107.

7. *Ibid.*, Vol. II, 67.

8. *Ibid.*, Vol. II, 73.

9. T. Ryle Dwyer, *Eamon de Valera* (Dublin: 1980).

10. Mulcahy Papers, P7/c/148; Comments, Vol. II, 262.

11. Mulcahy Papers, P7/a/210.

12. Comments, Vol. II, 123.

13. *Ibid.*

14. *Ibid.*, Vol. II, 250-251.

15. *Ibid.*, Vol. II, 114-115.

16. Mulcahy Papers, P7/a/210.

17. *Ibid.*

18. Mulcahy Papers, P7/c/128.

19. *Ibid.*

20. Mulcahy Papers, P7/c/21.

21. Mulcahy Papers, P7/c/144.

22. Joseph Curran, *The Birth of the Irish Free State* (Alabama: 1980), 182.

23. Mulcahy Papers, P7/c/140.

24. Mulcahy Papers, P7/c/127.

25. Mulcahy Papers, P7/c/128.

26. Comments, Vol. II, 114-115.

27. Mulcahy Papers, P7/c/119.

28. Mulcahy Papers, P7/c/127.

29. Mulcahy Papers, P7/c/128.

30. Mulcahy Papers, P7/c/130.

De Valera in 1917:
the Undoing of the Easter Rising

David Fitzpatrick

The 1916 Rising left Irish politicians of all parties with a pretty problem. As a dramatic pageant it had been a spectacular success, quickly generating a popular cult of the dead which politicians would ignore at their peril. Yet as a military enterprise it had been a spectacular failure, which even the most bloodthirsty Republicans were reluctant to see re-enacted. Former opponents of violent Republicanism were faced with four choices, all hazardous. They might condemn both the rebels and the consequences of their acts; praise the rebels while denouncing the consequences; praise both rebels and consequences without becoming Republican; or become Republican. Since most Nationalists were anti-Republican in 1916 but Republican by 1919, it is clear that the fourth course (conversion) was eventually the most popular. A substantial minority of Nationalists, including many members of parliament, remained steadfast in their condemnation of the Rising and of the vision of its creators; but already by mid-1917 even John Redmond had lost hope of carrying the country with him along the road of consistency and common sense. Inconsistency and ambivalence proved increasingly frequent responses, as politicians sought to exploit the popular mood of veneration for the dead in order to promote policies which the dead would have deplored. Colonel George O'Callaghan-Westropp, the Clare Unionist, provided a startling example of zestful ambivalence, for he delighted in both the spirit of the Rising and its immediate political consequences while remaining His Majesty's loyal servant. Unionists should be 'grateful' to the Republicans 'for smashing the villainous "Nationalist" Party Machine with its Tammany methods, class-hatreds, and intolerance, which soured Irish life, corrupted Parliament, and hustled King Edward into his Grave'. He found it expedient to deplore the 'Sinn Féin policy which is unpractical', while praising the 'Sinn Féin spirit which contains much that is beautiful'.[1]

More common, however, was the ambivalence of the politician who found the rebels 'brave but misguided' while urging their successors to be prudent and well-guided. Labour leaders such as Thomas Johnson, chairman of the Irish Trades Congress of 1916, sought to share a little of James Connolly's glory while avoiding commitment to either his

Socialism or his Nationalism. Johnson, though eager to advance Irish Labour's cause by applying pressure at Westminster, claimed 'Jim Connolly' as one of his own: 'We mourn his death, we honour his work, we revere his memory'. He further recalled the 'intense fervour' of another Labour martyr, Dick O'Carroll, who during a banquet in 1914 had foreshadowed the words of a later popular idol by crying 'Dublin, I love you!'[2] Johnson's ambivalence arose as much from his personal friendship with certain rebels as from political calculation. But for many churchmen and parliamentarians, the problem of reconciling admiration for rebel heroism with condemnation of its repetition was largely one of rhetoric. Thus Arthur Lynch, member for West Clare, tried to rally support for his 'Constitutionalist' revival by lauding 'the extraordinary courage, and devotion, of the young leaders. Whatever politicians may say of their wisdom or judgement, he added, they will inevitably take their place in the gallery of Irish heroes and martyrs beside Robert Emmet and Wolfe Tone.'[3] Similar sentiments were voiced just after the Rising by the Roman Catholic Bishop of Killaloe, who had been as deeply embroiled in Home Rule politics as any parliamentarian. Dr Fogarty 'bewailed and lamented their mad adventure; but whatever their faults or responsibility may be — and let God be their merciful judge in that — this much must be said to their credit, that they died bravely and unselfishly for what they believed — foolishly, indeed — was the cause of Ireland. Let their spirits rest for the present in peace in the silence of eternity.'[4]

The survivors and legatees of the Rising were scarcely less ambivalent in their response to the Rising cult than were their opponents. Exempt from the need to prove their Republican piety, they were burdened all the more with the duty of interpreting the Republican gospel in a political context much changed since the Rising. Mass martyrdom, as it was widely acknowledged, brought diminishing returns: one bloody sacrifice was enough for now. According to one 'turbulent' priest in July 1917, there was no danger of another Rising, since 'such incidents are like angels' visits — few and far between'.[5] Foremost among those who used their rebel prestige to guard against a precipitate revisitation of the angel of death was Eamonn de Valera. While still in Lewes Prison he deemed it his responsibility to act as custodian and interpreter of the martyrs' message: 'We feel that any important action of ours will, too, have a reflex effect on last Easter's sacrifice and on any advantages which have been secured by that sacrifice. To do anything which would be liable to be misinterpreted and misrepresented — to create a wrong impression as to the ideals, principles and opinions which prompted last Easter's action would, it seems to us, be a national calamity.'[6] His pre-eminence was scarcely challenged among Republicans. On 16 June 1917, the eve of his release from Lewes, he was sent a telegraphed summons to contest the by-election for Major Willie Redmond's seat of East Clare: 'To Comdg Devaltra 6 Harcourt St Dublin You are Sinn fein's selection for Clare'.[7] During the eleven subsequent months up to his rearrest and incarceration in Lincoln Gaol, de Valera became the most prominent Republican propagandist, touring the country on behalf of Sinn Féin and the Irish Volunteers and becoming president of both bodies in October 1917. During these months he developed the political strategy which was applied with such striking effect during the campaign against conscription in April 1918. The elements of his strategy were already evident during his successful campaign in East Clare, and undoubtedly helped mould Irish Republicanism into something the Easter martyrs would surely have distrusted: a vast, open, oddly respectable populist movement. How was this bizarre metamorphosis of a small, clandestine, radical élitist movement accomplished? How did the Hero of Ringsend set about turning the Easter tradition on its head?

Before de Valera could hope to turn the Easter tradition on its head, he had to perform some personal acrobatics: the teacher turned soldier became a politician. De Valera the politician seemed almost as incongruous a figure as de Valera the rebel commandant, yet his sense of dignity and indeed destiny shielded him from the sneers of those who saw only a gangling, awkward, scarcely articulate college teacher of mathematics. As Padraic Colum wrote, his 'ability to take himself and his position seriously, even solemnly, one reflects, was a potent factor in giving de Valera an ascendancy among the leaders of the Irish movement'.[8] Though aware of his defects, he considered them insignificant. Thus in October 1921, he admitted to Sinn Féin's Ard Fheis that 'I have been speaking practically the whole time — I am a very bad Chairman and nobody knows it better than myself'. Thereupon he continued speaking and remained chairman.[9] In similar vein, he protested in July 1917 that 'political platforms have little attraction for me, but in this case I considered that the principles for which my comrades died were at stake and that it was my duty, seeing I still adhered to these principles, to avail of every opportunity to vindicate and advance them'.[10] Though his admiring biographers observed that 'politics and soldiering were not yet fully sorted out in his mind' at the time of his release from Lewes, he proved a fast learner in the art of politics as public duty. By October 1917 he was eager to teach this art to the tenth Ard Fheis of Sinn Féin, a distinctly naïve assembly: 'We should have got beyond the stage when we regard politics as roguery and a politician as a rogue'.[11] De Valera had become a politician, and none dared call him a rogue.

The elements of de Valera's strategy were expressed plainly enough in his inelegant speeches, which John Dillon is reputed to have had reported *verbatim* in the *Freeman's Journal* in the hope of discrediting

their author.[12] Invariably de Valera avowed his adherence to the principles of the Easter martyrs, emphasising his own involvement by ap-
pearing in Volunteer uniform. But again and again he resisted attempts
to establish a formal élite of 1916 survivors, of whom there were not yet
enough to create the mass movement which he had in mind. In East
Clare he dragged Eoin MacNeill, who was regarded by the vulgar as
Judas to Pearse's Christ, from platform to platform in order to
demonstrate the oecumenical character of Sinn Féin. At the October Ard
Fheis, he rejected proposals that future election candidates should be attested Easter rebels: 'Speaking for my comrades I am sure they do not
want that there should be any special discrimination in their favour'.[13] De
Valera's decision to accept converts into his inner church manifested his
self-confidence, his openness of mind towards former opponents, and
perhaps also his reluctance to be surrounded exclusively by zealous pro-
ponents of physical force. For the soldier turned politician, former army
comrades might prove less comfortable associates than mavericks and
pragmatists with flexible outlooks.

De Valera remained an impassioned advocate of physical force, but his
advocacy was hedged about with debilitating qualifications. Like John
Dillon, who never publicly said 'one word against physical force when it
was used in a just cause and with some hope of success',[14] de Valera exalted productive violence and disparaged futile violence. During the East
Clare campaign he proposed several alternative conditions for undertaking 'revolution': 'the ghost of a chance', 'a fair chance of a military success', and 'a good chance of success'.[15] By implication, none of these conditions applied in the Ireland of 1917. In his concluding speech to the
1917 Ard Fheis, de Valera did his best, as one man of blood talking to
others, to urge restraint until Providence called for further carnage:[16]

> The rising up against the oppressor is not merely legitimate, but it is our duty
> as men provided we are able to accomplish it (Applause) . . . This government
> oppressing us at present is not a legitimate government and we are going to
> make up our minds to get rid of it and God grant that we will be able to get rid
> of it by physical force (Loud and prolonged applause) . . . It is a duty to
> prepare and do our best to do that if we get the chance of doing it successfully.

Thus violence should be employed if and only if success were possible,
credible, likely or certain. All these alternative stipulations conflicted
with the strategy of Pearse or Plunkett in 1916, for whom military defeat
resulting in renewed British oppression was prerequisite to the
reawakening of the Irish Nation. Had de Valera urged cessation of bloodshed until a new generation had grown up unsanctified by carnage, he
would have spoken in the spirit of the martyrs. By making military success the condition for undertaking armed protest, he broke away from
that spirit.

Pending the collapse of the British Empire or at least the end of the European war of attrition, which might conceivably create the conditions for a second rising, de Valera clearly recognised the necessity for the organised and aggressive expression of Nationalist opinion. The clandestine and conspiratorial tradition of the faction-ridden Irish Republican Brotherhood threatened to obstruct his strategy for grafting the ideals of the Easter rebels onto a new network of populist Sinn Féin clubs. Thus de Valera, like Griffith before him, allowed his allegiance to the Brotherhood to lapse in the hope of capturing a broader following. At the October Ard Fheis, de Valera was as vehement as Griffith in advocating the development of a vast body of parish clubs acting openly to impress the world with the popularity and unity of Republicanism. He denounced government attempts to persuade Britain's allies 'that this movement in Ireland is a movement of anarchists or, as some of them put it, that it was a Nihilist movement and not a National movement'. He did not demur when Griffith praised Sinn Féin's benefactors, some of whom had 'worked as generously in former years for the Parliamentary Party when they believed that Party honest and straight'. Nor had he any time for the purist sentiments of the militant Clare priest, Fr Pat Gaynor, who asked 'whether you are going to set up a political organisation or what will be in practice and in fact a Provisional Government. I am opposed to reorganising the United Irish League under another name'.[17] The architects of the new Sinn Féin were happy to model their organisation upon its execrated but once highly effective predecessor.

De Valera further departed from the 1916 precedent by insisting upon the clear separation of the political, military and governmental facets of the Republic. Whereas the 'Provisional Government' of 1916 had been the reincarnation of the Brotherhood's Military Council, the Republican parliament envisaged by de Valera in 1917 would comprise a democratically elected assembly. Sinn Féin would ensure that the right people were elected, while the Volunteers would protect Sinn Féin campaigners from molestation. The connections between these bodies were however less clear than their separation. De Valera stressed that 'we cannot allow Sinn Féin to take control of the military organisation. When the National Parliament is set up it will be a proper part of the activities of such an assembly to look after the National Army.'[18] In the meantime, as he told one hundred supporters in Ruane, Co. Clare, just before the Ard Fheis, it was necessary to keep both political and physical-force sides alive.[19] The division of functions was not, of course, intended to foster division of authority, and in due course de Valera became president of all three organisations. Its purpose was to allow the coexistence within Republicanism of a respectable political movement, a potentially disreputable army and a 'legitimate' assembly which could take its colour from either the respectable or the disreputable segments at will. The very complexity and imprecision of the relationships between the three major Republican institutions helped ward off collision between the advocates of passive resistance and the men of blood.[20] Furthermore, it enabled de Valera to carry through his celebrated stratagem of inviting the Republican parliament to do away with the Republic by means of a 'referendum'. In this respect his flexibility was fully in the tradition of John O'Leary and Joseph Mary Plunkett, both of whom found it possible to reconcile membership of the I.R.B. with preference for monarchical government.[21]

Sinn Féin could scarcely hope to win massive popular adherence and effective local organisation without the active aid of the Roman Catholic clergy. The great movements of the recent past — the United Irish League, the Ancient Order of Hibernians and the Irish National Volunteers — had all relied heavily upon the church for local leadership and provision of meeting places. In soliciting clerical support, the legatees of the Easter tradition had much to live down or explain away, since the Rising had been conducted by a coalition of members of a secret society and advocates of class struggle, both anathema to the church. As D.W. Miller has observed, de Valera 'demonstrated an acute sense of the difficulties he would face in leading a revolutionary movement without alienating the all-important support of the clergy'.[22] Indeed many of his more striking political affirmations during 1917 may be interpreted as messages of reassurance to the clergy. His separation from the proscribed Brotherhood, his close association with MacNeill (who had been strongly backed by the Clare clergy as Sinn Féin candidate for East Clare), and his quasi-theological justification of rebellion where success was likely, all helped to propitiate edgy bishops and priests.[23] His campaign leaflets in East Clare stressed the rift between the Parliamentary Party and the Bishop of Limerick, Dr O'Dwyer. Their titles included 'The Bishop of Limerick and John Redmond', 'Lynchites belying the Bishop of Limerick' and 'The Bishop of Limerick speaks: how the Irish prisoners are treated'.[24] Yet de Valera, either despite or because of his close association with priests as a teacher, did not employ the customary tone of whining deference used by Irish politicans in public intercourse with men of the cloth. At the 1917 Ard Fheis he firmly squashed attempts by Fr John O'Meehan, one of his supporters in East Clare, to qualify the constitutional preamble enabling Sinn Féin to 'make use of any and every means available' to free Ireland from British subjection. O'Meehan suggested that only means 'deemed legitimate and effective' by Sinn Féin's National Council should be admissible: 'As the rule stands it might cover anything from pitch and toss to manslaughter (Laughter). We do not wish our enemies to have to say that the banners of Sinn Féin would be sullied in any way by crime or murder.' A Sligo priest supported O'Meehan, asking if 'the young priests of Ireland' would 'support anything contrary to patriotism and religion'. But de Valera, his courage bolstered by 'loud and prolonged applause', declared that 'we are not going to truckle to people who insinuate things like that — We will not insult the Irish people by putting anything of that sort in any such clause.' A third priest backed de Valera, and Fr O'Meehan shamefacedly withdrew his amendment. Later in the debate, Fr Pat Gaynor made the mistake of patronisingly describing de Valera's scheme for Sinn Féin organisation as 'a business-like proposition'. Its author scornfully dismissed the priest's remarks, stating that 'Father Gaynor has managed to put us all into a knot. He is imposing his own ideas on mine.'[25] The de Valera of 1917 was no sycophant of clergymen. Yet he did more than any sycophant to render Republicanism innocuous to the church.

By late 1917 de Valera had formulated a political strategy which made a mockery of the precepts of Pearse. This strategy was put into effect with remarkable success. In East Clare Sinn Féin conducted a highly professional campaign to defeat a candidate who had 'defended one half of the murderers in Clare and is related to the other half'.[26] A Resident Magistrate complained that de Valera's canvassers included the Master of the Ennis workhouse, the Clerk of the Union, dispensary doctors, district nurses and even police pensioners.[27] Outside the major towns the canvassers often secured huge majorities for de Valera: in Meelick, home district of the influential Volunteer family of Brennans, 'things were so well organised' that only one out of 72 votes was unpledged by the time of the poll while 64 votes went to Sinn Féin; while in Gleninagh not one vote was missing, though 'people didn't rightly know what it meant at that time'.[28] The Clare county inspector reported that since the election 'all the young people have become Sinn Féiners as have also a great number of the older people', being under the impression 'that after the establishment of the Irish Republic people will be able to exactly as they please'.[29] The formal organisation of Sinn Féin in Clare grew most rapidly during September and October 1917, when de Valera again toured the county, and by the end of 1917 at least 64 clubs had been noticed in the local press. The existence of these clubs was not merely nominal, for 73 Clare clubs had been affiliated (at a price) with headquarters by 17 December 1917, while 63 clubs corresponded with headquarters between January and May 1918.[30] Thus in Clare, as in many other counties, the organisation of a vast network of parochial societies was largely accomplished months before the conscription crisis of April 1918. The threat of conscription was not crucial in the process of transforming Republicanism from an arcane profession to the most popular of Nationalist persuasions. As one Clare county councillor observed

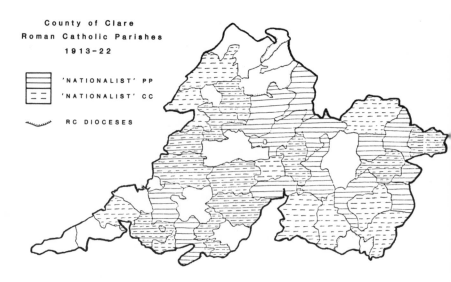

Map 1

County of Clare
Roman Catholic Parishes
1913-22

'NATIONALIST' PP
'NATIONALIST' CC

RC DIOCESES

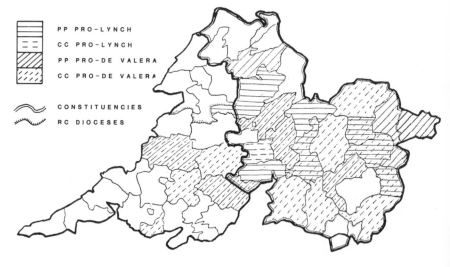

Map 2

County of Clare
Roman Catholic Parishes
East Clare Election Campaign
June–July 1917

PP PRO–LYNCH
CC PRO–LYNCH
PP PRO–DE VALERA
CC PRO–DE VALERA

CONSTITUENCIES
RC DIOCESES

in September 1917, 'I think they are nearly all falling into line'.[31]

De Valera's attempt to separate the political and military facets of Republicanism was imperfectly understood by the rank and file, who nevertheless obediently joined both organisations. But the formal separation undoubtedly facilitated the integration of clergymen, usually reluctant to join the Volunteers, into the Sinn Féin clubs. The history of clerical involvement in the East Clare campaign provides a fascinating example of the process by which the priesthood was induced to support the successors of the Easter rebels. Bishop Fogarty of Killaloe was widely believed to have voted for de Valera, though he kept 'strict silence' during the campaign and was a close friend of the most strident clerical supporter of the Home Rule candidate, Patrick Lynch.[32] Despite his prevarications over the Rising and his former embroilment in Home Rule politics, Dr Fogarty endorsed the proposal for Irish representation at the Peace Conference as early as March 1917.[33] On 30 September 1917, when the Clare county council greeted de Valera as 'the chosen Leader of the Irish Race', the bishop found himself unable to attend but praised 'the brave and honourable representative of East Clare'.[34] Bishop O'Dwyer, whose Limerick diocese overlapped with East Clare, was regarded as an even stronger antagonist of the Old Party than Fogarty. Only Bishop O'Dea of Galway remained aloof from politics in 1917.

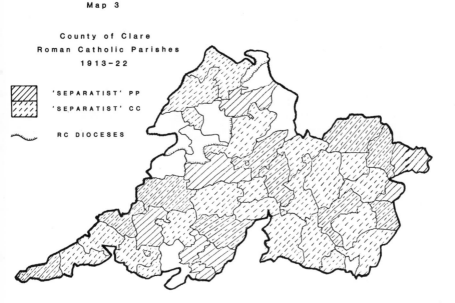

Map 3

County of Clare
Roman Catholic Parishes
1913–22

'SEPARATIST' PP
'SEPARATIST' CC

RC DIOCESES

The political stance of the bishop had a marked but by no means determinant effect on that of his clergy. Map 1 indicates that clerical support for Home Rule organisations between 1913 and 1922 was
widespread throughout both the major diocesan sectors of Clare. During
the East Clare campaign (Map 2), clerical involvement was virtually
limited to the Killaloe diocese, where priests in 19 of the 22 parishes
within the constituency are known to have participated in the campaign.
This applied to only one of the five East Clare parishes administered by
the Bishop of Galway.[35] But within the Killaloe parishes, there was considerable dissension among the clergy. Priests in eight parishes supported Lynch, but four of them found their curates campaigning for de
Valera. Dissension within parishes was concentrated in the eastern section of the constituency, where the tradition of clerical involvement in
Home rule organisations was fairly strong. De Valera was overtly supported by almost as many parish priests as was Lynch, and by far more
curates. Comparison of Maps 2 and 3 indicates that the incorporation of
the Killaloe clergy into the Republican movement was largely accomplished during the election campaign, though a continuing trickle of
clerical recruits 'came out' thereafter until all but three Clare parishes in
the diocese had thrown in their lot with Sinn Féin. Once persuaded of
Sinn Féin's respectability, the priesthood shamelessly transferred its
political affiliation to the new organisation.

Not all priests required proof of respectability. Just after the poll, Fr
O'Mara hoped to God that 'our day will come, and according to the signs
of the times, that day will soon be at hand when we will make them, the
British soldiers, run before us the same as they did at Fontenoy,
Castlebar, and Clontarf'. Later Fr Daniel Flynn, in execrating 'the
bloody old peelers', declared that 'we have our own Sinn Féin army who
are as solid as rock'; while during the conscription crisis, the irrepressible
Fr Gaynor remarked that if an attempt were made to conscript Irishmen,
'the fit resting place for an Irish bullet is in an English heart'.[36] For
curates like these, de Valera's carefully contrived reassurances seem
quaintly misdirected. But more moderate-minded priests required under-
takings that Sinn Féin would not, as predicted by Fr Slattery of Quin,
bring 'red ruin and revolution'.[37] They were doubtless happy to hear that
members of the Tulla Sinn Féin club had threatened to burn the effigy of
the dreaded Countess Markievicz; and (during 1918) to read de Valera's
frequent admonitions against precipitate radical action on the part of
Labour.[38] With remarkable aplomb, de Valera managed to calm the fears
of the prudent while retaining the enthusiasm of the wild curates. As Fr
Clancy expressed it in a poem published in the *Clare Champion*:[39]

De Valera had spoken in manly appeal,
To the gallant Dalcassians and up stood McNeill,

As his pleading for Erin with eloquence fell,
Hark, sweet came the tones of the Angelus bell.
A reverent pause as the sound reached his ears,
Then he called out aloud to a priest standing near,
"The Angelus, Father," and bowed was each head,
As the message of God in the old town was said.

De Valera's great contribution to Irish Nationalism in 1917 was to cajole the conspirators and men of blood into subsuming their energies into an open political movement. With astonishing success, he also persuaded a large part of the clergy and their flock that celebration of one Rising was not tantamount to preparation for another. Without his feats of legerdemain, a new populist movement would certainly have arisen; but it might well have found itself in conflict with a revived organisation of conspirators. As it was, the reorganised I.R.B. and the more warlike section of the Volunteers did not manage to resume the carnage until early 1920, and then on an unexpectedly small scale. In his centenary, let us celebrate the memory of Eamon de Valera not for his part in the making of the Easter Rising, but for his part in its undoing.

NOTES

1. Letter to *Irish Times* dated 18 July 1917, in his Letterbooks (now in National Library of Ireland).

2. Thomas Johnson, *The Future of Labour in Ireland* (I.T.U.C.L.P.: 1916).

3. Interview with *Saturday Record*, 19 August 1916.

4. Sermon reported in *Clare Champion*, 20 May 1916, and elsewhere.

5. Public Record Office (London), CO 904/23/3. The priest was Fr Tom Wall of Limerick.

6. Letter to Simon Donnelly, April 1917, quoted by Earl of Longford and Thomas P. O'Neill, *Eamon de Valera* (London: 1970), 55.

7. Telegram in Ennis Urban Museum (original spelling).

8. Padraic Colum, *Arthur Griffith* (Dublin: 1959), 203.

9. Public Record Office (Dublin), 1094/1/6.

10. Longford and O'Neill (1970), 64 (Draft of campaign speech in his hand).

11. Typed report of proceedings, N.L.I., Ms. 21523, p. 14.

12. Desmond Ryan, *Unique Dictator* (London: 1936), 223-4.

13. N.L.I., Ms. 21523, p. 57.

14. Letter published 10 November 1917, quoted by F.S.L. Lyons, *John Dillon* (London: 1968), 427.

15. *Saturday Record*, 14 July 1917; Longford and O'Neill (1970), 64; State Paper Office (Dublin), Press Censor's Correspondence, no. 34.

16. N.L.I., Ms. 21523, pp. 50-2.

17. *Ibid.*, pp. 5, 13.

18. *Ibid.*, p. 56.

19. P.R.O. (London), CO 904/23/3.

20. The constitutions of the Irish Volunteers and Sinn Féin were not altered to give allegiance to Dáil Éireann until about March 1920 and October 1921 respectively.

21. Marcus Bourke, *John O'Leary* (Tralee: 1967), 165-6; F.X. Martin, 'The 1916 Rising', *Studia Hibernica*, 8 (1968), 106.

22. David W. Miller, *Church, State and Nation in Ireland 1898-1921* (Dublin: 1973), 393.

23. Miller (1973), 393; Michael Brennan, *The War in Clare* (Dublin: 1980), 24-5.

24. Leaflets in O'Brien Gift, N.L.I., P 116.

25. N.L.I., Ms. 21523, pp. 10, 33. No amendments were accepted by the Ard Fheis, which had been warned in advance that all resolutions on the agenda had been 'agreed to *unanimously*' by the Executive: see Notices of Motion, copy in N.L.I., P 1891.

26. Annie O'Brien to Redmond, 19 June 1917, Redmond Papers, N.L.I., Ms. 15263/2, quoting reports of 'a Sinn Féin conversation'.

27. Report by George McElroy, S.P.O., R.P. 17396/1917, dated 14-15 July 1917.

28. Information from Austin Brennan and Con O'Donoghue.

29. Monthly Confidential Report, July 1917, P.R.O. (London), CO 904/103.

30. Reports of meetings in *Clare Champion* and *Saturday Record*; G.N. Plunkett Papers, N.L.I., Ms. 11405; Précis of Sinn Féin Correspondence, N.L.I., Ms. 10594. See also my *Politics and Irish Life* (Dublin: 1977), chapter 4.

31. *Clare Champion*, 29 September 1917.

32. Patrick Gaynor, *Kilmihil Parish* (typescript, 1946), now in N.L.I., p. 368.

33. Miller (1973), 352.

34. *Clare Champion*, 6 October 1917. For newspaper reports of this and other letters and speeches of the period, see Kevin J. Browne, 'A Man and a County', *Clare Champion*, 1971-2 (*passim*).

35. The Bishop of Galway was also Bishop of Kilmacduagh and Apostolic Administrator of Kilfenora, so that his territory covered much of north-west Clare. The maps are based on data already analysed statistically in my *Politics and Irish Life*, Appendix.

36. P.R.O. (London), CO 904/23/3; Gaynor (1946), 383-5.

37. *Saturday Record*, 7 July 1917.

38. County inspector's Monthly Confidential Report, November 1917, P.R.O. (London), CO 904/104; see my *Politics and Irish Life*, chapter 7.

39. Issue of 7 July 1917, quoted in Browne, *loc. cit.*, 13 November 1971.

De Valera, Lemass and Irish Economic Development: 1933-1948

Raymond James Raymond

For nearly 60 years Eamon de Valera was the most dominant, influential, and controversial figure in Irish politics. Prime Minister for a total of 21 years, President for 14, he was Ireland's best-known international statesman. Indeed, of all the great Irish political leaders of the past 200 years — Daniel O'Connell, Charles Stewart Parnell, Michael Collins — de Valera was the master; he was the archetype. Through the refractions of his life we can see many of the causes for Ireland's continuous development throughout the twentieth century.

Eamon de Valera was highly intelligent, charming, compassionate, vindictive, volcanic and cold, vicious, and generous. He played every part; he left out no emotion. The pulsings within him, his will, daring, guile, and lust for power, were phenomenal, a continuous astonishment. De Valera was not an idealist, but he served ideals when it suited and pleased him. He was not a reactionary, but he fanned reaction when it helped him advance himself. De Valera's career was one person's experience of nearly everything important in Irish public life since 1916, and he was as personally responsible for Irish history between 1917 and 1959 as any other man of his time.

These five clustering decades from Pearse to Lemass are best understood as the de Valera period because de Valera, more than any of the other Irish politicians of the time, helped generate the values and participated in and then presided over the trends that ultimately prevailed. He was himself in his origins, his ambition, his ambivalent attitude towards Britain, the embodiment of the events and the shapes of power that have become Ireland's present reality.

This is as true of economic as it is of political development. Eamon de Valera was a man with the capacity of mind to reappraise old assumptions, and it was during World War II that de Valera took the first decisive political steps towards economic planning. This view of de Valera is at odds with the view to be found in the earlier works of Bromage, McArdle, Longford and O'Neill, Morrisson and Fitzgibbon, and most recently, T. Ryle Dwyer.[1] The view of de Valera which this earlier generation of scholars held is of a man whose political interests were limited to a narrow range of diplomatic and constitutional issues. Beyond this, the existing scholarship holds that in economic and social matters de Valera was content to leave policy to Sean McEntee, Sean Lemass, and Sean T. O'Kelly, who were credited with shaping the Government's economic priorities. In fact, de Valera turned his attention towards economics more than is commonly supposed and together with Sean Lemass formed an unlikely partnership whose work marked the beginning of the decisive impetus towards the full blow economic planning of the 1960s. Lemass drew up the first Keynesian blueprint for Irish economic development as early as 1944; de Valera provided the political mechanism two years earlier in 1942. Together, de Valera and Lemass precipitated a revolution in economic policy and consequences with which Ireland is still coming to grips.

I

Today, governments in the industrialized nations account for a high proportion of national expenditures and investment enterprise. It is now widely accepted by politicians and administrators that governments have an obligation to manage and even plan the economy in accordance with a series of prescribed objectives. The Republic of Ireland is no exception. Between 1958 and 1970, two successive 'Programs for Economic Expansion' helped transform the Irish economy and revitalize society.[2] These programs not only initiated sweeping reforms in the civil service, but also stimulated the competitiveness of the private sector and took the first steps towards a comprehensive incomes policy. Espousing the philosophy that the economy could be engineered away from stagnation towards rapid economic growth, these development plans appear to mark a watershed in twentieth century Irish history. Or do they?

Little or nothing has been written on the long-term origins of the Whittaker revolution and, as a result, two key points have been ignored.[3] First, the developmental philosophy of the Whittaker revolution owed much to the pioneering work of De Valera and Lemass whose courage and endurance made the need for rational economic and social planning visible in the bitterly hostile environment of the late 1930s and early 1940s. The very *raison d'etre* of the Whittaker program, the concern to make a better tomorrow, and the assumption of a vast new array of economic and social responsibilities by the state in order to create full employment and economic growth, took root in the years between 1937 and 1945.

Moreover, far from having to create its own administrative mechanisms, Dr Whittaker was faced with the simpler task of rationalizing an already complex administrative network in which government departments and semi-state bodies were already carrying out the functions which the first and second programs would later coordinate. This was no fortuitous occurrence. It, too, represented the culmination of a generation of change and innovation during which the whole administrative machine was overhauled at the behest of de Valera and Lemass. Indeed, it might even be argued that the Irish planning revolution was little more than the logical result of a new consciousness which began to develop during and after the 'Emergency' that the Irish economy could be directed into the desired channels.

This development was, of course, symptomatic of a broader European trend. In Ireland, as all over Europe, war planning brought about deep structural changes in the economy. In the broad sense, war planning not only altered parts of the economic system, but also created fundamental changes in the role of the government in the economy. It precipitated the rise of economic planning, state capitalism, and the increased power of the bureaucracy. Above all, however, World War II delivered a great impetus to the general trend within the European economy towards a more rational, a more efficient, and a more managed deployment of resources. Extension of state control was resorted to only when unavoidable and was dictated primarily by considerations of the optimum deployment of resources rather than more radical social aims.

The kind of state planning implemented in Ireland after 1958 was 'coordinative' planning. Under coordinative planning, government influences the economy's performance by focusing its economic power towards certain strategic points: it manipulates but does not control the economy. In this sense, coordinative planning complements private enterprise. The government uses its policy instruments to influence all the key variables which singularly and collectively determine the level of economic activity.[4] Coordinative planning of this kind requires a political environment that gives the government the necessary powers and functions to plan; a developed state statistical apparatus to manage aggregate data; and a heightened awareness of the potentiality of economic planning. The partnership of de Valera and Lemass helped create these preconditions between 1938 and 1948. The creation of the political environment and administrative mechanism will be examined in this first half of the essay; the development of the new awareness of economic planning through the promotion of Keynesian economics will be discussed later.

Irish politicians and administrators had long been concerned by the economic impact on Ireland of any European war. As a result, the years from 1937 through 1939 witnessed a formidable intensification in the pressure and strain of public business. This was not at all surprising because throughout the 1930s the Irish government had begun to play a more vigorous role in promoting growth and development. It was natural, therefore, that the state, as the single most powerful economic actor, would play the decisive role in Irish war planning.

The immediate prewar years had also witnessed an impressive extension of the scope, organization, and range of activity of Irish Cabinet committees. In order to conserve resources, ration precious foreign exchange, and obtain a fair distribution of the limited supplies available, the Irish Cabinet system was overhauled. The contingency plans which it produced cannot be defined as 'planning' in any meaningful sense of the term, however. Nevertheless, they did mark the beginning of a crude form of objective forecasting.

During the war, the very word 'planning' experienced a rehabilitation. From the fall of 1942 through the summer of 1944, there was considerable discussion in professional journals, in the quality press, and among interest groups about the need for rational economic and social planning. Indeed, the development of a new vocabulary was the surest sign that large elements of Irish society had entered into secure possession of a new concept.[5] By 1943, the term 'planning' began to be freely used for the first time in Ireland in a recognizably modern sense. Yet, while the public debate went on, no one was aware of the extent of the planning in process in government buildings in Merrion Street. Fewer still could have imagined that the political initiative had come from Eamon de Valera, a man whom historians have generally portrayed as indifferent to economic and social policy.

The conventional view of de Valera is of a man whose political interests were limited to a narrow range of constitutional issues. Beyond this, the conventional wisdom holds that in economic and social matters, de Valera was content to leave policy to Sean Lemass, Sean McEntee, and Sean T. O'Kelly, who were credited with shaping the government's economic priorities.[6] The myth has even grown up that de Valera distrusted industrialization and was fully content with the austere vision of rural frugality. By contrast, Sean Lemass has been portrayed as the progressive architect of the modern Irish economy. Indeed, one noted scholar has recently observed that 'there are few Irishmen of whom one can feel as confident tht further research will enhance rather than diminish their stature'.[7] Doubtless, Lemass did great things, but the personality cult always detracts from reality. Earlier we have seen how de Valera took personal charge of all war planning and how Lemass's role was essentially subordinate. Indeed, it is often difficult to see Lemass as anything other than the sub-contractor. It was only in 1944, when de Valera finally began to relinquish exclusive control of the reins of power, that Lemass began to emerge as the architect of the modern Irish economy, introducing Keynesian thinking to Irish economic policy. This was no coincidence. By 1944, Lemass had completed his tutelage in economics under John Leydon, the permanent secretary of the Department of Supplies. By then, Lemass was finally ready to emerge, not only as a developmental thinker, but as the decisive political force in shaping Irish economic development.

Doubtless, de Valera harboured his engaging fantasies of bucolic bliss throughout the 1930s, but he was never distrustful of industrialization. He was too astute to ignore the fact that rural Ireland was already doomed, strangled by its own innate sterility. But while he never fully abandoned his dream of a self-sufficient rural utopia, de Valera had the calibre of mind to re-examine his assumptions in the light of changed circumstances. The desperate crises of 1941 and the collapse of his economic foreign policy created a whole new situation. By the late spring of 1942, he was ready to begin a process which would bring a revolutionary turnabout in Irish economic policymaking. Under de Valera's leadership, new mechanisms for long-term planning began to evolve. These can legitimately be regarded as the first step towards securing the full coordination of policies and activities throughout the public sector which would later characterize the first and second programs for economic expansion in the 1950s. The 'Chief' provided the decisive initial impetus towards the creation of the managed economy in Ireland.

The move towards a managed economy came about primarily because of the crisis of legitimacy created by the 'Emergency'. The economic crisis of 1941 brought about massive emigration and acute shortages of supply; the symbolic system of de Valera's state was losing its efficacy. The state that had been founded on symbols of Catholicism, Gaelicism, and Republicanism could not withstand the economic shock waves of war, nor could it hold its own people within its borders. De Valera was, above all, a consummate politician, a political survivor. He realized that to ensure the future of the state which he had established in the 1930s, he needed to refound it in a new economic formula: state capitalism and coordinative planning. De Valera's move towards planning was, therefore, a direct response to the revolution in Irish socio-economic aspirations brought about by rampant inflation and supply shortages. Irish economic policy became politicized because it was now necessary to redefine the legitimacy of the state in economic terms.

De Valera launched the initiative on 30 June 1942 at a Cabinet meeting when, at his instigation, a lengthy discussion was in progress on the need for systematic planning to develop Irish agricultural and industrial capacity to meet the needs of the postwar world. During the meeting, the Cabinet decided that de Valera, in consultation with Sean T. O'Kelly, Sean Lemass, and Sean McEntee, should examine the social and economic problems likely to arise after the emergency and the measures which should be prepared to deal with such problems, and he should arrange for the preparation by the departments concerned of developmental proposals.[8]

Four days later, Sean T. O'Kelly received a memorandum from de Valera outlining his ideas. In this first draft of the memorandum, the Irish leader demonstrated an acute awareness of the problems which would beset the economy at the end of the war.[9] The unemployment problem, he knew, would present particular difficulties with the return of over a quarter of a million ex-servicemen and workers from overseas and the demobilization of the defense forces at home. De Valera had no illusions either of the difficulties confronting Irish agriculture and industry. The Taoiseach was acutely aware of the need for further industrial development and the need to assist those industries which were being seriously affected by supply shortages during the war, while, with the fall in the value of Irish external assets, the prospects for the balance of payments looked decidedly grim. De Valera, therefore, concluded: 'The position, indeed, is likely to be so serious that well-thought-out plans prepared in advance by the government and put into execution under government supervision can help us to tide over the period after the war.'[10] Accordingly, the Taoiseach recommended that each government department should immediately start to examine the matters within its own province and prepare its plans for collation through the Department of Finance. The situation was so serious that De Valera emphasized that financial considerations should be subordinated to the necessity of getting the work under way.

Following consultations with O'Kelly, de Valera redrafted his memorandum to provide for two programs of public works; one a two-year program, the other a five-year program. The Taoiseach also envisaged that Maurice Moynihan, Secretary to the Cabinet, should serve as Chief Executive Planning Officer working in close collabortion with a special planning official in each department. Nevertheless, in view of the seriousness of the nation's economic problems, de Valera proposed that he himself whould act as supervisor and coordinator of all plans.[11]

John Leydon, the Permanent Secretary of the Department of Supplies, was unhappy with this proposed planning structure. On 22 September 1942, he wrote Maurice Moynihan enclosing a short personal memorandum for the Taoiseach.[12] In the memorandum, Leydon argued that if economic planning were to prove successful, it should be directed by men who were in close contact with the trend and development of government policy, the Permanent Secretaries of the Departments of Finance, Industry and Commerce, and Agriculture. In order that they could make rapid progress with the task, Leydon argued that they should be relieved of all their normal routine duties. Moynihan brought the matter up with de Valera two days later on 28 September, but the Taoiseach had grave doubts about Leydon's proposals, and he ultimately rejected them.[13]

De Valera's reasoning is not hard to fathom; on the one hand, he may have been concerned that given the grave supply and shipping difficulties then besetting the Irish economy, that Leydon and McElligott should, in the national interest, give their whole attention to these problems. On the other hand, it was clear that in the difficult postwar years, de Valera's political future could well depend upon his ability to handle the economy, particularly the thorny problem of unemployment. He may, therefore, have wished to personally control the program with the assistance of his two closest confidantes, Sean Lemass and Sean T. O'Kelly. Moreover, the whole concept of planning was a politically sensitive issue suggestive of social engineering, and, therefore, not to be left in the hands of civil servants.

The degree to which the need for postwar planning preoccupied the minds both of the Taoiseach and the business community was clearly manifest in de Valera's speech to the Dublin Chamber of Commerce on the evening of 28 October 1942:

> The nature of the present war organization is such that it is bound to leave a permanent mark on the character — the outlook and the ideals of the individual and on the social organization of which he is part. State control and state intervention will tend to remain and entrench itself in many spheres where formerly private enterprise alone held the field. The state will continue to accept responsibility where formerly it accepted none. International trade will tend to become more and more directly an inter-state affair and be operated and controlled in bulk by several states each in the national or community interest to which private interests will be definitely subordinated.[14]

De Valera continued:

> The training we are receiving in trying to solve the problems of the present emergency is the best training for meeting the problems we must face after the war. What we plan and execute now we should plan and execute as far as possible with a view to permanency.[15]

The acceptance of the need for rational economic planning implied significant changes in the procedures for long-term economic and social decision making. It was not at all surprising, therefore, that at the next Cabinet meeting on 24 November 1942, de Valera suggested that a Cabinet Committee on Economic Planning be set up to plan for postwar reconstruction.

This Cabinet Committee held its inaugural meeting on 2 December 1942, when it reviewed the departmental replies received in response to de Valera's letter in July.[16] The Taoiseach envisaged that the state should and would play a crucial role in Irish economic and social development. Accordingly, throughout the remainder of 1942 and most of 1943, the Cabinet Committee on Economic Planning received departmental proposals which were operational in character and which concerned methods for achieving a general social goal about which there was little basic policy controversy. That goal embraced the alleviation of unemployment through short-term public works and through developmental schemes in agriculture, industry, and investment in the economy's infrastructure.

By 10 January 1944, de Valera and Moynihan, the two chief planning executives, had collated all the existing departmental proposals into a development program costing some 86·6 million pounds, a small figure by the standards of the 1980s, but extremely significant in the 1940s.

The nature and purpose of the plans evidence a revolution in Irish socio-economic aspirations and in the government's willingness to meet them.[17] It is easy to argue that 'total war' inevitably brings social and economic change because in order to ensure its survival, the state must retain the allegiance of its citizens, and the greater the demands it makes on them, the more they will seize the opportunities to make demands on it. But the process surely depends on the receptivity of government, and it is more plausible to contend, as Arthur Marwick does, the common economic, social, and psychological experience of war produces a change in the climate of social consciousness.[18] Lest the reality of this changed climate be doubted, it need only be remarked that in Ireland at the height of the 'Emergency', the Cabinet Committee on Economic Planning was examining plans for the alleviation of unemployment, sweeping reforms in housing, education, social welfare, and massive infrastructural investment.[19] Of the 86·6 million pounds budgeted for in the de Valera 'plan', 52 million, or more than half, went for slum clearance, improved hospitals and schools, and rural electrification.[20]

To sum up then, planning activities in the Irish war economy did not begin and end at the center. Both in logic and time, the planning decisions of the Cabinet Committee on Economic Planning had to be preceded by corresponding planning decisions in each of the major spending departments. The latter had to decide how much labor, capacity, and materials they would require in order to develop the necessary projects which the Taoiseach demanded. From this perspective, the planning acts of the Cabinet Committee were often little more than decisions to reconcile the claims to resources advanced by individual departments for long-term expansionary programs. After July 1944, the Cabinet Committee refocused its attention towards more broad policy review and the preparation of the necessary legislation to implement the various programs.

De Valera's commitment to development 'planning' clearly required a new emphasis on data management skills. In order that his various policies could be coordinated in accordance with the general plan, it was necessary that the state's statistical apparatus be reasonably developed. Unfortunately, this did not occur.[21] No real attempt was made to reorganize or improve the statistics branch until 1949, however, when, because of Ireland's participation in the Marshall Plan, the whole statistical apparatus of the state was restructured.

Before World War II, the Irish statistical service lacked both system and skill. Although several quantitative approaches were made to the nation's economic problems in the 1930s, their methodological assumptions were sometimes little better than makeshift guesses. The 'Emergency' did precipitate some changes, but what existed within the Irish administration at this time was a form of crude elementary recasting and the rigid control of resources, combined with a definition of priorities which excluded most of the priority choices available in peacetime, including the relation of statistics to policymaking.

In no sense, therefore, was the de Valera development program an economic plan. The work which de Valera and his aides were engaged upon did not bear comparison to even the initial phase of the construction of an economic plan. For example, there was no attempt to formulate objectives as interrelated quantitative targets or to attempt to link these targets with available policy instruments. Moreover, the Taoiseach and his fellow 'planners' had no knowledge of econometrics or of model building, both essential to the process of development planning. Quantitative economic planning in this sense was a closed book to de Valera and his advisers. Nevertheless, the Cabinet Committee on Economic Planning did promote administrative efficiency in key areas, and a greater coherence of central government when faced with the daunting and unprecedented challenges of total war. It proved a vital liaison between the various departments and what was not in effect, a War Cabinet. Its tone was bureaucratic and collectivistic; it embodied a real continuing need to reinforce the Cabinet in running a complex and increasingly collectivised society with the help of a specialized policy and planning mechanism. Indeed, by its very commitment to a bureaucratic, corporatist approach, the Cabinet Committee on Economic Planning (and to a lesser degree the other Cabinet economic committees) provided a vital model for the evolution of postwar economic policymaking, one that has left an indelible stamp on Irish economic life ever since. Under de Valera's aegis, Ireland began to move towards a managed economy.

II

Another precondition for economic planning is that there must be a widespread capacity for making decisions and assuming responsibility. A planned economic system must depend on the capacity and industry of many thousands of individuals if it is not to bog down. There must be general consent to the main directives and objectives which are chosen; otherwise the plan will be sabotaged at important points. There must, therefore, be a change in prevailing economic ideas towards a heightened awareness of development possibilities.

There is, of course, great difficulty in assessing precisely the influence of economic thought upon economic policy at any given time. It is often impossible, for example, to determine the extent to which the one is the consequence or alternatively the inspiration of the other. But insofar as the influence of economic doctrine was substantial, possibly even decisive at this time, Keynesian economics was responsible for encouraging much-needed remedial action by de Valera's government which now had the power, the resources, and the administrative capacity to begin to take effective action.

De Valera, Lemass, and their advisers needed the stimulus of new ideas, for although the acceptance of a new vocabulary evidenced acceptance of the concept of planning among the policymaking elite, it is clear that the concern for long-term development was not held by the majority of the rural population. Ireland during the 'Emergency' was still a stable society rooted in a peasant agricultural economy, taking as given fixed horizons and a rigid hierarchical ranking of statuses based on birth, land, and localism. This was a system of ideas which powerfully mobilized sentiments for traditionalism and continuity as against change, mobility, and innovation.

Curiously, prevailing notions of corporatism seemed to have had little practical influence in the formulation of Irish developmental planning.[22] As an organizing principle, corporatism had become very fashionable in many circles in the 1930s. The basic idea was to substitute a form of industrial self-government for the self-regulating market system: to avoid the extremes of laissez faire capitalism or of totalitarian central control by establishing self-governing corporations which would cooperate in the regulation of supply and price of goods, thereby protecting their members from exploitation by individual capitalists or by the state. In Ireland the de Valera government had initially shown some interest in this notion and had established a Commission on Vocational Organization in 1939. After four years of investigation, the Commission presented an ambitious report which was strongly opposed both by de Valera and Lemass. As Joseph Lee has written: 'It [the Commission] criticized civil servants for doing too much. Lemass criticized them for doing too little. The Commission wanted a corporate society, Lemass a corporate state.'[23]

De Valera's conception was much less ambitious. The Taoiseach strongly disapproved of the government planning the actions of others.

In his view, the state should simply plan its own policies, attempting to maintain some consistency over the range of its economic and social policies rather than of public and private sector investment programs.[24] Although de Valera envisaged that the state should and would play a crucial role in Irish economic and social development, there was a distinctive role for private enterprise, too, in the Taoiseach's philosophy. He made this abundantly clear to the Fianna Fáil Ard Fheis on 27 September 1943. De Valera declared: 'We believe in encouraging the development of industries by private enterprise, above all those industries best suited to our requirements and our national resources.'[25] But, the Taoiseach continued:

> We cannot rely entirely on private enterprise. For example, in seeking to promote the development of our mineral resources the state has found it necessary to provide by special legislation for the establishment of two companies . . . . There are other directions also in which it is necessary to provide for active participation in development work by the state . . . in long term planning we have new projects.[26]

As is clearly evidenced by this and other speeches, de Valera's 'planning' was not guided by any theoretical framework. Indeed, despite the need, despite the prestige of the Keynesian voice, and the ready acceptance of most Keynesian ideas by British economists, Keynesian economics had no significant impact on Irish economic thinking until the autumn of 1944. In fact, as de Valera's speech quoted above makes clear, the idea which seems to have had the widest support both in the Cabinet and in the Department of Industry of Commerce was contra-cyclical public works spending to provide direct employment.

The failure of Keynesian economics to influence Irish economic thinking until 1944 is not at all surprising. In the first place, there were very few Irish academic economists, and fewer still with any real sympathy for the 'new economics'. Even the two most brilliant young economists, Patrick Lynch and Louden Ryan, did not fully accept the principle of government intervention until the spring of 1945.[27] Indeed, as we shallsee later, the decisive academic influence in the genesis of Irishdevelopmental planning was Professor George O'Brien, the economic historian. O'Brien's incisive essays on full employment and Keynesian economics in the Jesuit periodical, *Studies*, were read avidly by de Valera and other members of the Cabinet.

The second reason why Keynesian economics failed to influence Irish economic thinking can be found in the attitudes of the Department of Finance. Finance, still the most powerful government department, clung tenaciously to the tenets of classical economics. Indeed, it was not until their mentors in the Treasury produced the now famous *White Paper on*

Full Employment in May 1944 that the Irish Department of Finance began to seriously reconsider its basic theoretical assumptions.

This in itself points up a third factor in the reluctance of Irish policymakers to embrace the 'new economics'. Keynesianism was simply an idea untested by actual experience and was, therefore, not to be trusted. This was a theme which was emphasized not only by the Finance Department, but also by de Valera's personal economic advisor, Professor T.G. Smiddy.[28] In a confidential memorandum for the Taoiseach on 7 July 1944, Smiddy lost no time in denouncing the British proposals for counter-cyclical public works, low interest rates, adjustable tax levels, and a prices and incomes policy. His analysis concluded by arguing that 'the whole emphasis is on consumption goods and not on production goods. The penalty of inadequate production of real wealth in the present is inadequate growth of consumption goods in the future. From this there is no escape.'[29] De Valera was unhappy with Smiddy's negative attitude towards the new development policies. Six days later, he raised the matter at a meeting of the Cabinet Committee on Economic Planning.[30] After a discussion with Lemass and O'Kelly, de Valera instructed the Department of Finance to furnish its observations on the British proposals for full employment.

Throughout the summer and early fall of 1944, as Allied armies began their advance towards Berlin, Finance Department officials carefully analyzed the British White Paper. The results of their analysis were embodied in a long memorandum for the Cabinet Committee on Economic Planning on 31 October 1944.[31] In the foreword, the department of Finance emphasized what it saw as the three main considerations which should shape the government's thinking on full employment: first, that to prevent emigration preparations for increased employment should be put in hand at once; second, that the Irish unemployment problem was different in character to that existing in the United Kingdom in that fluctuations in capital investment were of less importance in Ireland than the more basic problem of domestic underinvestment in Irish agriculture. Consequently, the Irish Finance Department believed that employment could best be increased by developing Irish agriculture through maximizing its efficiency and increasing its productivity. The third consideration which the Department of Finance emphasized was the need to avoid the burden of excessive direct employment of returned emigrants. Although the British government envisaged increased control over employment, Finance argued that they did not envisage the state embarking on expensive programs of direct employment, and that Ireland should follow suit.

Overall, the Treasury's proposals for full employment involved a decisive break with two of the main principles of financial orthodoxy so well loved by the Irish Department of Finance, the balanced budget and the reduction of government expenditure. Not surprisingly, Finance cast a jaundiced eye on the Treasury's proposals for central funding. While none of the Treasury's proposals involved deliberate planning for a budget deficit in depressed years, and much of the capital expenditure was likely to be commercially remunerative, the general line of policy involved additions to the British public debt. The Treasury readily admitted that much of the additional debt would be dead weight and that the ultimate success of the policy would depend on the adequacy of the arrangements to eliminate at least part of the debt during boom periods.

The Irish Department of Finance was quick to seize upon this aspect of the policy to restate its long-held view that a large proportion of the Irish national debt had been incurred for non-productive purposes. The debt was a continuing direct burden on production and a factor in maintaining high interest rates. Accordingly, the Irish Finance Department recommended that if the Cabinet wished to adopt the Keynesian policy of full employment, then 'it would be a considerable advantage if future arrangements involving the creating of public debt were accompanied by provisions for amortisation within the shortest possible period. It is equally desirable, of course, that debt created for revenue producing schemes should be amortised within the lifetime of the assets to which it relates.'[32] Whatever international circumstances might emerge after the war, the Irish Finance Department argued that there were a number of key factors which were of special importance if the Cabinet contemplated a policy of full employment. First, that agriculture production must be maintained at maximum output, and that the policy of land division be reviewed to determine whether or not it was impeding efficiency in production and increased employment. Second, The Finance Department recommended that a comprehensive review of all existing controls and tariffs should be made with the object of removing unnecessary restrictions on trade. Finally, the government should eliminate all Emergency services as quickly as possible and should avoid any further commitments in the sphere of social security measures.

On 21 November 1944, Sean Lemass presented a vigorous rebuttal to the Finance Department's proposals to Maurice Moynihan, the Cabinet Secretary, requesting that his personal memorandum be forwarded to the Taoiseach immediately. In this personally drafted memorandum, Lemass took issue with virtually every point raised by the Department of Finance against the British White Paper proposals.[33] This document is particularly important, not only because it signalled Lemass's emergence as a decisive force in Irish economic development, but also because it evidenced the beginning of his conversion to Keynesian thinking. As a result, it deserves special attention.

The aim of Sean Lemass's memorandum was to show that full

employment was not only practicable, but was in line with modern economic thinking and involved no departure from democratic ideals. His two fundamental principles were that total public and private expenditure on Irish products should always be high enough to set up a demand for such products which could not be satisfied without using the maximum output capacity of the country; and second, that the national output capacity should be expanded so that it would require all available manpower. Lemass's proposals fell in three parts: agricultural reorganization, industrial reorganization, and the framing of a new budgetary strategy for demand management. Each part will be reviewed in turn.

Obviously, the farming community had a particularly important role to play in any strategy aimed at full employment. Lemass argued, however, that although agriculture was of special importance to the Irish economy, and expansion of the volume of agricultural output would not necessarily involve a proportionate expansion in employment, the aim must be to relate the number employed in agriculture to the requirements of the industry; to reduce the effect of seasonal fluctuations in the demand for labor; and to prevent industrial unemployment producing undue competition for agricultural employment.

Drawing on the work of Keynes and Beveridge, Lemass went on to argue that the price mechanism was an effective means of regulating the supply and demand of primary produce, and that this was substantiated by the Irish experience during the war. An increase in expenditure on agriculture would not of itself result in an expansion of production sufficient to create significant additional employment in the industry. Before increased demand could produce increased production and employment, radical changes would have to be made in the organization of the industry.

Consequently, Lemass proposed that a six-point program for agriculture reorganization should be implemented. This program was to embrace the elimination of all incompetent farmers; the reduction of farmers' costs through the abolition of local rates on all agricultural land and buildings; increased mechanization; improved technical instruction; and lower veterinary costs. Lemass also proposed the provision of long-term capital for the purchase of new equipment; the provision of guaranteed prices through the elimination of all private competition, with farmers selling directly to the state at a fixed price determined by the farmers' costs; and finally, that state organizations would take over the agricultural export trade in order to ensure standardization of quality and continuity of supply. Lemass concluded:

> Emphasis is placed on the need for changes in the organization of the agricultural industry because in a predominantly agricultural economy, full

employment cannot be promoted merely by expanding outlay on the products of industry, but requires positive action by the state to ensure the enlargement of output capacity, but the improvement of productive equipment, better management, the reorganization of distributive methods, etc. can be expected to follow on the stimulation of private demand, but a community of small farmers cannot organize themselves for these purposes and only the state has the power and resources to do the job thoroughly.[34]

Conditions in other industries did not require state regulation to such a level under the Lemass program. In regard to manufacturing industry, Lemass proposed that the state should help provide long-term capital in order to expand industrial capacity by repatriating Irish investments abroad. He also recommended that some form of price commission be established so that the expansion of demand would not be met by an increase in prices in lieu of an increase in output. In order to cope with the other problems impeding Irish industrial development, Lemass proposed the following program: (1) That the Trade Union movement be invited to participate in industrial management through works councils and in return get their acceptance of a mandatory incomes policy supervised by a public authority. (2) That in order to ensure efficient productive methods that Trade Union regulations which restricted the number of new entrants to a trade and limited worker participation should be banned by law and that the state should be given powers to insist upon the introduction of new machinery. (3) That the income tax code be overhauled so as to provide the maximum inducement to industrialists to accumulate funds for the replacement of obsolete plants. (4) That steps should be taken to establish new large-scale industries capable of competing successfully in international markets. Lemass proposed that these steps should embrace the provision of a state guarantee to assist in raising capital; exemption from corporations profits tax and local rates in proportion to the total output exported; the provision of free factory sites convenient to suitable port facilities; the granting of free import of materials; and the granting of shift work permits if desired. Finally, Lemass also proposed that a new state export corporation be established with agencies around the world to obtain information on all potential export markets and facilitate the making of contracts.[35]

Turning his attention to the pivotal question of finance, Lemass contended that overall demand could be maintained at a sufficiently high level to ensure full employment by increasing state expenditures from borrowing, and the reduction of taxation. The most effective way in which the state could increase outlay was by increasing its own expenditure on public works, capital investment, subsidizing exports, and increasing social service payments. This, of course, involved a new kind of budget based not on exchequer requirements, but on estimates of the total outlay on industrial products necessary to maximize output capacity, and on the estimate of expenditure on industrial products at the existing level of taxation. If actual outlay was estimated to fall short of that necessary to maintain full employment, then the state would finance additional expenditure out of borrowing. Lemass conceded that such a policy might involve a large increase in the national debt, and that the annual appropriation from revenue for the service of the debt would involve a heavy burden of taxation. Nevertheless, the Minister of Supplies argued that an increase in public borrowing would be less than the increase in public expenditure since the higher expenditure would increase the yields from existing taxation.

It is not at all surprising that these revolutionary proposals met with a hostile reception in the Department of Finance. In a series of detailed notes on the Lemass proposals, McElligott, the Permanent Secretary, witheringly observed:

The condition stated to be necessary for full employment would involve a control of all economic processes so complete and detailed that it probably could not be realised without the full socialization of industry and the suppression of freedoms which no western people would sacrifice without a bitter struggle . . . . In manufacturing industry as in agriculture, the less State regulation there is the better for the national economy . . . . As for the full employment policies of the British and American governments, they are merely paper schemes, and their practicability and effectiveness remain to be seen.[36]

McElligott concluded with one final parting shot: 'To a layman these proposals suggest that the "vicious spiral" which was so unpopular a few years ago has lost its terrors. The authorities cited in support of this policy (Keynes, Beveridge, and Kaldor) all appear to belong to the escapist school of economics.'[37]

The two memoranda by Lemass, the rebuttals by the Department of Finance, and the essays of George O'Brien framed the terms of the debate which took place within the Cabinet Committee on Economic Planning throughout the Spring of 1945. De Valera, whose interest had been originally fired by O'Brien's writings on the 'new economics', favoured the new Keynesian approach, but it was Lemass who was now providing the decisive impetus.[38]

At weekly meetings between February and June 1945, the Cabinet Committee on Economic Planning discussed each memorandum paragraph by paragraph in what was undoubtedly the most far-reaching debate on Irish economic policy in the history of the state. Unfortunately, the Committee's records do not contain verbatim transcripts of its proceedings. It is, therefore, impossible to follow the terms of the debate as closely as we would like. Nevertheless, for the first time the tenets of classical economics were seriously questioned, and Keynesian strategies found new protagonists among the members of the Cabinet, who de Valera now involved in the debate by enlarging the membership of the Committee to embrace all ministers in the government.

The end of the war in Europe brought this debate to an inconclusive end with no decisions taken. The Cabinet Committee on Economic Planning did not meet again until the end of 1946; the revolutionary new doctrines which, if implemented, would have created the necessary control mechanisms to influence economic development remained in the files of the Department of the Taoiseach. The prevailing concept of the budget was still that of a national bookkeeping exercise determined by the requirements of the exchequer. The reason is not hard to find. The end of the war confronted the de Valera government with an unparalleled shortage of raw materials. The European economy was devastated. The immediate problem was not one of shortage of assets, despite the heavy destruction, but a severe scarcity of essential supplied including food and a weakened and undernourished population. Imports were urgently needed in Ireland as all over Europe, but because of a low export potential the European nations had not the means to pay for them. Ireland's position was aggravated by diplomatic isolation, large public debts, new waves of inflation, and unfavourable terms of trade. The magnitude of these short-term difficulties overwhelmed Irish policymakers and precluded serious consideration of long-term planning. All of these difficulties facilitated the Department of Finance in winning its bureaucratic battle with the Cabinet. Nevertheless, the days of financial orthodoxy were numbered, for Sean Lemass had called in question the validity of the assumptions that had underpinned Irish economic policy for 25 years.

Indeed, Lemass's own program was probably the most significant development arising out of the 'Emergency'. The Lemass plan was revolutionary in character, for it was comprehensive, rational, and coherent. It embraced the whole economy; it argued from a clearly defined set of economic principles, and each of its component parts was consistent with the other and subordinated to the overriding goal of economic development. Despite its flaws and omissions — particularly concerning the role of the Central Bank — it was a systematic attempt to subject Irish underdevelopment to modern economic analysis. As such it was unprecedented.

To sum up, the work of de Valera and Lemass in promoting development planning falls into three phases. The first covers the period from the Munich crisis of September 1938 through December 1940; the second phase runs from the introduction of the British economic squeeze in January 1941 through June 1942; the third and final phase from June

1942 to the end of the war. During the first period, de Valera dominated the partnership taking complete charge of all war preparations. Given de Valera's relatively conservative leanings, it was not surprising that this period was characterized by an intense bout of chaotic planning during which the orthodoxies of classical economics were occasionally questioned but rarely violated. Under de Valera's supervision, Irish officials focused their energy on the creation of an economy whose dominating purpose was survival; not to maximize its war potential, but as a neutral, to minimize the risk of war damage. The result of this apparent clarity of purpose was an attempt to create a form of economic organization for the duration of the war which was sharply different from that of the preceding to succeeding periods of peace. Unfortunately, what was lacking in de Valera's case was a sophisticated understanding of war economics and an unambiguous answer to the question of what war to prepare for and when. Irish war planning was haphazard, uncoordinated, and misinformed.

The climacteric second phase of development planning was a result of the failure of de Valera's war preparations; the impact of Anglo-American economic pressure; and the increasing influence of Sean Lemass. Since 1939, Lemass had been pressing for comprehensive planning, but it was not until June 1942 that Lemass compelled de Valera to reassess some of his economic assumptions. The seriousness of Ireland's economic difficulties during this period brought about a sudden multiplication of government activities and an extension of state controls into shipping, technological research, as well as other areas of national economic life. This expansion was chaotic but permanent. The centralization and the seeds of supervision led to some degree of planning, if only to establish priorities in expenditure. The mechanism which coordinated this dramatic expansion of state activity was the Cabinet Committee on Economic Planning which was established by de Valera in June 1942. Doubtless, Lemass had been pressing for the establishment of such a mechanism for some time, but to attribute this remarkable innovation to Lemass's pressure alone is to oversimplify. De Valera was a man with the calibre of mind to reexamine his assumptions in the light of changed circumstances. The desperate crises of 1941-42 brought abut massive emigration and acute supply shortages; the symbolic system of de Valera's state was losing its efficacy. The state that had been founded on symbols of Catholicism, Gaelicism, and Republicanism could not withstand the economic shock waves of war, nor could it hold its people within its borders. De Valera, therefore, realized that the state needed to be refounded on the new economic formula of state capitalism and coordinative planning.

The establishment of the Cabinet Committee on Economic Planning ushered in a new phase in the the de Valera-Lemass partnership. By now, Ireland's neutrality was no longer in danger, and de Valera began to give Lemass more scope to exercise his initiative. The development program devised by de Valera and Lemass cannot be regarded as a 'plan' in any meaningful sense of the term. But it can legitimately be regarded as the first step towards securing that vital coordination of policies and activity so essential in economic planning.

Perhaps the most significant development of all was the beginning of a deliberate and successful attempt to preserve full employment which was to last for nearly 30 years. This development is entirely attributable to Lemass. His emergence as a developmental thinker and as the decisive political force within the Irish Cabinet on economic policy after 1942, brought with it the first impact of Keynesian economics. Lemass's ideas on full employment and deficit financing, shared to some extent by de Valera, were decisively shaped by his reading of the works of Sir William Beveridge and John Maynard Keynes. Lemass's radical ideas challenged the very assumptions upon which Irish economic policy had been based for over 20 years. They not only caused the most far-reaching debate on Irish economic policy since the foundations of the state, but foreshadowed the whole developmental strategy which Lemass would implement after 1959 when he himself became Taoiseach.

Eamon de Valera and Sean Lemass together had brought about the first stirrings of the Irish planning revolution. Three features in their work are especially noteworthy. For the first time 'economic planning' was being used in a recognizably modern sense. Next, this happened under direct economic and political pressure from the Irish people. Finally, a great body of data had been collected on a subject hitherto widely canvassed but not really known. In short, the 1960s were foreshadowed.

ACKNOWLEDGEMENTS

The author has been granted access to certain official documents and permission for the publication of quotations therefrom by the Department of the Taoiseach and by the Department of Finance. The author alone is responsible for the statements made in this essay and the views expressed therein.

NOTES

1. Mary Bromage, *De Valera and the March of a Nation* (Dublin: 1956); Dorothy McArdle, *The Irish Republic* (New York: 1967); Lord Longford and Thomas P. O'Neill, *Eamon de Valera* (Dublin: 1970); Constantine Fitzgibbon and George Morrison, *The Life and Times of Eamon de Valera* (Dublin: 1973); and T. Ryle Dwyer, *Eamon de Valera* (Dublin: 1978).

2. Department of Finance, *Program for Economic Expansion*, Pr. 4796 (Dublin: 1958); Department of Finance, *Economic Development*, Pr. 4803 (Dublin: 1958); Department of Finance, *Second Program for Economic Expansion*, Part I, Pr. 7239 (Dublin: 1963), and Part II, Pr. 7670 (Dublin: 1964). See also: P. Lynch, 'Escape from Stagnation', *Studies* (Summer: 1963), 50-63.

3. Dr Ronan Fanning's magisterial volume *The Irish Department of Finance 1922-1958* (Dublin: 1978) does contain a fascinating account of the immediate background to the publication of *Economic Development*. See Chapter 6. Other works which touch briefly on the antecedents of planning are: John L. Pratschke, 'Business and Laoour in Irish Society 1945-1970', in J.J. Lee (ed.), *Ireland 1945-1970* (Dublin: 1979), 40-41; Garret Fizgerald's *Planning in Ireland* (Dublin: 1968), 1; and Lorraine Donaldson, *Development Planning in Ireland* (New York: 1965), p. 1. See also: John A. Murphy, *Ireland in the Twentieth Century* (Dublin: 1975), 123-124.

4. This distinction is drawn by Patrick George Brady, 'Towards Security: Postwar Economic and Social Planning in the Executive Office, 1939-1946', unpublished Ph.D. dissertation, 1975. Rutgers University, New Jersey.

5. See the lengthy series of articles in the *Irish Independent* throughout 1942 and 1943. For a discussion of the need for rational planning in agriculture, see *The Beet-Grower's Record* for 1943 and 1944 (National Library of Ireland Pamphlet IR 05). For a sample of the literature advocating economic planning and proceedings of conferences which discussed planning, see the reports from the United States Legation and Consulate during this period: Record Group 59, 841D.5017/8-644; 841D.50/37; 841D.50/38, National Archives, Washington, D.C.

6. See Brian Farrell, *Chairman or Chief* (Dublin: 1971), 27-29; J.J. Lee, 'Sean Lemass', and 'Continuity and Change', in Lee (ed.) *Ireland 1945-1970* (Dublin:1979).

7. J.J. Lee, 'Lemass and His Two Partnerships', *The Irish Times*, 19 May 1976.

8. Irish Cabinet Minutes, 30 June 1942, Cab. Sec. S 12882, SPO.

9. De Valera's memorandum is on Cab. Sec. S 13206A, SPO.

10. *Ibid.*

11. The revised memorandum is also on Cab. Sec. S 13206A, SPO.

12. Leydon to de Valera, 22 September 1942, Cab. Sec. S 12882, SPO.

13. Ms. note by Maurice Moynihan, 29 September 1942, on Cab. Sec. S 12882, SPO.

14. The full text on the speech is on Cab. Sec. S 13206A, SPO.

15. *Ibid.*

16. Minutes of the meeting, 2 December 1942, Cabinet Committee on Economic Planning, Cab. Sec. S 13206A, SPO.

17. The revolution in the government's willingness can be seen in the relevant policy documents in many areas of state activity. For the development of national health insurance, see Cab. Sec. S 13688; for plans to cope with returning emigrants, see Cab. Sec. S 11582; for plans for rotational employment schemes, see Cab. sec. S 9600; and for the evolution of Irish labour policy, see Cab. Sec. S 12882A, SPO. A careful analysis of these files reveals that de Valera, Lemass, and Moynihan were acutely aware of the desperate plight of the people and of their demands for better living conditions, stable employment, and a reasonable income.

18. *Britain in the Century of Total War: War, Peace, and Social Change 1900-1967* (London: 1967), *passim.*

19. The collated program is on Cab. Sec. S 13206A, SPO.

20. *Ibid.*

21. For background on this period of the Irish statistics service, see Maurice Hickey, 'An office that Makes Statistics Attractive', *The Irish Independent*, 14 October 1954.

22. For an analysis of some aspects of Irish corporatist thinking, see Joseph Lee, 'Some Aspects of Corporatist Thought in Ireland: The Commission on Vocational Organization, 1939-1943', A. Cosgrove and D. McCartney (eds.), *Studies in Irish History Presented to Robert Dudley Edwards* (Naas: 1979).

23. *Ibid.*, for de Valera and Lemass see Department of the Taoiseach, S 13645; Cab. Sec. S 13101, SPO. See also J.J. Lee, 'Lemass: His Two Partnerships', *The Irish Times*, 19 May 1976. For Lemass's conception of the role of state in Irish economic development, see his two memoranda for the Cabinet Committee on Economic Planning dated 21 November 1944 and 17 January 1945, cab. sec. S 13101A, SPO.

24. For de Valera's overall conception, see his memorandum for the Cabinet 3 July 1942, Cab. Sec. S 1320-6A, SPO.

25. This speech was drafted jointly by Maurice Moynihan and de Valera himself. The full text is on Cab. sec. S 13206A, SPO.

26. *Ibid.*

27. See the Minutes of the meeting of the Statistical and Social Inquiry Society, 27 April 1945, published in the *Journal of the Statistical and Social Inquiry Society*, **XVII**, 438-459. The Society was a particularly important forum for public servants and academics to meet and discuss ideas informally.

28. The memorandum is on Cab. Sec. S 13101A, SPO.

29. *Ibid.*

30. Minutes of the meeting, 13 July 1944, Cabinet Committee on Economic Planning, Department of the Taoiseach S 13645.

31. The memorandum is on Cab. Sec. S 13101A, SPO.

32. *Ibid.*

33. The memorandum is on Cab. Sec. S 13101A, SPO.

34. The memorandum is on Cab. Sec. S 13101A, SPO.

35. *Ibid.*

36. Memorandum for the Cabinet Committee on Economic Planning, 29 January 1945, Cab. Sec. S 13101A, SPO.

37. *Ibid.*

38. See O'Brien's essays and reviews, *Studies*, September 1944, 305; June 1944, 210; and 'New Views on Unemployment', *Studies*, March 1945. For his influence on de Valera, see Moynihan to Editor, *Studies*, 28 March 1945, Cab. Sec. S 13101A, SPO; P.O. Cinneide to Private Secretary to all government ministers, 31 March 1945, Cab. Sec. S 13101A, SPO.

De Valera, the Catholic Church and the 'Red Scare', 1931-1932

Dermot Keogh

In the 1930s, an interesting book appeared bearing the somewhat improbable title, *Could Ireland become Communist?* This little work was
remarkable in many ways. It was written by a Professor of History at
University College, Cork, James Hogan, and displayed the quality of
mind expected from a man holding such an academic post; it was vastly
superior in style and content to what one might associate with such a
literary *genre*. *Ireland's Peril* by the prolific Father Edward Cahill, S.J. is
an example of less gifted reflection.[2] Indeed, in the Ireland of the 1930s
one of the most common themes to be found in devotional literature was
a fixation with Communism. There were the most meticulous searches
carried out to detect the first signs of 'contagion'. One might be forgiven
for reflecting that in the 1930s some of the more obsessional local writers
on that theme must have believed that when Joseph Stalin woke up each
morning his first thoughts turned inexorably towards the subversion of
Catholic Ireland. That attitude was not altogether surprising. World
Catholic opinion had been mobilised by Pius XI who regarded the defeat
of international Communism as one of the primary pastoral objectives of
his pontificate. Moreover, popular imagination was fed on a diet of
reports of anti-clerical antics under the second Spanish Republic and the
harassment of the Catholic Church in Mexico.

Therefore, the implications of the title *Could Ireland become Communist?* would not have sounded either improbable or extraordinary in
Catholic Ireland of the 1930s. Apart from the obviously superior quality
and style, what singled James Hogan's book out from the others in that
genre was the use of a question-mark in the title. In the more popular
literature there was no room for subtlety. It was assumed that Ireland
was drifting towards Communism. Such intellectual crudity was not to
be found in Hogan's work. Another clue to the more enduring quality of
this book can be found in the sub-title: *The Facts of the Case*.
Indeed, *Could Ireland become Communist?* contained a richness of
detail which could only have been assembled by somebody with access to
the upper echelons of Cumman na nGaedheal when that party was in

Government. It is probable that the official sources on which this article is based were also made available in the early 1930s to James Hogan. Had the book been published in 1931, its political and popular impact would have been all the greater. By 1935, its contents sounded a little jaded.

Even the redoubtable Alfred O'Rahilly, an academic colleague of Hogan was lukewarm in his response to the manuscript. Basically, he regarded the work as too highbrow for the majority of the Irish who lacked a grounding in philosophy and who held views that were 'largely a hotch-potch derived from the movies, novels and imported papers'. The result was national 'mental chaos'. However, O'Rahilly was convinced that 'Ireland will not *become* Communist, but it may very well *slide* imperceptibly and gradually into something indistinguishable from Communism — though, of course, that nasty word will be carefully avoided. . . . Better be alarmist, therefore, than somnolent.'

If O'Rahilly regarded the book as 'alarmist', it is because it reflected a perception of political reality by Cumann na nGaedheal with which he did not agree. O'Rahilly knew full well that *Could Ireland become Communist?* was virtually an official history of the fall of Cumann na nGaedheal. It was in the run-up to the 1932 General Election that Alfred O'Rahilly publicly parted company with Cumann na nGaedheal. The invitation to comment on a manuscript, encapsulating a general perception of political reality which O'Rahilly did not share, placed him in a rather delicate position. But he managed to extricate himself with a deftness which one has come to associate with the man.

In 1932, Alfred O'Rahilly — one of the most prominent Catholic laymen in the country — publicly declared his intention to vote for Fianna Fáil. He was disillusioned by the strident manner in which Cumann na nGaedheal had run their campaign. He opposed what he believed was a vulgar attempt to harness Catholicism exclusively to Cumann na nGaedheal. When he read *Could Ireland become Communist?*, a few years after the 1932 election, he does not appear to have been persuaded to have second thought about the fear of a major communist threat to political stability in Ireland.

Both Hogan and O'Rahilly were leading Irish Catholics. They worked in the same university. They were both outstanding academics. More importantly, in this context, they shared a common allegiance to Cumann na nGaedheal throughout the 1920s, yet, at the 1932 general election both O'Rahilly and Hogan parted political company. The former voted for Fianna Fáil while the latter almost certainly did not.

This chapter will look at the documents and events on which *Could Ireland become Communist?* is based. It will analyse the bases on which a 'conspiracy' of the Left was revealed in 1931 and the implications that had for Cumann na nGaedheal's electoral strategy. It will show how

well-briefed Eamon de Valera was on internal government policy —
despite the official veil of secrecy. It will also explore the way in which
Eamon de Valera and Fianna Fáil outflanked Cumann na nGaedheal at
the hustings, neutralised all charges of being involved in a Left Wing
conspiracy, successfully countering with their own smear campaign.
Another example of de Valera's growing popularity will be seen in the
way that he handled the Catholic Church during the period. This contribution will analyse how de Valera managed to win the vote of people
like Alfred O'Rahilly's in 1932. Conversely, it will show Cumann na
nGaedheal lost Alfred O'Rahilly and held on to Professor James Hogan,
one of the key factors in that process was the general reaction to the pro-
priety of implicating Fianna Fáil in the 'politics of Red Conspiracy'.

Smouldering Subversion

In the early months of 1931, the Garda Commissioner, General Eoin
O'Duffy, had every reason to be extremely concerned about the
deteriorating political and social situation in the countryside. On 30
January, Patrick J. Carroll, a police agent who had infiltrated the Dublin
I.R.A., was found shot dead in the capital. On 14 February, the I.R.A.
admitted responsibility for the 'execution'. Two months after the first
murder, on 20 March, Superintendent Curtin — who had begun a case
against suspected local I.R.A. men — was shot dead beside his home.
Another garda was also shot.

In July, a worried O'Duffy, wrote to the Secretary of the Department
of Justice outlining the deterioration in public order:

> Members of the Irregular Organisations and their followers treat the gardai
> with absolute contempt; criminal suspects refused to answer any questions
> and the ordinary citizen in the effected areas who, under normal conditions,
> would assist the gardai to the utmost of his ability is through fear driven into
> silence. Since the murder of Superintendent Curtin and of Ryan the position
> has become much worse. As I stated in my last report the harassing tactics
> adopted towards the enemies of the state had good results, but since these are
> no longer permitted and since the courts have pronounced such methods il-
> legal, the Irregulars have the field to themselves.[3]

O'Duffy was unconvinced, along with other senior serving officers, that
a mere increase in the strength of the S Branch unit 'however formidable,
will meet the situation created by the limitations imposed on the gardai in
the prevention and detection of crime'. He was supported in that view by
the sergeants from the more disturbed areas. He said that the '*Poblacht* —
the I.R.A. newspaper — was widely read in "disturbed areas" and that its
propaganda was believed and that it was 'poisoning the minds of the
youth of the country against the state and state institutions'. But he was
convinced that if a determined stand was taken 'even now I believe the

problem is a comparatively simple one, one which the garda can deal with'. He said incidents occurred every day which underlined 'the folly of the present position'.

> A man known to the authorities — and for that matter to the public — as a member or a leader of a treasonable organisation, and as such to have organised, planned or sanctioned crimes, even murder, if detained in the garda station for an unduly long period — possibly for the deliberate purpose of preventing the commission of a further crime — can on his release, and ordinarily does, take action against the particular garda concerned and claiming his constitutional rights, secure a verdict and damages against that member. The law takes no cognisance of the fact that the member decreed had but one object in his act, and that, the protection of the public.

O'Duffy still regarded the problem as 'a comparatively simple one'. He sought a radical change in the law:

> Since it is clear that an organisation exists, the members of which are conspiring to overthrow the constitution by force it is, in my opinion, an obvious necessity — and perfectly just — that these persons should be deprived of the protection which enables them to endanger the security and peace of the state, by placing them outside the protection of a constitution, which at the same time they are attacking and sheltering behind, and placing them in a position uninfluenced by the constitutional rights of citizenship where their activities can be met by suitable action. There is no good reason why an organisation making war on the state should be afforded the protection which the state affords its loyal citizens.[4]

A Department of Justice report, dated August 1931, estimated that there were approximately 1,300 officers and 3,500 rank and file in the I.R.A. The names, addresses and ranks of practically all the men involved of any importance were known to the police but 'for reasons which will appear it is not possible to bring them to justice'. The I.R.A. had been responsible for the murder of 'one Minister of state, one state witness, many police officers, and several of its own followers who were suspected of treachery or cowardice' over the past four years. The same memorandum mentions a number of associations where people held dual membership with the I.R.A. whose 'object is the bringing about in this country of a revolution on the lines of the Russian revolution . . . a "working class republic" '[5]

The Department of Justice Memorandum for August stated that all the 'leading spirits' were 'well known to the police'. They were also aware of visits to Russia by these associations and by the I.R.A. 'by the former for training in revolutionary techniques, by the latter for military training and the purchase of arms. One of the principal I.R.A. leaders has recently shown a distinct tendency to adopt the Soviet principle formally as his model.'[6]

The Department of Justice became very alarmed in July 1931 following the arrest of Sean MacBride. He was described in official reports as the 'principal travelling organiser of the Irish Republican Army'. The police found a pamphlet on him entitled, *Saor Eire*, which set out the aims and constitution of a new organisation: 'Its object, put shortly, is to turn the Free State into a Soviet republic, in which manual workers, only, will have any rights.' As far as the Department of Justice was concerned, their memorandum argued that 'this development appears to mark the definite union of the Irish Republican Army with Communism in this state; the Irish Republican Army lend the support of their military organisation to the Communists and in return the Communists supply to the Irish Republican Army as a potential recruit every man who, whether from poverty or principle or mere love of agitation, is anxious to see the system of private property and private enterprise destroyed in this state.' It saw that 'union' as elevating the I.R.A. to a new plane of subversive effectiveness.[7]

The memorandum stated that there was reason to believe that Russell, or MacBride, T.J. Ryan, Sean O'Farrell and other members of the Irish Republican Executive had been 'gained over to the Communist movement'. Sean MacBride was reported to have taken up residence in Paris at one stage and there got into touch with the Soviet delegates. Another key figure in the union of I.R.A. and Communism was said to be Peadar O'Donnell who 'handpicked six youths in 1929 to attend the Lenin College in Moscow'. It was also stated that Communist money had found its way to Ireland.[8]

How well informed was the Department of Justice about the socialist activities of the I.R.A.? How good was the intelligence work on which recommendations were based? While it is not of central importance to pursue this line of inquiry here, a number of points have to be made if for no other reason they might help explain the respective positions taken up by both de Valera and Cosgrave on the matter. The latter part of 1931 saw the government presiding over a country in the midst of a major economic and social crisis. The I.R.A. had become very active again towards the end of the 1920s and O'Duffy was finding it increasingly difficult — under existing legislation — to deal with the problem. There was widespread intimidation of jury members in 'political' cases. O'Duffy wanted a radical change in the law. It was in his sectional interest to represent the situation in the country as rapidly getting out of hand. Coupled with that particular interest, it would be fair to say that O'Duffy was not the most sophisticated of thinkers. In the 1920s, he had imbibed many of the anti-communist fears associated with fascism as practiced by Mussolini.

There were also highly placed members of the Department of Justice who were more learned than O'Duffy but equally alarmist and concerned about the advance of international communism. Their views were supported by the brilliant propaganda work of Peadar O'Donnell, who was a 'communist in the strict sense of the word if ever there was one', according to James Hogan.[9]

According to the same source, the 'sidelong and serpentine propaganda favoured by Mr O'Donnell is entirely in keeping with the spirit and methods of the Communist international'.[10] If O'Donnell and his tiny band of followers had as profound an impact on the rank and file of the radical republican movement as they had on the thinking of O'Duffy and some members of the Department of Justice then the summer of 1931 could have marked a major switch in Irish politics. No such revolutionary change occurred. There was a proliferation of revolutionary groups in the early 1930s. But they were very often Dublin based; there was over-lapping membership and they often had fewer adherents than initials in their names. The subversive groups referred to most regularly were, the I.R.A., Cumann na mBan, Fianna Eireann, Saor Eire, Irish Friends of Soviet Russia, Irish Working Farmers Committee, Workers Revolutionary Party in Ireland, the Irish National Unemployed Movement, the Workers' Defence Corps, the Irish Labour Defence League.

In electoral terms, the Communist party had never been particularly popular in Ireland. At the local elections in 1930, the Revolutionary Workers Group put up two candidates: Jim Larkin Junior got 967 first preference votes and won a seat but Mrs McGregor only got 129 first preference votes and failed to gain election.[11] Big Jim Larkin's Irish Workers League put up 12 candidates but only one, the leader, was elected.

But the discovery of Saor Eire documents on Sean MacBride confirmed the suspicions held by the gardai, senior civil servants and members of the government. They had proof that an organisation which was growing in popularity was attempting to turn the Free State into a Soviet republic. The means they were to adopt were as follows:

(1) To organise Committees of Action among the Industrial and Agricultural workers to lead the day-to-day struggle of the working-class and working farmers against exploitation, and to secure a revolutionary leadership for their common struggle.

(2) The mobilisation of the mass of the Irish people behind a Revolutionary Government for the overthrow of British Imperialism and its allies in Ireland, and for the organisation of a Workers State.[12]

In retrospect, it might be rather fashionable to regard Cosgrave and his front bench as the victims of some form of conservative paranoia. But it must be remembered that one of the most active members of Cosgrave's Executive Council, Kevin O'Higgins, had been murdered by the I.R.A.

in 1927. In the early 1930s there had been recrudescence of I.R.A. violence. A deteriorating economic situation, provided subversives with a favourable social climate in which to contemplate a radical new departure. The I.R.A. lurch to the left, may well have taken place, to a great extent, only in the rhetoric and the mind of Peadar O'Donnell and his close associates. But that was not how it appeared to the government in the summer of 1931. Out of office, and not in the confidence of the government, de Valera could afford to take a more philosophical and school-masterish view of developments.

Saor Eire went public at their first Congress in September 1931. About 150 delegates attended.[13] A month earlier, the government had decided to introduce special legislation to deal with the threat and had taken the unusual step of enlisting the support of the hierarchy directly to deal with the situation. Cosgrave felt it would be very important for the hierarchy to make a public statement in support of the government's intended policy.

Joseph Walshe, Secretary of the Department of External Affairs, had made contact with Cardinal MacRory in August to brief him about the situation. William Cosgrave met the Cardinal in Dublin to discuss the situation. Less than a month later a confidential memorandum regarding the activities of certain organisations was sent to every bishop in the country. Cosgrave stated that a 'situation without paralel as a threat to the foundation of all authority has arisen'. The memorandum sent to the hierarchy spoke of 'the existence of a conspiracy for the overthrow by violence of state institutions'. Class war was being organised. There was 'definite evidence of contact with the International Communistic Organisations which have their headquarters in and are controlled from Russia'.

De Valera was very interested in the contemplated course of action. He, too, had been made privy ,unofficially, to the contents of the memoranda sent to the hierarchy. Naturally, he was anxious to ensure that Fianna Fáil would not be mentioned either explicitly or implicitly by the hierarchy in the contemplated pastoral. De Valera met the Cardinal in Maynooth and they had a long conversation. It is idle to speculate on what views were exchanged. But de Valera appears to have come away relatively content. Fianna Fáil had an opportunity to make its position clear regarding 'the conspiracy'.

On 18 October 1931 a joint pastoral was read in every Catholic church. Saor Eire was condemned by name as a 'frankly communistic organisation' trying to 'impose upon the Catholic Dáil of Ireland the same materialistic regime, with its fanatical hatred of God, as now dominates and threatens to dominate Spain'. When the Dáil had reassembled, on 14 October, after the summer recess, a bill which inserted Article 2A (a

Public Safety bill) into the Constitution was introduced. Three days later, the Bill became law. Twelve organisations were immediately banned including the I.R.A. and Saor Eire. Military tribunals were introduced. At last, O'Duffy had at his disposal fuller powers to detain suspects. Hundreds were arrested.

But the combined opposition were less than impressed by the stated reasons for introducing such draconian measures. The former leader of the Labour party, Thomas Johnson, felt the move was politically opportunistic and the powers were liable to be extended to other groups in the country, possibly the trade union movement.

Johnson did not trust Cumann na nGaedheal's sense of justice, and he wrote to R.J.P. Mortished at the Irish International Labour Organisation official in Geneva:

> . . . and in the times that may come if Europe goes smash, or if unemployment extends and prices rise at home, I don't trust them to refrain from using the new powers against normal civil agitation. Neither the present government nor their successors can be trusted with those powers. The introduction and the passage of the bill was accompanied by an anti-communist, anti-Russian rampage — attacks on the church — anti-God, look at Spain, our beloved faith in danger, etc., etc.,[14]

In fact, Johnson saw a positive side to the Saor Eire-I.R.A. 'link up'. He mentioned that O'Donnell was planning to use key social issues to agitate for school meals and free books

> . . . quite in line with the Bolshevik tactic. I don't think he has any great success outside the I.R.A. followers but the I.R.A. appears to have been captured by the communist wing. As the Russian communists are not anarchists and do not rely upon assassination as a useful method, this change would lead away from the secret army of the republic notion and the fanatical "partitionism" of the past. The new tactic might be more dangerous to the established order but it would be healthier albeit wasteful and costly and probably futile into the bargain.[15]

De Valera and Fianna Fáil were as sceptical as Tom Johnson and completely opposed to the new measures.

During the debate on the Constitutional (Amendment No. 17) or Public Safety Act on 14 October 1931, de Valera claimed that the government's proposals failed to address the fundamental causes of the trouble. They were in themselves unnecessary and unwise.[16] In his speech, de Valera laid stress on the resolution of the social and economic situation, recognising 'that if men are hungry, they will not be too particular about the ultimate principles of the organisation they would join, if that organisation promises to give them bread'. De Valera said that one had to 'remove the breeding ground of attachment to the false principles. That breeding-ground is there in the present economic situation.'

The Fianna Fáil leader then spoke speculatively about the present political situation in the country:

> Suppose I accept for the present that, let us say, a Russian organisation of some kind is beginning to interfere here. Why would the eye of Russia turn upon Ireland at present? Because of the fact that there are social conditions here that make it possible for people to work on these lines; because there is a natural invitation wherever there are people out of work and people homeless and the rest of it. They naturally seize upon the situation, and it would not be too great a stretch of the imagination to think that a movement of that sort would be very glad to try and link up, if they were able, the political movement with the economic movement on the lines they would like to have. There is ground for thinking that that is not impossible. I do not think it is a fact but suppose we assume it to be so. Again, the way to deal with it is to remove the causes which make the present situation one which is attractive to people who want to preach doctrines of that sort. The way to deal with it is to deal with the conditions and see that people who are anxious to work will get work, that people who are entitled to have decent houses will get these houses, and organise the community to end the evils that are about them — and not simple to say, "there must be no movements of this sort in our midst, we do not want them". We may say that as much as we like. We may have as many laws to prevent it as we have public safety acts and the rest here on the statute book. All the laws in the world are not going to prevent it unless you remove the causes.[17]

In the speech, de Valera left no room for ambiguity as far as his adherence to Catholic principles was concerned; he was at pains to point out that he was anxious 'that that principle or that doctrine (*Bolshevism*) should not be preached here or spread here'.[18] Earlier, he had taken up the economic side of the government's argument specifically:

> What is the problem we have to deal with there? We have had all these problems in the past — doctrines which are subversive of the social order that we stand for. The President has indicated certain principles. I accept them. I do not think they are denied by any one in this House. The right of private property is accepted as fundamental, and, as far as Catholics are concerned, there has been definite teaching upon it — the right of private property and the right, on the other hand, of society, insofar as the common good is concerned, of dealing in a proper way with the relations between the community and the private individual. We accept that. There is nobody on these benches but is just as anxious as the people opposite that these principles will be the ruling principles as far as our social organisations here are concerned. My own belief is that there is no immediate danger whatever of these principles being undermined — none whatever.[19]

Arguably the timing of the 1932 general election had a considerable bearing on its outcome. Cosgrave need not have gone to the country until the autumn, October at the latest. Traditionally, two reasons have been advanced for such a decision. The Eucharistic Congress was due to take place in Dublin in June and the Imperial Economic Conference was scheduled to meet in Ottawa the following month. It has been suggested that the Dáil was dissolved on 29 January 1932 and the general election held on 16 February in order that a government could be firmly installed before those two important events took place. It is certain that both considerations were of particular concern to Cosgrave personally. There was the possibility that an October election would run the risk of turning the Eucharistic Congress into an occasion for unseemly politicking. But that is precisely what might have recommended the latest date to the political strategists in Cumann na nGaedheal. The party was very badly divided on the question of timing. In the final months of 1931, some T.D.s favoured an early election; to allow the Dáil run its full term was only to the electoral advantage of Fianna Fáil. The opposition had more time to prepare, and they could also choose the ground on which to fight the campaign. But the recent bishops pastoral, coupled with the need for tough anti-I.R.A. legislation, provided the government with an opportunity to shift electoral ground and fight a campaign on a law and order ticket.

However attractive and obvious such a tactic might be for Cumann na nGaedheal, it seems that as late as November 1931 the party had rejected the idea of an early election. The adverse economic situation was considered to outweigh the advantage of surprise. On 5 November, Ernest Blythe told a party meeting that the Executive Council had given consideration to the views of deputies expressing the desire for an 'early general election' and had come to the conclusion that until the economic and other difficulties 'with which we are faced' had been dealt with, a general election would be undesirable. He said that it was intended to introduce a supplementary budget immediately.[21]

In fact on 30 October 1931, the executive council had decided to introduce the supplementary budget: this was the decision revealed to the Cumann na nGaedheal parliamentary party meeting on 5 November. The Irish public were very quickly made aware of the details of the emergency measures. Petrol went up 4d a gallon and income tax by 6d in the pound.[22]

Beset by economic difficulties, Cosgrave was so overwhelmed by the deteriorating economic and social situation to think at that point in politically opportunistic terms. But the arguments in favour of a snap election — to be fought on law and order — must have become quite compelling because the Dáil was suddenly dissolved on 29 January 1932.

While Cosgrave may have been personally exercised by the risk of the possible 'politicisation' of the Eucharistic Congress, there were others who had less altruistic motives for wanting to go to the polls as soon as possible. But in many ways the timing could not have been more helpful for Fianna Fáil. The most appropriate moment for Cumann na nGaedheal to have gone to the country was in mid-November, when the 'red-republican conspiracy' was deemed to be most dangerous and the national pastoral was fresh in the minds of the electorate. But ,by February, the credibility of a conspiracy seriously threatening the country had worn somewhat thin.

Cosgrave had the political advantage. In theory he could have decided to go to the country whenever he considered it electorally opportune. But in practice, he needed time to allow the unpopularity of certain corrective economic measures to abate. The workings of the Military Tribunal and the crack down on subversion had further increased Cumann na nGaedheal unpopularity in the short-term. The government needed time. They had until October, 1932; they could have held out. But when Cosgrave finally took the decision, he was left with very little political choice other than to fight upon a law and order ticket. The bitter memories of the recent supplementary budget — and the prospect of even more severe cuts if Cumann na nGaedheal were returned to power — left the President very little choice. Despite the obvious threat from subversion, the challenge from a Moscow inspired left wing republicanism was not so easily perceived by the 'plain people of Ireland'.

From Bodenstown to Bolshevism

Cumann na nGaedheal electoral strategy had a strong 'civil war' tone. This was reflected in the pages of the handbook, entitled *Fighting Points*, distributed to speakers and workers of the Party.[23] The 1932 Cumann na nGaedheal *vademecum* did not implicate Fianna Fáil directly in a left-wing plot to subvert the state. But there was a strong emphasis on the 'slightly constitutional' and 'crypto socialist' tradition of de Valera and his followers. Under the heading, 'points against Fianna Fáil', there was the suggestion that if de Valera got into office, his party would be soft on 'the gunmen', destabilise the economy by provoking hostility with Britain, embark on a ruinous policy of nationalisation, and play into the hands of the I.R.A. and international Communism by not treating the dangers to the state from those quarters seriously.

Under the heading, 'Fianna Fáil encourage and support the gunmen', appropriate de Valera texts were cited with chapter and verse:

> The fight has to go on.
> — de Valera, 9 January 1922, after the Treaty had been ratified.

The People had never the right to do wrong.
— de Valera, March, 1922.

If they accept the Treaty . . . THEY WOULD HAVE TO WADE THROUGH IRISH BLOOD, through the blood of the soldiers of the Irish Government and perhaps the blood of some members of the Government.
— Mr de Valera at Thurles, St Patrick's Day, 1922.

The handbook argued that 'the gunman menace originated in the pernicious doctrines taught by Mr. de Valera and his colleagues in 1922 and succeeding years'. When de Valera allowed himself to be nominated 'President' of a 'Government' which 'had no mandate from the people' he gave 'countenance to a fundamental error that is responsible for the gunman mentality'.[24]

That mentality was actively cultivated, according to *Fighting Points*, by the actions and words of Fianna Fáil. In June 1931, they had marched '*behind* the gunmen at Bodenstown', while a Roscommon delegate to the last ard fheis on 28 and 29 of October in the same year was quoted as saying that 'These men (the I.R.A.) are all right; they have our sympathy.'[25] But there was nothing particularly new in the political accusations about Fianna Fáil's ambivalence towards violence. There was, however, in the suggestion that some sections of the I.R.A. had advanced from Bodenstown to Bolshevism and Fianna Fáil were also travelling that road. Cumann na nGaedheal instructed its speakers and workers in '*the real facts*':

> The Communist organisation is international and its aim is to gain control in every country where it can. The only country where it has so far been successful is Russia. Is is now fighting for supremacy in Spain. The country, however, which Communists regard as the ideal ground for their experiment is England, and it is because of Ireland's proximity to England that they are interested in Ireland.[26]

The handbook went on to emphasise that although the membership of the small number of communistic organisations in the country is low, there was considerable danger because of the 'gradual' linking up of Bolshevism with the physical force Republican movement. The handbook then itemised details from the various memoranda cited earlier in relation to the 'red plot', and includes two quotations from the October Pastoral. In the face of what Cumann an nGaedheal perceived as a serious threat from the international Left, the handbook depicted Fianna Fáil, and de Valera in particular, as adopting one of three methods of dealing with Communism in Ireland.

(a) They deny its existence.
(b) They say it is only a Government scare.
(c) They blame the government for its existence.

On 12 November 1931, de Valera was quoted as saying: 'it passes my comprehension why anybody should feel that Communism has the slightest likelihood of winning any measure of acceptance here'. De Valera was also quoted in support of position (b):

> I was not afraid that Communism was going to be suddenly taken up by the Irish people. The only danger I can see to social order in this state is one springing from circumstance within this country and nowhere else. I am prepared to deliberately suggest that Mr. Cosgrave was by no means loath to make up circumstances that he found at hand into a scare suitable to give him back power for the next five years.

The Fianna Fáil leader was also quoted as blaming the government for the existence of the plot: 'Why would the eye of Russia turn upon Ireland at present? Because of the fact that there are social conditions here that make it possible for people to work of these lines because there is a natural invitation wherever there are people homeless and the rest of it. They naturally seize upon the situation and it would not be too great a stretch of the imagination to think that a movement of that sort would be very glad to try and link up, if they were able, the political movement with the economic movement on the lines they would like to have.'[27]

If there was no suggestion of direct Fianna Fáil involvement in the communist plot then, apart from being ambivalent towards 'the gunmen', the social radicalism of de Valera and his followers tended 'more and more towards State Control of Industry and of Agriculture'. Examples of interference with free enterprise were the Fianna Fáil proposals to set up a Wheat Control Board, a National Housing Board and an advisory council to deal with questions of agriculture and industry. The ard fheis motion to secure the unification under state control, of all transport services was also sited. The danger of Fianna Fáil's policy of nationalisation was confirmed in the quotation of de Valera that '*Until the State came in on behalf of the community and made it impossible for the individual to practise selfishness* they would have to get from those who saw the truth in these matters a readiness to make certain sacrifices'.[28]

The handbook gave a number of examples of the losses caused in Britain, Germany, Australia, New Zealand, and Russia by nationalisation and also made a further point about the fact that Fianna Fáil wanted a land tax. In this section of the handbook, party workers were provided with certain inferences which impugned the goodwill of Fianna Fáil towards farmers generally. The Fianna Fáil philosophy of land-ownership was summed up as follows:

(a) That the farmer is not absolute owner of his land.
(b) That if he is not absolute owner of his land he must enjoy his ownership at the pleasure, or by the goodwill of some superior power which can be none other than the State.

(c) That the State should levy a land tax (or State rent) on the farmer for his land.

(d) That whilst the farmer does not owe anything to the people who lent him the money to buy his land, he must continue to pay *the State* for the privilege of using it.

The handbook concluded that 'Fianna Fáil's theory can mean nothing else but that the owner of a holding is tenant-at-will to the State. And this is State socialism.'[29]

In summary, the Cumann na nGaedheal handbook said that 'Fianna Fáil would like to erect a Chinese wall around this country — develop a sort of a Hermit Nation — adopt a policy of non-co-operation abroad and eternal disorder at home and wind up in the complete effacement of our Nations'.[30]

But Cumann na nGaedheal was not the only party to make good use of this handbook in the 1932 election. De Valera and a number of other prominent frontbenchers either had a copy of the *Fighting Points*, or else

THE DISSOLUTION

had access to its contents. However, the Cummann na nGaedheal electoral message was developed much more graphically in a series of highly professional posters which left little to the imagination. The handbook had only gone so far; it had provided a liberal supply of quotations which was designed to provide party workers with the evidence that a Fianna Fáil victory would lead to economic ruin, widespread social and political unrest, and plunge the country into an unnecessary confrontation with Britain. No interest group in the country would survive unscathed in the bruising confrontations: the army, gardai, farmers, industrialists, publicans etc.

Poster Power

If *Fighting Points* tended to stress the 'crypto-socialist' nature of Fianna Fáil, then the Cumann na nGaedheal election posters proved to be even

more strident. Where the handbook relied upon suggestion and innuen-
do, the handbills and posters wre based on 'social realism'. One of the
posters in an effect to exploit most obviously the 'red-I.R.A.-Fianna Fáil'
alliance, showed a card game between a Saorstat citizen, William T.
Cosgrave, de Valera and a criminal type complete with half face mask
and a cap with Saor Eire written on it. The unsuspecting W.T. Cosgrave,
has his eyes on his cards while de Valera is stretching under the table to
slip the joker, which he has between his toes, to the Saor Eire gunman.
The caption on the poster read: 'Fianna Fáil's game. Don't let them cheat
you. Vote for Clumann na nGaedheal.' Another poster, entitled 'His
master's voice' showed de Valera being prodded along by the same

ORPHANS OF THE STORM

THE ONLY HOPE
MR. COSGRAVE: Look, look, that life belt may save us!

Ex-Unionist (after the election): Mr. Cosgrave has not been returned, but our money has been well spent. As you will see, it has been employed by Cumann na nGaedheal to defame the natives far better than we used to do it.

criminal type with a gun in his back. But his face portrayed the complicity between Fianna Fáil and the gunman. Yet another poster took up the Sean O'Casey title 'Shadow of the gunman'; the country was menaced by his dark shadow, while another poster had the red flag being superimposed on the tricolour and carried a warning against the possibility of communism taking over in Ireland.[31]

In retaliation, the recently started *Irish Press* — which was tried for criminal libel on four counts before the military tribunal — ran a series of high quality cartoons. The Fianna Fáil paper demonstrated that it, too, could throw mud. In the circumstances, it is probable that the masonic/unionist tag was more likely to stick to Cumann na nGaedheal than the red-I.R.A. tag was likely to damage de Valera and Fianna Fáil. The day following Cosgrave's decision to go to the country, the *Irish*

ALONE HE DID IT!

LADY EX-UNIONIST: Look, only our William is in step.

Press depicted Cumann na nGaedheal as a dissolving jelly.[32]

Another cartoon showed a shipwrecked Cumann na nGaedheal about to be swept off their rock by the wave of the general election while Cosgrave was about to make a dive for a battered, patched life buoy, tagged 'aid from ex-unionist'.[33]

But the cartoon which used the unionist — masonic motif most explicitly appeared in the *Irish Press* on 15 February 1932. It shows a meeting of ex-unionists, in obvious good humour, after the election. At that monied gathering, the walls portrayed the various Cumann na nGaedheal posters: Devvy's circus, the shadow of the gunman, his master's voice, etc. The group were obviously pleased because the speaker was preening himself that despite the defeat of William Cosgrave their money 'had been employed by Cumann na nGaedheal to defame the natives far better than we used to do it'.[34]

Another cartoon showed the people of Ireland striding in to vote for Fianna Fáil while a solitary W.T. Cosgrave was the only one going to vote for Cumann na nGaedheal. This scene was watched by an ex-unionist lady who was saying to her monocled-companion 'look, only our William is in step'.[35]

As might be deduced from the tone of the handbook, the posters and the cartoons, the election rhetoric was wild on occasions. In Castlebar the Minister for Justice, Mr Fitzgerald-Kenny warned that 'the Civil War that would follow a Fianna Fáil attempt to govern would be worse than anything that came before'. Terrible danger, he said, threatened the country if Fianna Fáil got into power:

> The government had mastered those bodies who had stained their hands with human blood, and had put down those persons who wished to create

The Ship whose Captain forgot to look at his chart for ten years!

disturbance in the state. If Cumann na nGaedheal were returned the problem of armed subversion would be resolved.[36]

The Minister for Justice said that de Valera felt that no force was to be used against the I.R.A. and Saor Eire. He would allow them to carry out their own sweet will in any fashion they liked and would taken no step to deter them except that Deputy de Valera promised he would reason with them:

> Do you think that people who are deaf to the call of conscience are deaf to the voice of the bishops, who are willing to put the stain of murder, as they have done upon their souls, will suddenly be convinced by a few words from deputy de Valera?[37]

CUMANN NA nGAEDHEAL STATES ITS POLICY.

Although the threat from subversion was a prominent theme in Cumann na nGaedheal Election rhetoric, Cosgrave was more restrained in his speeches than some of his Executive Council colleagues. He referred, in more moderate tones, to the threat from subversion in most of the speeches. In Cork, he said there used to be a phrase in the country, '*A Dhia Saor Eire*', 'but somebody removed the word of God: We do not remove it. We trust in God, and as long as we have the power and are entrusted with the responsibility of administration we will not remove the proclamation declaring Saor Eire and the friends of Soviet Russia, and such other similar organisations as illegal associations.'[38]

He vigorously defended the setting up of the military tribunals: 'We won't stand these attacks against the liberties and rights of our people. Now, having adopted a jury that will not be subject to their acts they are whining. Gallant, patriotic Irishmen never whined in difficulties; they took their medicine like men, and if the cause were worthy of it, the means adopted to get what they want are not worthy of the people of this country, they are alien to us and to our religion, our nationality, and our judgement, and, as I said before, we will not have any such intimidation here.'[39]

Cosgrave was quick to repudiate the repeated charges by Fianna Fáil that Cumann na nGaedheal were dominated by Freemasons or by ex-Unionists:

> If that be so, I want to know whether the Freemasons are responsible for the Irish language policy of this government; if they are responsible for our flag, if they are responsible for our National Anthem, under the Constitution of this state there is no discrimination either for or against any citizen whatever his religion is or whatever his political alliances . . . We are satisfied that on a platform such as ours, broad-based on the people's will, and anxious to improve the condition of this country and its own people, that there will never be in the city of Cork any consideration for those who would endeavour to outlaw any section of the community because of its religious opinions.[40]

Such admonitions to uphold the liberal spirit of the Free State constitution were respected by de Valera during the campaign. But some of his close political associates — as in the case of Cosgrave's own front-bench — were not given to exercising a close reign on their over-heated imaginations. But no election speech ever quite matched the vitriolic tone of one 'Catholic' journal.

In one political obituary for Cosgrave following the defeat of Cumann na nGaedheal in 1932, the rabidly pro-Fianna Fáil journal, *The Catholic Bulletin*, wrote:

> Mr William Cosgrave, like the late Mr John Redmond, being a broad minded man, accommodated himself in a generous way to the requirements of alien

institutions. He will be remembered by the Masonic brethern as one who struggled "manfully" to make Capitalistic Imperialism and English Protestantism respectable to the Irish people. He will be remembered in British history as a great statesman who made "a damned good bargain" over the enslaved bodies of 420,000 Irish nationalists, sealing the said bargain with an annual tribute of five and three-quarter millions. He will hold an affectionate place in the memory of the board of Trinity College, and his name will be recalled with pleasure by the Royal Dublin Society. He will be spoken of with acclaim by Ranchers and Rotarians, and Veneration will be his crown in the imperial chambers of commerce. He will continue to be hailed as statesman in the columns of the Times, the Irish Times and the Irish Independent, while ex-soldiers of the great war and pensioners of the civil war will salute him ere as a true patriot and benefactor. Last, but not least, in this exalted album of memories, will be the grateful recollection of the sportsman of Britain for the hunting and fishing facilities he placed at their disposal. William Cosgrave's full and faithful admeasurement may be laid down in this, that he won the respect and gratitude of every man and woman whose flag was the Union Jack, and whose motherland was England . . . Mr Cosgrave and his party received many golden and academic appreciations during the ten years of "good" government, but perhaps the one that will be cherished most was the last to be received. On the Sunday preceding the election the usual prayers in all Protestant churches, for his majesty, the royal family, the army and navy, were supplemented by zealous petitions for the success at the polls of "the government party". And so, inflated by masonic gas, Mr Cosgrave soared into oblivion![41]

That was a most unfair political obituary. At a personal level, Cosgrave had fought a clean campaign. The Cumann na nGaedheal reaction to that growing threat was quite understandable in the summer of 1931. The introduction of emergency legislation to cope with I.R.A. violence was also a practical response to a deteriorating situation. But there was a fundamental miscalculation when the conspiracy became the basis on which the election was to be fought and Fianna Fáil were implicated in the plot — de Valera was to slip Saor Eire the ace under the table. Armed with the national pastoral denouncing Saor Eire, Cumann an nGaedheal went to the hustings not realising that de Valera had long since come out from under the shadow of the gunman as far as many in the key sectors of Irish society were concerned.

The respectability of de Valera and Fianna Fáil was gradually recognised by the most influential section of the community. Many members of the clergy and bishops had gained a new-found respect for de Valera. Since the 1927 election, Fianna Fáil had worked hard to win the support of elites. The bishops and clergy have already been mentioned. The fact that de Valera was *persona grata* in that quarter is reflected in his visit to see MacRory in Maynooth at the height of rumours about the 'red scare'.

But he had also managed to neutralise fears inside the army, the gardai and the civil service about the possible adverse consequences of a Fianna Fáil takeover. Liberal assurances were given that there would be no victimisation — and that was important to the security forces and the civil service — many of whose members had parted company with de Valera at the time of the Civil War.

The degree to which Cumann na nGaedheal depicted de Valera and Fianna Fáil as politically unreliable, reflected the extent to which, Cumann na nGaedheal as a party, had allowed itself to drift into the realms of defective political analysis.

The 'Red Scare', when applied to de Valera was just as relevant as charges of masonic and ex-unionist manipulation were to the activities of Cosgrave and his party — but probably less effective politically

Throughout the two-week campaign, Cosgrave personally did not electioneer with the virulence of some of his government colleagues. He defended his administration's time in office and attacked Fianna Fáil on many grounds. But his campaign was not personalised and anti-de Valera. He did not provide the strong leadership which might have prevented the use of graphics and rhetoric which was seen as being 'too clever by half'. Had he taken de Valera into his personal confidence in the summer of 1931 about the gravity of the political situation — de Valera found out about the situation anyway and had access to all the documents — he might have forced the leader of the opposition to moderate his remarks in relation to the Public Safety Act. Philosophically, Cosgrave and de Valera were much closer together on this issue than either ever fully realised. The bitterness of the Civil War clouded judgements even in 1932.

Pardoxically, the increased police powers had a doubly advantageous impact on the outcome of the election for Fianna Fáil. Many members of the I.R.A. were locked up, giving Fianna Fáil the opportunity to play the emotive republican card — put us in to get them out — a slogan which had echoes of earlier Sinn Fein days. Whatever animosity and hostility between the I.R.A. and Fianna Fáil existed — and it was considerable — was lost sight of in the common campaign to get Cumann na nGaedheal out.

The second way in which Fianna Fáil were helped by the Legislation is a little more complicated to explain. Dozens of the most active and militant republicans were put behind bars before a bitter election campaign where their presence on the streets could only have provoked incidents resulting in violence with Cumann na nGaedheal supporters. In the relatively peaceful climate which surrounded the campaign, Fianna Fáil had no reason to have to take a stand on strong-arm electioneering tactics.

Although most of the Fianna Fáil lobbying of elite groups in Irish

Society had been carried out prior to the campaign, members of the clergy, civil service, gardai and army had little reason to have second thoughts about the rise of Eamon de Valera. (O'Duffy and some dissident elements in the army and police force were not so easily reconciled to the possible change and contemplated extra-constitutional measures to halt the rise of Fianna Fáil.)

Cosgrave had not underestimated the threat from subversive groups in Irish society, but he had been misled by both O'Duffy and the Department of Justice over the communistic nature of the threat. His actions in suppressing the I.R.A. were as warranted then as were de Valera's use of the same powers two years later against the same organisation.

Cosgrave was not a politician to be easily panicked. He was presented with highly coloured and — on the surface — convincing evidence concerning the new turn taken by the I.R.A. in 1931. A colder appraisal of the facts might have resulted in memoranda of a different tone being written. In their anxiety to make the case for tough legislation to be introduced — in a climate of growing violence — there was a tendency to schematise and reduce complex patterns of events to the most simplified format. The result was an intelligence evaluation indicating that a 'communist conspiracy' had reached an advanced stage in the country.

Following the victory of Fianna Fáil, the satirical magazine, *The Dublin Opinion*, ran a cartoon which showed a meeting of grim-faced Russian Commisars, presided over by the president of the Supreme Soviet Council, and slamming the table with his fist, demanding, 'What I want to know is, where did the Communists in Ireland get the hundred pound deposits to forfeit?'[42] If some members of the Department of Justice had as strong a hold on political reality as the *Dublin Opinion* cartoonist, then the country might have been saved a detour into the realms of 'Red Scare'. Who knows, Alfred O'Rahilly might not, then, have had reason to change his vote in 1932 and *Could Ireland Become Communist?* might never have been written.

NOTES

1. James Hogan, *Could Ireland Become Communist: The Facts of the Case* (Cork: n.d.).

2. Edward Cahill, *Ireland's Peril* (Dublin: 1931).

3. Eoin (O'Duffy) O Dubhthaigh, to Secretary, Department of Justice, 27adh Iul 1931 (State Paper Office SPO 5864B). The most affected areas were Tipperary, Kerry, Leitrim and Donegal.

4. *Ibid.*

5. Department of Justice Memorandum, August 1931 (SPO 5864B): associations named are the Friends of Soviet Union, the Workers Union of Ireland, the Irish Working Farmers Committee, the Workers Revolutionary Party in Ireland.

6. Report submitted to government by Department of Justice on alliance between Irish Republican Army and Communists (SPO 5864B).

7. *Ibid.*

8. *Ibid.*, funding for *An Phoblacht.*

9. Hogan, *op. cit.*, p. 44; Hogan referred, on the same page to the action which O'Donnell took against the editor of the *Irish Rosary*, Fr Vincent-Casey OP for libel resulting from the publication of an article in which it was alleged that O'Donnell went to Moscow in 1929 to study anti-religious propaganda, which was 'the cornerstore of the Soviet technique of revolution' *Irish Rosary*, April 1932. The offending editorial was entitled *A Dhia Saor Eire* (God free Ireland) O'Donnell lost the action. Hogan did not express any surpise at the outcome.

10. *Ibid.*, vii.

11. Anon., *Communist Party of Ireland: An Outline History* (Dublin: n.d.), 9.

12. Department of Justice memorandum, Appendix 1 (in my possession).

13. Tim Pat Coogan, *The I.R.A.* (London: 1970), 59 and J. Bowyer Bell, *The Secret Army: A History of the IRA 1916-1970* (London: 1972), 110-113 and S. 5864B.

14. Tom Johnson to R.J.P. Mortished, 1 November 1981 (Mortished papers, papers in possession of Mrs Margaret Vanek, Ballinderry House, Rathdrum, Co. Wicklow). See also Mortished to Johnson, 11 November 1931 (Tom Johnson papers, M.S. 17, 243 N.L.I.) Mortished considered the Russian scare in Ireland quite funny in view of the growing Soviet respectability in Europe of the early 1930s.

15. *Ibid.*

16. Maurice Moynihan (ed.), *Speeches and statements by Eamon de Valera 1917-1973,* (Dublin: 1980) 182.

17. Moynihan (ed.), 187-188.

18. Moynihan (ed.), 188.

19. Moynihan (ed.), 187.

20. McCracken, J.L., *Representative government in Ireland: a study of Dáil Éireann 1919-1948* (London: 1958), 77.

21. Cumann na nGaedheal Parliamentary Party Minutes (uncatalogued), Archives Department, U.C.D.

22. Ronan Fanning, *The Irish Department of Finance 1922-58* (Dublin: 1978), 210-215). *Cork Examiner* 6-11 November 1931; 'The Paper' was a strong supporter of the government but it still regarded the measures taken as harsh.

23. *Fighting Points for Cumann-na-nGaedheal Speakers and Workers* (General Election 1932), published by Cumann-na-nGaedheal, 5 Parnell Square, Dublin, 1932.

24. *Ibid.*, 120-122: the quotations from de Valera and sources cited above are as they appear in the handbook.

25. *Ibid.*, 123.

26. *Ibid.*, 139-140.

27. *Ibid.*, 136-139.

28. *Ibid.*, 146-7; quoting de Valera at Aonach na Nodlag, 12 December 1931.

29. *Ibid.*, 118-119.

30. *Ibid.*, 158.

31. Proclamations File, National Library of Ireland, Dublin.

32. *Irish Press,* 30 January 1932.

33. *Irish Press*, 27 January 1932.

34. The Cumann na nGaedheal poster entitled 'Devvy's circus is probably one of the most famous from the 1932 campaign. It read 'absolutely the greatest road show in Ireland today' and 'the world famous illusionist, loth-swallower and escapologist. See his renowned act escaping from the straitjacket of the republic'. McCracken, *op. cit.*, 83.

35. *Irish Press*, 6 February 1932.

36. *Cork Examiner*, 5 February 1932.

37. *Ibid.*

38. *Ibid.*, 8 February 1932.

39. *Ibid.*, 5 February 1932.

40. *Cork Examiner*, 1 February 1932.

41. Kevin, 'Far and near the general election', *Catholic Bulletin*, vol. xxii, April, 1932 (no. 4), 255-256.

42. *Dublin Opinion*, March, 1932.

'The Rule of Order':
Eamon de Valera and the I.R.A., 1923-40

Ronan Fanning

On 27 April 1923 Eamon de Valera, in his capacity as the head of the self-styled 'Government of the Republic' established in October 1922, issued a proclamation laying down his principles for a negotiated end to the civil war. That his proposals were rejected out of hand by the government of the Irish Free State is irrelevant to our present purpose for the simple reason that, as I shall show, it was irrelevant to de Valera's subsequent perception of their significance. His first three principles were:

(1) That the sovereign rights of this nation are indefeasible and inalienable.
(2) That all legitimate governmental authority in Ireland, legislative, executive and judicial, is derived exclusively from the people of Ireland.
(3) That the ultimate court of appeal for deciding disputed questions of national expediency and policy is the people of Ireland, the judgement being by majority vote of the adult citizenry, and the decision to be submitted to, and resistance by violence excluded not because the decision is necessarily right or just or permanent, but because acceptance of this rule makes for peace, order and unity in national action and is the democratic alternative to arbitrament by force.[1]

The conflict between these first two principles — majority rule and the inalienability of national sovereignty — has been recognised (by de Valera's official biographers among others) as fundamental to an understanding of his political position in his years in the wilderness: for him '*that* was the dilemma of the "Treaty", the dilemma that made civil war inevitable unless, somehow, a way out of it could be found and patience and mutual understanding triumphed over feeling and partisanship' — so de Valera told his audience in the La Scala theatre at the inaugural meeting of Fianna Fáil in 1926. The third principle, however, has attracted less attention notwithstanding de Valera's assertion to the same audience that it 'was intended as a partial solution of the fundamental difficulty introduced by the "Treaty" — the difficulty regarding majority rule. Republicans admit that majority rule is an inevitable *rule of order* — a rule that cannot be set aside in a democracy without the gravest consequences' (pp 137-8). But if the republicans who followed de Valera

into Fianna Fáil might so admit, the republicans of the I.R.A. did not.
That this difference of opinion about the 'rule of order' forms the context
in which de Valera's attitudes to the post-1923 I.R.A. may most appropriately be considered is the subject of this paper.

It was not, as de Valera admitted to the first Fianna Fáil *ard-fheis* later
in 1926, that he argued

> that force is not a legitimate weapon for a nation to use in striving to win its
> freedom. I know that in history it is seldom that foreign tyrants have ever
> yielded to any other, I have believed, and still believe, that if a nation held in
> subjection by a foreign power were to exclude altogether the idea of using
> physical force to free itself, it would in effect be handing itself over as a bound
> slave without hope of redemption . . . But a nation within itself ought to be
> able to settle its polity so that all occasion of civil conflict between its
> members may be obviated, and no nation which even pretends to freedom
> will suffer a foreign power to impose conditions which make the adoption of
> such a polity impossible.   (p. 144)

De Valera returned to the theme in 1929 when accused of ambivalence
in his attitude towards the I.R.A. and when he vindicated Fianna Fáil's
entry into the Dáil (as contrasted with the I.R.A.'s continued rejection of
parliamentary authority) in the following terms:

> We came in here because we thought that a practical rule could be evolved in
> which order could be maintained; and we said that it was necessary to have
> some assembly in which the representatives of the people by a majority vote
> should be able to decide national policy. As we were not able to get a majority
> to meet outside this House, we had to come here if there was to be a majority
> at all of the people's representatives in any one assembly.
>   As far as I am concerned, the only constitution I give "that" for, the only
> thing I think I am morally obliged to obey in this House, is a majority vote,
> because you are all elected by the Irish people. As a practical rule, and not
> because there is anything sacred in it, I am prepared to accept majority rule as
> settling matters of national policy, and therefore as deciding who it is that
> shall be in charge of order.   (pp 162-3).

But, just as de Valera stopped short of denying the legitimacy of force for
a nation seeking independence, so he explicitly refrained from any other
complaint about those from whom he had parted in 1926. Indeed in one
critical area he went out of his way in that same Dáil speech in 1929 to
confer legitimacy upon them when he said that 'those who continued on
in that organisation which we have left can claim exactly the same continuity that we claimed up to 1925. They can do it. I differed with them
because . . . I had to recognise there was some body who would have to
keep order, that there was a *de facto* position created'. Such a distinction
between *de facto* and *de jure* in a speech larded with references to the

events leading to the establishment of the Irish Free State in 1922 as a *coup d'etat* added to the ambiguity and it is hardly surprising that many within the I.R.A. assumed that their differences with de Valera were a mere matter of tactics.

But the closer de Valera came to power, the more apparent became his differences with the I.R.A. on the 'rule of order' and the wider the implications of those differences. In October 1931, for example, when the Dáil debated the innocuously entitled Constitution (Amendment No. 17) Bill — which became more commonly known as the Public Safety Act — de Valera did not oppose it as a champion of civil rights in the abstract, let alone as a champion of the I.R.A. (pp 182-8). His opposition was pragmatic rather than principled: that there was no 'immediate urgency' for so draconian a measure which he pictured as an attempt on the part of the government to play upon 'national anxiety . . . in order to prepare a favourable atmosphere for the coming election'. Their common opposition to the bill at a time when Fianna Fáil and the I.R.A. still made a joint annual pilgrimage to Wolfe Tone's grave at Bodenstown together with their co-operation in the ensuing election campaign seems to have obscured a realistic appraisal of how far de Valera had already advanced down the path of recognising the necessity for such measures as the Public Safety Act even before he entered government. Although de Valera disputed that the I.R.A. could be correctly described as a secret organisation and argued that 'the right way of proceeding is to end the necessity for such organisations' by ending the conditions which bred them, he also categorically denied that any authority outside the Dáil

was entitled to take human life . . . Our position in the matter is this — that there must be some authority in the country . . . I have to admit that ultimately authority does want the sanction of force. Unfortunately we have not got to the stage when force is not to be the ultimate sanction, but it ought to be reserved as the ultimate sanction.

If Fianna Fáil were in government, de Valera continued more ominously for the I.R.A.,

and were called upon to deal with a case where there was a serious attempt to interfere with the general will of the people, having made it quite possible for that will to be expressed, then we would have to come along and say, "Very well, we understand such and such, we are prepared to do so and so; but we have, however, to be the judges of policy in the long run." Having decided what was the national policy on the basis of majority rule, we too, if we were driven to it, in the last resort would have to say, "Very well, we are the last word upon national policy; the majority of the people have spoken and entrusted us with the present responsibility, and we are the judges of what must be done."

Neither the convoluted syntax nor the plethora of 'very wells', 'such and suchs' and 'so and sos' could disguise what was, in fact, a clear statement of intent.

Within five months Fianna Fáil *were* in government and the very first decision recorded in the Executive Council minutes[2] after they took office was an order releasing under a free pardon seventeen I.R.A. men held under the Special Powers Act whom the newly appointed Ministers for Defence and Justice, Aiken and Geoghegan, had already visited in Arbour Hill military prison the previous day.[3] De Valera himself had earlier indicated his the government's intentions in a radio broadcast to the United States some days before the Dáil reassembled when he envisioned 'internal peace without coercive legislation' and spoke of the removal of the oath of allegiance — the first plank in Fianna Fáil's election manifesto — as enabling 'every section of our people . . . without coercion of conscience or sacrifice of principle . . . to send their representatives to the people's assembly, where national policy can be determined and the direction of the national advance decided on authoritatively by majority vote',[4] a subject upon which he elaborated in his Dáil speech on the Constitution (Removal of the Oath) Bill a few weeks later.

The larger political landmarks of Fianna Fáil's early years in office — the dramatic deterioration in Anglo-Irish relations and the polarisation perceived in domestic politics between Cumann na nGaedheal and the Blueshirts on the one hand and Fianna Fáil and the I.R.A. on the other — has militated against an early appreciation (either by contemporaries or, later, by historians) of the gulf which had already opened between de Valera and an I.R.A. which, oath or no oath, continued to look outside de Valera's Dáil for the source of legitimate authority. Contemporary press and public opinion, moreover invariably focusses upon what governments do rather than upon what they fail to do and so sets a snare into which historians are subsequently prone to fall headlong: that de Valera's government did *not* repeal the Public Safety Act proved of far greater historical significance than his apparently making common cause with the I.R.A. by releasing the prisoners. That de Valera first invoked the powers available under the act, in August 1933, against the Blueshirts has compounded the confusion, both at the time and afterwards. Indeed it may well be that the principal contribution of the Blueshirts to Irish history was to postpone the moment when de Valera came to grips with the I.R.A. Yet it is in his speech replying to opposition criticisms of this use of the act that the phrase 'rule of order' rang like a refrain which sounded no less sinisterly for the I.R.A. His policy, de Valera declared, was to permit

every nationalist who had any aspirations for the independence of the country to pursue these aspirations in a peaceable way, in a way in which he could settle his differences with his neighbour by the only *rule of order* that human beings have been able to discover.

I have been attacked for want of consistency. It has been suggested that my devotion to majority rule is quite a new thing. I deny that. There is absolute, positive documentary evidence in the last ten or twelve years since these differences began that I have recognised the fact that every sensible person must recognise, that either we have got to settle our political differences by force or settle them by some *rule of order*. I never suggested that there was in majority rule anything more than a *rule of order*, but that it was a precious *rule of order* I have held at all times . . .

It is not human that we should all think alike. It is not human no matter how sincere we may be in advancing the country's interest that we should all have the same methods of trying to secure the country's interests. We are bound to differ, and as we are bound to differ it is necessary to have in the general interest this *rule of order*. We wanted to get it and we founded the Fianna Fáil organisation in order to get it. We were satisfied that if we could get rid of the oath, we would have ninety-nine per cent of those who stood against the Treaty, at the time of the Treaty debates, with us in the future (pp 239-40).

The weakness in de Valera's strategy was not in his calculation that the great majority of those who had opposed the treaty would follow him — so much was incontestable — but in the tacit assumption that those who rejected his leadership would nevertheless accept his political philosophy and turn their backs on the use of force. His method of dealing with the I.R.A. was essentially paternalistic, if not pedagogical. He spoke of them much as a benevolent schoolmaster might speak of a spirited but naughty schoolboy. 'There is a far better way of dealing with the Irish people [the terminology is instructive: de Valera avoided the use of the term 'I.R.A.' whenever possible] than trying to coerce them', he told the Fianna Fáil ard fheis in 1932, 'and that is to lead them on the right path'; hence, he explained, his government's decision not to search out those with arms in their first year in office. But benevolence was coupled with a warning that his government were also 'mindful of their duty to see that order is maintained' and would proceed vigorously against any one found in the possession of arms in public. (p. 225).

Privately, de Valera's patience was already wearing thin as the following extraordinary outburst in a letter of January 1934 to Joe McGarrity abundantly illustrates:

You talk about coming to an understanding with the I.R.A. You talk of the influence it would have both here and abroad. You talk as if we were fools and didn't realise all this. My God! Do you not know that ever since 1921 the main purpose in everything I have done has been to try to secure a basis for national unity. How can you imagine for one moment that I don't realise what division in the Republican ranks means at a time like this. But is this need and desire for unity to be used as a means of trying to blackmail us into adopting a policy which we know could only lead our people to disaster? It has taken us ten long years of patient effort to get the Irish nation on the march again after a devastating civil war. Are we to abandon all this in order to satisfy a group who have not given the slightest evidence of any ability to lead our people anywhere except back into the morass?

We desire unity, but desires will get us nowhere unless we can get some accepted basis for determining what the national policy shall be and where leadership shall lie. What is the use of talking any more with people who are too stupid or too pig-headed to see this . . . The oath was the barrier which made this basis impossible until we removed it. I do not believe the wit of man will discover any other basis. No one has attempted to suggest any substitute. If this country is not to be a Mexico or a Cuba, a basis must be found, or else the party that has got the confidence of the majority here will have to secure order by force. There is no alternative. We have undertaken a responsibility to the people at present living, to the future and to the dead. We will not allow any group or any individuals to prevent us from carrying it out.[5]

Although the ruthlessness which de Valera was ultimately to bring to the task of suppressing the I.R.A. is here laid bare, the internal logic of his position demanded that he first strip the state of all those elements which *he* deemed repugnant to right-minded republicans, a process which culminated in the enactment of the 1937 constitution and the return of the ports in 1938. In the meantime 1935 saw a series of episodes which contributed to the growing sense of confrontation such as the More O'Ferrall murder in February, the I.R.A. involvement in the Dublin transport strike which began in March and the April announcement that Fianna Fáil would no longer sell Easter Lilies, 'the symbol of "an organisation of whose methods they disapprove" '.[6] The Catholic hierarchy had also become increasingly trenchant in their public criticism of the I.R.A. as their traditional antagonism was reinforced by the so-called 'Red scare' attendant upon the formation of the Communist Party of Ireland in 1933 and the Republican Congress in 1934. The upshot was the Lenten pastoral of 1935 prohibiting membership of the I.R.A. De Valera, by contrast, although an earlier target of 'Red scare' tactics particularly at election time, seemed increasingly respectable in the hierarchy's eyes. Indeed the Fianna Fáil government had taken pains to stress their commitment to catholicism. An early cabinet meeting in April 1932, for instance, favoured the suspension of sittings of the Oireachtas on church holidays, the opening of Dáil sittings 'with an appropriate form of prayer' and displaying a crucifix in the Dáil chamber,[7] to say nothing of their whole-hearted participation in the Eucharistic Congress of 1932.

Church disapproval and the increasing isolation of the I.R.A. may have weighed with de Valera when, in May 1935, he publicly admitted in the Dáil something of what he had earlier expressed so forcefully to McGarrity. He was disappointed, he said, 'that the Republican section which is not in Fianna Fáil' — a classic devaleraism — had not co-operated with him after the removal of the oath; he expressed particular disappointment that they had not developed 'a sense of respect for law because it was home law' as opposed to foreign law. 'There must be order', he again intoned, and 'if the ordinary operations of law cannot be relied upon to maintain order and secure justice — if there is to be government at all — the Government have to seek and use the powers which will make law operate'. He went on to say that if his government 'were introducing a new constitution tomorrow . . . we would have to introduce in that constitution certain emergency provisions which would give power to the executive, in case the ordinary courts were set at defiance, to bring those who were acting in an unlawful and illegal manner before courts which could not possibly be intimidated'.[8]

But the time for a new constituion was not quite yet and in the meantime, in November 1935, de Valera turned down the demand of William Norton in the Dáil to revoke article 2A of the 1922 constitution — the Public Safety Act — on the grounds that 'organised crimes of violence are still occurring' and he explicitly denied Norton's contention that the act amounted to 'tyranny . . . worse than any crime against the people's liberty that has been committed'.[9]

More armed murders by the I.R.A. soon followed, notably retired Vice-Admiral Somerville in March 1936 and Garda John Egan in April. De Valera hesitated no longer and on 18 June 1936 his government made an order under the Special Powers Act declaring the I.R.A. an unlawful association. The imprisonment of many I.R.A. leaders, including chief of staff Maurice Twomey, swiftly followed. The use of the Public Safety Act prompted opposition charges of inconsistency which, as always, stung de Valera into an elaborate restatement of all the arguments we have already rehearsed. His disappointment that the I.R.A. refused to recognise that there was no longer 'any reason whatever for the maintenance of an armed organisation' — although he still conceded that 'they had reason in the past for their attitude' — was now tempered by a public expression of regret if his own policy towards the I.R.A. in the early thirties had 'led in any way to the murder of individuals in this state'.[10]

The next eighteen months saw rapid progress in de Valera's policy of creating a state which would satisfy republican aspirations. The abdication crisis of December 1936 occasioned the deletion from the constitution of all mention of the King and the Governor-General, and de Valera's constitution, which made the state as much of a republic as he wished it to be, was enacted in 1937. That constitution duly provided, as de Valera had anticipated, for the establishment of special courts (Art. 38(3)) 'by law for the trial of offences in cases where it may be determined in accordance with such law that the ordinary courts are inadequate to secure the effective administration of justice, and the preservation of public peace and order'. The rigidly restricted definition of treason in the constitution may also be related to the evolution of de Valera's 'rule of order' (Art. 39):

> Treason shall consist only in levying war against the state or assisting any state or person or inciting or conspiring with any person to levy war against the state, or attempting by force of arms or other violent means to overthrow the organs of government established by this constitution, or taking part or being concerned in or inciting or conspiring with any person to make or to take part or be concerned in any such attempt.

De Valera spelt out the significance of this article when he introduced the Treason Bill in the Dáil in 1939. 'The moment the constitution was enacted by the people', he argued, 'treason had a new meaning. The constitution was the foundation of a state' and the definition of treason had been definitely limited 'to make it clear that treason must no longer be understood in terms of allegiance to foreign powers . . . Once the constitution was passed, treason was defined as an act of treachery against this state, and nothing else'. Now that 'the Irish people had established freely a state in accordance with their wishes, those who tried, by violent means, to overthrow that state should be held here, as in other countries, to be guilty of the most terrible crime of a public character which is known in civilised society'.[11] The baldness of de Valera's words contrasts starkly with the labyrinthine language of so many of his earlier utterances on the subject. The reason why ambiguities were at an end, of course, was that, after 1937, the state was no longer the Irish Free State detested by all republicans but de Valera's 'Ireland'. The framework for the application of the 'rule of order' was now complete.

At first, however, de Valera seems to have nurtured the hope, albeit briefly, that all republicans would become reconciled to his new state. 'I have never been more satisfied or happier about the situation than I have been for the last couple of years', he told the Dáil in March 1939.

> I felt that what I had said and what I had prophesied had come true; that the moment we had got a constitution freely accepted by the Irish people themselves in a free plebiscite, and the moment we had got a government elected or selected by representatives of the people who were freely chosen, all the difficulties which we had here in the past would disappear.[12]

But it was rather the last of de Valera's illusions about the I.R.A. that had disappeared, blasted by their 1939 bombing campaign in Britain, and the occasion of these remarks was his coming to the Dáil to seek the sweeping powers which were to be embodied in the Offences Against the State Act which provided, among other things, for imprisonment without trial. The very title of the act underlined the significance which de Valera attached to the 1937 constitution as justifying his taking the most draconian powers to deal with the I.R.A. There had been 'a change of position in this country', as he was later to tell the Dáil:

> the methods which were used to try to defeat a foreign power in this country ought not to be used against an Irish government freely elected here under a free constitution . . .
>
> Some of these people do not understand. We were willing to do everything we could to make allowance for them and to try to wean them off; but they have resisted every effort of ours to induce them to obey the law and to accept the constitutional position of the Irish people. If they take up that position and are going to rely upon force, there is no other way of meeting it but by the full force of the state — no other way . . .
>
> If one-half of the efforts that are made to hold the hand of the government when justice has to be done were made to convince these people that they are wrong and show them the right way, how much better it would be. If you cannot do that with them, then tell them: "Very well, if you are not going to be advised, then you are going to come up against a power which will be much stronger than you are".[13]

Paternalism it may still have been, but paternalism which had become more authoritarian than benevolent. The Emergency — the quaintly indigenous description of World War II is in this context at least entirely appropriate — greatly accelerated the trend towards authoritarianism. De Valera's Emergency Powers Act was even more stringent than the British act upon which it was modelled in respect of the trial and punishment of offences. The explanatory memorandum drafted by de Valera's legal advisers at the time of the Munich crisis explained why: the British 'don't even contemplate the possibility that juries will be perverse. In our view the same reliance cannot be placed on juries here and least of all in cases involving charges of disaffection or subversive activities or attempts against the state'.[14] That all the major political parties in the state supported de Valera's neutrality policy throughout World War II immeasurably enhanced his authority and, for the first time since 1921, gave him a genuine claim to that position of national leadership which he had so desperately sought to retrieve. Under these circumstances it was not, perhaps, surprising that de Valera should see fit, in 1940, to address a radio broadcast to the nation on what he described as 'the basic question of authority'. Although he accepted that the ambition to realise Irish unity was lawful — the I.R.A., in 1939 and subsequently, focussed their attention on partition — he insisted that it fell to the single sovereign authority of the state to regulate by what mode of action such unity may be sought. It is not the moral right of any individual or group of individuals to choose a means that is contrary to the public good or general justice. The claim to choose such means can never be substantiated by an appeal to the facts or conditions of Easter Week 1916 — nor to the sentiments of the leaders. We can conceive of these men as wishing only the true good of their country, and in the altered conditions of our days it cannot possibly make for the good of the nation to refuse due obedience to the freely elected and Irish government which now controls the major portion of our land.[15]

But it was not merely in respect of the growth of authoritarianism that World War II altered the perspective of de Valera's attitude towards the I.R.A.; much more serious was the threat their campaign might pose to his primary aim as wartime head of the Irish government: the preservation of Irish sovereignty. The I.R.A.'s 1939 declaration of war on the United Kingdom, acting as the self-styled 'Government of the Irish Republic' was an intolerable affront to de Valera, coming, as it did, so soon after the British had returned the ports under the terms of the 1938 defence agreement which he saw as recognising and finally establishing Irish sovereignty over the twenty-six counties and so soon, also, after he had publicly and categorically reiterated his pledge that his government would not permit its territory to be used as a base of attack on Britain. De Valera's response was the Offences Against the State Act but even that was deemed inadequate to meet the menace of a war in Europe in which the Irish government was determined to keep Ireland neutral. De Valera's reaction to the I.R.A. hunger-strikes of 1939-40 revealed his hardening attitude when he spoke of events having taken a 'new turn' since the I.R.A. had

definitely proclaimed itself as entitled to exercise the powers of government here, to act in the name of our people, even to commit our people to war. Now, we are in a time of peril. We have a war being waged around us, the outcome of which no man can tell. We have seen already in this war nations, comparatively large nations, losing their freedom. Is the government of this country to be deprived of the only power that it has to prevent things taking place here . . . to rob us of the independence . . . and . . . the fruits of all the efforts that have been made for the last twenty-five years? That is what is at stake . . .

The government have been faced with the alternative of two evils. We have had to choose the lesser, and the lesser evil is to see men die rather than that the safety of the whole community should be endangered.   (p. 421-22).

And see men die they did, the protests of Senator Margaret Pearse, among others, notwithstanding.[16]

But de Valera suffered his greatest humiliation at the hands of the I.R.A. on Christmas Eve 1939 when it became known that, in a raid on the Magazine Fort in Phoenix Park, they had seized over a million rounds of ammunition which they took away in thirteen lorries. The Dáil met in special session in the first days of 1940 and passed an amendment to the Emergency Powers Act enabling the government to intern on suspicion and without trial in detention camps at the army's headquarters in the Curragh. The measure was necessary, claimed de Valera, because the I.R.A. were ready to use armed force 'against the organised forces in this state. They are prepared to embroil this state, if they think it accords with their purposes, with neighbouring states'.[17] The Goertz episode and other clear evidence in 1940 revealed I.R.A. links with Germany at a time when de Valera, with good reason, felt that Winston Churchill's government were looking for an excuse to invade Ireland. The gun-fight in Holles Street between the I.R.A. and armed detectives thought to be bringing dispatches from the United Kingdom Representative in Dublin, Sir John Maffey, to the Department of External Affairs prompted similar fears and was the occasion of a special radio broadcast by de Valera when he spoke of his government's 'excessive patience' and warned that 'the policy of patience has failed and is over'. He warned further that the I.R.A.

> will not be allowed to continue their policy of sabotage. They have set the law at defiance. The law will be enforced against them. If the present law is not sufficient, it will be strengthened; and in the last resort, if no other law will suffice, then the government will invoke the ultimate law — the safety of the people.[18]

A litany of later incidents making up what has been described as the 'pattern of provocation, retaliation and vengeance'[19] between government and I.R.A. forces would be redundant. The outcome was predictable. Ultimate law, the policy of executions carried out after trial by military tribunal, the policy of internment in the Curragh, prevailed. Victory, as de Valera had foreseen, went to the stronger power.

A Unionist observer, looking at Dublin from Stormont at the end of 1938, remarked that 'the Southern Irish voter is always "agin the government" and it suits de Valera that they should be against the British government rather than against himself'.[20] His observation is, I believe, helpful in understanding the ultimate impotence of the I.R.A. when confronted with de Valera, not as an ally, but as an enemy. That he was so persistently represented by the British government as *their* enemy, whether in the twenties or during the economic war or in his confrontations with Churchill during and after the second world war, was his greatest strength. What I have described elsewhere as his successfully playing the Green Card redounded to the disadvantage of the I.R.A. no less than to the disadvantage of his constitutional political opponents. While de Valera was withholding the land annuities, tearing up the oath, degrading the office of Governor-General, taking the crown out of the constitution, getting back the ports and defending neutrality against all comers, the I.R.A. had scant hope of winning ground among the unconverted. As one of their number was later to observe it was not that the I.R.A. leaders were individually inferior to de Valera's own front bench — he listed, among others, Moss Twomey, Sean MacBride, George Gilmore, Peadar O'Donnell, Tom Barry and Frank Ryan — but that they 'lacked a "plan of campaign" in the de Valera sense of the term'.[21]

The I.R.A. were at a further disadvantage in that they did nothing to bridge the gap between their *de facto* position and their *de jure* claim that their republic had never ceased to exist, whereas de Valera was spectacularly successful in that regard and did, in effect, what he set out to do. But then the fundamental difference between de Valera and the I.R.A., ever since the civil war, was his conception of politics as the art of the possible; he had even made reference in his celebrated message to the 'Legion of the Rearguard' to the republic's already having been destroyed, the implications of which escaped those for whom it was primarily intended.

There are curious similarities between the reactions to de Valera in power of pro-treaty constitutionalists on the one hand and anti-treaty revolutionaries on the other. Both were slow to realise that he meant what he said and that his programme for future action was in large part spelt out in his speeches. Both denied that his goal could be attained and, when it was, reacted with frustrated bafflement. Both failed to appreciate the impeccable conservatism of his political philosophy and seemed strangely surprised when he proved as willing to order the execution of erstwhile political allies in defence of his state as Cosgrave's government had been in defence of the Free State. Both failed, in short, to understand the depth of his commitment to the 'rule of order'.

NOTES

1. Maurice Moynihan (ed.), *Speeches and statements by Eamon de Valera 1917-73* (Dublin: 1980), 113. All otherwise unattributed references are to this source.

2. SPO G2/10/1-2.

3. J. Bowyer Bell, *The secret army — the IRA 1916-79* (Dublin, revised ed., 1979), 99.

4. Moynihan (ed.), 191.

5. Sean Cronin, *The McGarrity papers* (Tralee: 1972), 157-8.

6. Bell, (1979), 121.

7. SPO CAB 1/4/47-8.

8. Moynihan (ed.), 263-6.

9. D.E., 59, 1535-6.

10. Moynihan (ed.), 278-9.

11. D.E., 74, 966-7; 23 Feb. 1939.

12. D.E., 74, 1379.

13. D.E., 95, 1460-2; 1 Dec. 1944.

14. See Ronan Fanning, *The Irish Department of Finance 1922-58* (Dublin: 1978), 308-9.

15. Moynihan (ed.), 424.

16. Margaret Pearse to Eamon de Valera, 15 Nov. 1939, SPO S 11515.

17. D.E., 78, 135-6.

18. Moynihan (ed.), 433-4.

19. Bell, (1979), 183.

20. Sir Wilfrid Spender to Major-General H.M. de F. Montgomery, 23 Nov. 1938, PRONI D.715/11/73-4.

21. Cronin, (1972), *loc. cit.*

Article 50 of Bunreacht na h-Eireann and the Unwritten English Constitution of Ireland

John F. O'Connor

In 1975, the Supreme Court reminded us (if we needed reminding), that the Constitution is a legal document, but a fundamental one which expresses not only legal norms, but basic doctrines of political and social theory.[1]

The written provisions of Bunreacht na h-Eireann clearly set out the basic principles for the legal, political and social arrangements of the State. In relation to our legal order, Article 15,2, 1° provides:

> The sole and exclusive power of making laws for the State is hereby vested in the Oireachtas: no other legislative authority has power to make laws for the State.

This sole and exclusive power is limited by Article 15, 4, 1°.

> The Oireachtas shall not enact any law which is in any respect repugnant to this constitution or any provision thereof.

To the extent that the Oireachtas does enact any law which is repugnant to the Constitution, such law is invalid (Art. 15, 4, 2°).

The question of the constitutional validity of any law is ultimately decided by the Supreme Court established under the Constitution (Art. 34, 4, 4°).

These constitutional-legal provisions are typical of 'written constitution' States, such as the United States of America or the Federal Republic of Germany, and they contrast strongly with the 'unwritten' British Constitution where the legislative power of Parliament is legally unlimited and the Courts have no power to declare Acts of Parliament invalid by reference to fundamental constitutional norms.[2]

There is no doubt that the changes introduced by the Constitution of 1922, and the further changes introduced by the Constitution of 1937, radically altered the legal-constitutional position of Ireland as part of the United Kingdom of Great Britain and Ireland. The precise international status of Ireland, as a sovereign independent Republic is beyond question, and it is also beyond question that the Oireachtas is a sovereign legislature, with power to make new law and unmake old law, subject only to the constraints of the written Constitution. Any statutory or common law rule of the pre-1922 era can be altered by legislation, or will not be enforced by the Courts if inconsistent with the Constitution.

In that sense, what Johnston J. said in *The State (Burke) v. Lennon* in 1940 is certainly correct:

> The Constitution of 1937 represents a fresh start in respect of fundamental principles that are to be the guide of this country for the future, and I do not think that a further Constitution — an unwritten one — was intended by the people of Eire to exist side by side with this written constitution or even — perhaps it would be more correct to say — outside and beyond the present Constitution.[3]

In the same sense, it is of course correct, as Walsh J. said in *Byrne v. Ireland* in 1972, that English common law practices, doctrines or immunities cannot qualify or dilute the provisions of the Constitution.[4]

But it is also true that the people of Ireland remain subject to a very large body of English common law and pre-1922 statutory rules by virtue of Article 50 of our present written Constitution. Article 50 (its predecessor was Article 73 in the 1922 Constitution), has the effect of continuing all the pre-1922 law, except to the extent to which that is inconsistent with the Constitution, and that pre-existing law continues to be of full force and effect until repealed or amended by the Oireachtas.

The Oireachtas has repealed or amended the pre-1922 law in many respects, and the Courts since 1922 have held that particular rules, both statutory and common law, have not continued as the law in force because they were inconsistent with the Constitution. But a vast number of rules of the pre-1922 era remain as part of the legal order by virtue of the continuance provisions of the Constitutions of 1922 and 1937. It is these rules, these legal norms (which in themselves reflect basic doctrines of political and social theory) which constitute our 'unwritten' constitution. It is submitted that our 'unwritten' constitution, in that sense, has not received the attention which it deserves, and any discussions to change or amend the Constitution should, in my view, also include consideration of our unwritten constitution.

The Significance of Continuance of the Law in Force in 1922

Continuing the law in force in a new State is not only, or merely, a technical device to avoid a legal vacuum. The law in force broadly reflects the socio-political and socio-moral views which are prevalent in the society in question and the continuance provision in the Constitution of 1922 (Article 73) was, in effect, an affirmation and confirmation that the pre-1922 society was to continue with the least possible change.

O'Byrne, J., (who was a member of the Committee which drafted the 1922 Constitution) explained the purpose of Article 73 in *The State (Kennedy) v. Little* in 1931 as follows:

> It seems to me to have been intended to set up the new State with the least possible change in the previously existing law, and that Article 73 should be so construed as to effectuate this intention . . . I am of opinion that the fullest possible effect should be given to Article 73, and that the previously existing laws should be regarded as still subsisting unless they are clearly inconsistent with the Constitution.[5]

In 1949, nearly 30 years after the new Irish State was established and more than a decade after the 1937 Constitution came into effect, the consequences of continuing the law in force (now by Article 50 of Bunreacht na h-Eireann, 1937) were strikingly illustrated when Conor Maguire, C.J., stated in *Boylan v. Dublin Corporation* that a decision of the House of Lords of the former United Kingdom of Great Britain and Ireland, given in November 1922, was binding on the Supreme Court.[6] Six months later, Murnaghan, J., said that he understood the position was that decisions of the House of Lords upon law common to England and Ireland given before the coming into operation of the Constitution of 1922 are of binding force in the Courts until their effect has been altered by our legislature.[7] The question of the merits or otherwise of particular rules of the pre-1922 law, though obviously important, is not the principal issue here. The principal issue is that the whole of the pre-1922 law (save where clearly constitutionally inconsistent or altered by subsequent legislation) continues to be the law of the State. This means that many areas of Irish national life continue to be governed by rules of law, which may or may not be conducive to the welfare of the people of modern Ireland, but which *must* be applied by the Courts and observed by the people as part of our 'unwritten' Constitution. The continuation of pre-1922 law for an indefinite period was particularly unfortunate and inappropriate in the Irish situation because the system which was continued as 'the law in force' was the common law system and therefore itself 'unwritten'. The Irish Constitution, in the larger sense of the legal norms which actually govern modern Ireland, is therefore very largely unwritten, and in practice it may be difficult, even for lawyers and judges, to establish what these norms are.

The Nature of the Law continued in force

The law in force in Ireland, immediately before the coming into operation of the Constitution of 1922, was the common law, as declared and developed by English and Irish Courts, supplemented by the Statutes in force.

The common law (in fact the laws of England), according to the official and traditional belief, arrived in Ireland in the twelfth year of the reign of King John (1210).[8] On the modern view that the law follows the flag, it arrived about 40 years earlier when Henry II planted his standard in Ireland in 1171.[9] In any case, Sir Edward Coke, whose life and writings had so large an influence on the place which the common law achieved in British constitutional theory, said that the just and honourable laws of England were joyfully received and obeyed by the Irish.[10] On the other hand, Edmund Spenser with more local knowledge, admitted that in Ireland the laws of England 'worke not that good which they should, and sometimes also that evill that they would not', the reason being, apparently, that the Irish as a people were very stubborn![11]

The truth of course was that English law — the common law — was originally extended to Ireland solely for the benefit of the colonists in the twelfth century and it was not until the sixteenth century that the King's writ, and with it the common law, ran throughout the country.[12] The common law in Ireland was never the common law in its original English sense of the standardisation and development of the native customs so as to form a law 'common' to the whole of the kingdom.

On the contrary, the customs of the Irish, used time out of mind, were declared to be abolished by the introduction of the common law of England into Ireland.[13]

By 1922, the common law, as developed by the Courts in England and Ireland, was the foundation of the socio-legal structure of Ireland as part of the United Kingdom of Great Britain and Ireland. Common law rules determined the nature and extent of property rights, testate and intestate succession to property, contractual relations of all kinds (including the relations between employers and employees), our system of criminal justice, and our system of compensation for injuries caused by the fault of another.

The normal process of development of the common law did not (and could not) meet all the challenges of change in society, and especially in the nineteenth century, the Parliament of the United Kingdom changed and supplemented the common law in many areas. But it is important to emphasise that in the common law system, the Courts proceed upon the premise that Parliament legislates against the background of an all-embracing customary or common law. As recently as 1974, Lord Scarman said 'the modern English judge still sees enacted law as an exception to, a graft upon, or a correction of the customary law in his hands'.[14] What he said of modern English Law is equally true of modern Irish Law. The Oireachtas, like its counterpart in Britain, legislates to change and supplement the common law. It has done so, for example, in such important Acts as the Civil Liability Act, 1961, The Succession Act,

1965 and the Sale of Goods and Supply of Services Act, 1980. But, as Lord Scarman said of the similar situation in Britain 'every one of these limited codes is enacted in a scene of which the back-cloth is the customary law, developed by the courts and in which the principal actors are the judges and the legal profession, educated in and loyal to the principles and attitudes of that customary law'.[15]

The Oireachtas (and the expert who drafts the Bill which the Oireachtas considers) accepts this fact. The Acts mentioned above (which have direct and far reaching social consequences) do not pretend to be full statements of the law of civil liability, or succession, or sale of goods and supply of services. They must be considered against a vast background of unwritten rules — the common law.[16] Again, what Lord Scarman said of English Law might be quoted here; it is equally applicable to Irish Law:

> This system of lawyers' law, conceived, developed, and from time to time adjusted by the judges and the legal profession through the forensic process, has had great consequences for the substance and administration of English law. Its shape and content are lawyer-made: its home-made principles, concepts and classifications dominate the education and the thinking of the profession and control legal practice in and out of court. They are preserved and perpetuated by a strict system of precedent . . .[17]

The effect of Article 50 was not only that it carried over particular rules (which might in time have been considered and dealt with by the legislature) but also an entire system of legal thinking and a judicial approach to socio-legal problems which, I believe, had, and continues to have, a fundamental impact on modern Irish Society. In the last 20 years, and particularly in the last 10 years or so, the people of Ireland have become increasingly aware of the legal, as distinct from the political dimension of the *written* constitution. The wide publicity given to such cases as *McGee v. Attorney General* (contraception case),[18] *De Burca v. Attorney General* (Women and juries),[19] *Murphy v. Attorney General* (married couples and taxation),[20] and *Blake and Madigan v. Attorney General* (Rent Restriction Cases)[21] has given a high profile to legal aspects of the written constitution. It should be noted that all of these cases dealt with the constitutionality of legislation passed since 1922, in other words, they were concerned with the obvious fundamental change introduced by the Constitution, viz. the institution of judicial review of legislation. Significantly less publicity has been given to the far more numerous cases, decided at all levels of the Courts, on the basis of the 'unwritten' constitution. Yet these cases were, and are, none the less important for the parties and society generally. To use the words of the Supreme Court, they established, or rather confirmed, not only legal norms, but basic doctrines of political and social theory and they were decided on the basis of the law in force before 6 December 1922 and carried over as the unwritten constitution of modern Ireland. It would not be possible, within the confines of a short paper, to consider all the important cases decided on the basis of the law carried over — what I have identified here as the substance of our unwritten constitution. Some examples must suffice; but perhaps the examples given will provide some indication of the actual and potential social significance of our unwritten constitution.

The first example concerns a matter which received great attention in Bunreacht na h-Eireann — the Family. As is well known, Article 41, 3, 2° provides that no law shall be enacted providing for divorce. Article 41, 3, 3° goes further in protecting marriage, (on which the legal family depends), by providing that no person who has obtained a divorce elsewhere but whose marriage is a subsisting valid marriage under Irish law, shall be capable of contracting a valid marriage in the State.

Under the law in force in Ireland before 1922, a divorce obtained outside Ireland in a country where the petitioner was domiciled, was entitled to recognition by the Irish Courts. In 1971, the Irish High Court confirmed that this pre-1922 law was still the law of Ireland by virtue of the carry over provision of the Constitution, so that a recognised foreign divorce meant that there was no longer a valid marriage under Irish Law.[22]

The obvious difficulty of reconciling the clear constitutional duty of the State to uphold the institution of marriage, and the constitutional obligation of the Courts to apply the law carried over is compounded in this particular case by the peculiar problems created by the old English rules on the legal concept of 'domicile'. By these rules, e.g., men and women who have had no real connection with Ireland for many years may still be legally domiciled in Ireland. On the other hand, foreign nationals who have lived in Ireland for many years may not be legally domiciled here. An attempt by Barrington J. in the High Court in 1980 to reconcile the difficulty led to a decision to refuse recognition to a French divorce, obtained 22 years before, to a couple who, even under the peculiar Anglo-Irish rules, were clearly domiciled in France. The divorce, although it could not have been set aside in France, was refused recognition in the High Court for two reasons, one being that there had been collusion between the parties amounting to a fraud on the French court, and the other that it would be hard to reconcile the recognition of the divorce with the constitutional duty of the State to uphold the institution of marriage.[23] The result of that decision was hardly typical. The defendant's stately home in the West of Ireland was classified as a family home within the meaning of the Family Home Protection Act, 1976 and he was ordered to pay his long cast off wife maintenance of £300 per week! But the rules applied in that case also apply — by virtue of Article 50 of Bunreacht na h-Eireann, to the far more typical case of ordinary Irish married couples separating, the husband going abroad and perhaps remaining abroad for many years, obtaining a divorce abroad and re-marrying abroad with a 'wife' left behind in Ireland.

The proliferation of limping marriages and the increasing likelihood of disputes about maintenance, family homes and succession to property is one example of the undesirable consequences of continuing the old law in force in this area by Article 50.

Another example might be mentioned, in this area of marriage and the family, of the unfortunate consequences of continuing our unwritten English Constitution. As the Memorandum on the Law of Nullity prepared in the office of the Attorney General in 1976[24] points out, until 1863 marriages in Ireland between two Roman Catholics were left to the operation of the common law. In that year, an Act provided for the registration of marriages between Roman Catholics, but did not affect the law relating to the validity of the marriage — this was left to the common law.[25] The marriage law of members of other religious faiths was regulated by various Statutes.[26] All of this tangled web of common law and statute was continued as the law of modern Ireland, even though in 1922 it was clearly in need of reform. Not surprisingly, the problems since 1922 have increased considerably, particularly in relation to nullity of marriage. Five years ago, the Attorney General's Memorandum stated that an examination of the law relating to nullity leads to the conclusion that there is a real and pressing need for reform.[27] Nothing has been done. The unsatisfactory law carried over since 1922 still governs this fundamental area of Irish life.

Two other areas of the law carried over, the general rules of contract and tort, are almost exclusively judge-made. Their potential significance in the day to day activities of all citizens hardly needs emphasis as they deal respectively with the whole area of legally enforceable agreements for sale of land, goods and services and liability for general civil wrongs such as trespass, nuisance, negligence and defamation. Although the Oireachtas has intervened with important amending legislation in some of these areas notably the Civil Liability Act, 1961 and the Sale of Goods and Supply of Services Act, 1980, the vast majority of the rules here are still those which have been carried over from the pre-independence era. It is highly questionable whether some of these rules are suitable for the conditions of modern Ireland, but leaving aside the merits of individual rules, the blanket continuation of *all* of these rules has perpetuated prac-tices of litigation which are surely not in the public interest.

The rules of negligence in the law of tort, for example, as applied to ac-tions for personal injuries in road accidents or in the work place are conducive to unnecessarily protracted court hearings involving expert witnesses and layman juries.

In the important matter of buying and selling houses and land, it is little short of ludicrous that a Statute of 1695 and decisions of the English and Irish Courts of the last century related to that statute, should still cause problems for modern Irish courts and, of course, considerable unnecessary expense and worry for the citizens affected. But that is the situation in relation to cases of land bought 'subject to contract' and the Statute of Frauds 1695. After several High Court decisions in recent years and two Supreme Court decisions last year,[28] the problems here are still unresolved.[29]

Continuing all the law in force, as a constitutional obligation, is a national liability when the nature of that law is examined critically. The apparently soft option taken in 1922 and 1937 to avoid a legal vacuum has contributed more to an inefficient, unresponsive and unnecessarily expensive legal system than is generally realised.

Consideration of Bunreacht na h-Eireann, with a view to its replacement or major revision, should include a review of Article 50. In particular, some thought should be given to a new constitutional requirement that the State should establish a Commission with the task of producing a comprehensive written code of Irish Law. The existence of an unwritten Constitution side by side with a written constitution should not be perpetuated.

A continuance provision to avoid a legal vacuum until a new code is enacted would of course be necessary, but it should not be one like the present Article 50: this encourages excessive and indefinitely prolonged reliance on the unwritten laws of the political order which Mr de Valera and the Founding Fathers of Bunreacht na h-Eireann, and a majority of the Irish people, rejected 60 years ago.

NOTES

1. *In re Article 26 and the Criminal Law (Jurisdiction) Bill, 1975,* [1977] Irish Reports (hereinafter I.R.) 129 at p. 147.

2. The British constitutional practice of safeguarding the rights of the subject by statutory enactment, e.g., *Magna Carta, Habeas Corpus, The Bill of Rights* and the *Act of Settlement* gives rise to documents which enjoy a special 'constitutional' aura, but as all such written constitutional norms can be legally abrogated by Parliament as easily as 'ordinary' legislation, they lack the entrenched character of true written constitutional norms. For a recent critical summary of the British constitutional position on fundamental rights see Sir Leslie Scarman, *English Law — The New Dimension* (The Hamlyn Lectures), (1974), pp. 10-21.

3. [1940] I.R. 136 at p. 179.

4. [1972] I.R. 241 at p. 281.

5. [1931] I.R. 39 at p. 58.

6. [1949] I.R. 60 at p. 65. The decision in question was *Fairman v. The Perpetual Investment Building Society*, reported [1923] A.C. 74.

7. *Minister for Finance v. O'Brien*, [1949] I.R. 91 at p. 116.

8. See W.J. Johnston, 'The First Adventure of the Common Law', *The Law Quarterly Review* [No. CXLI, Jan. 1920], p. 10.

9. *ibid.*

10. *ibid.* For Coke's influence on the common law see Holdsworth, *A History of English Law*, Vol. V, pp. 423-493.

11. Johnston, *op. cit.* p. 10.

12. On the gradual introduction of the common law into Ireland, see *The Case of Tanistry*, Davies Reports, (ed. 1762), pp. 101-108.

13. *ibid.* p. 101.

14. Scarman, *op. cit.* note 2, p. 3.

15. *ibid.*, p. 5.

16. For example, Part III of the *Civil Liability Act, 1961*, although it purports to be a codification of the law on concurrent fault (see Explanatory Memorandum on the Bill, p. 4) refers to the torts of conspiracy, libel, nuisance, fraud and negligence without any explanation of what these are, or where the rules relating to them might be found.

17. Scarman, *op. cit.* p. 5. In 1965, the Supreme Court relaxed the strictness of the system of precedent to some extent for itself. (*See A.G. and Another v. Ryan's Car Hire Co. Ltd.* [1965] I.R. 642.

18. [1974] I.R. 284.

19. [1976] I.R. 38.

20. Unreported. Supreme Court, January, 1980.

21. [1981] ILRM, 34.

22. *In re Caffin*, [1971] I.R. 123.

23. *L.B. v. H.B.* (High Court, unreported, 31 July 1980).

24. *The Law of Nullity in Ireland*, (Prl. 5628).

25. *ibid.* p. 2.

26. The most important of these were (and are) the *Marriages (Ireland) Act*, 1844 and the *Matrimonial Causes and Marriage Law (Ireland) Act*, 1870.

27. *The Law of Nullity in Ireland*, introduction VII.

28. *Joseph Kelly v. Irish Nursery & Landscape Co. Ltd.* [1981] ILRM 443; Carthy v. O'Neill & O'Neill [1981] ILRM 443.

29. The present confused state of the law and the recent Irish cases are dealt with by Robert Clarke in two articles in *Dublin University Law Journal*, (1979-80), pp. 42-51 and (1981), pp 105-109.

Eamon de Valera: Seven Lives

Notes on the biographies by Gwynn (1933),
O'Faolain (1933, 1939), Ryan (1936), MacManus (1944),
Bromage (1956), and Longford and O'Neill (1970)[1]

John Bowman

> Fanatical, ruthless, self-centred, and self-sufficient, this man is
> dangerous. But to none is he more dangerous than to whatever
> cause he attaches himself, for the fates which guide his destiny
> have given him a genius for destruction which is his and his
> country's curse.[2]

This editorial comment from the *Morning Post* on 22 February 1932 is
not untypical of the British press response to Eamon de Valera's victory
in the 1932 Irish general election. Nor was this perception of de Valera
confined to Fleet Street; it was also widespread in Westminster and
Whitehall.[3] The British hoped that General Smuts's sympathetic con-
dolences from South Africa would prove prophetic and that de Valera
would be merely 'a transient apparition'.[4] De Valera's failure to oblige his
critics on this score was presently manifest and as he consolidated his
position as the leader of Irish nationalism, British publishers were
prompted to commission biographies of him. The first three biographies
here considered were products of this initial interest: Sean O'Faolain's
first biography and those by Denis Gwynn and Desmond Ryan.

Considering their provenance and content, what one may ask is the
value of the early biographies? If they have been superseded by Longford
and O'Neill's life, why disinter them now when they are mainly forgotten and long out of print? Admittedly the biographical data of the early
volumes is of little interest since more complete and accurate information
is now available. But there are a number of reasons why these early lives
are worthy of some attention: the contemporary critical reception accorded them provides some indication of how de Valera was perceived during
the course of his lengthy and controversial career; there is some evidence
of how these authors worked which reveals something of de Valera's attitude towards his biographers; also there are important questions to be
raised about the most important of these books, the Longford and
O'Neill 'authoritative' biography, based on de Valera's papers and written with his co-operation.

Throughout his political career de Valera was preoccupied by the verdict of history. This was part of his own psyche but was reinforced by two considerations: self-doubt about his behaviour during the Treaty period and the need to reply to the criticism of what he must have seen as — and not without justification — his detractors and calumniators in the 1920s. He was also preoccupied by Irish historical grievances. Numerous witnesses attest to this. Ramsay MacDonald confided his impression of de Valera after his talks with him in 1932. 'He begins somewhere about the birth of Christ and wants a commission of four picked solely to give individual opinions to explore the past centuries and all he demands is a document, a manifesto, a judgement as from God himself as to how the world and more particularly Ireland should have been ruled' in the past.[5] In Ireland, de Valera repeatedly called for an 'Historical Commission of Inquiry' into the Treaty and Civil War periods. When he became head of the government in the 1930s, he proposed to W.T. Cosgrave that the latter should nominate three members of such a commission, 'say a Judge, or constitutional lawyer, a Professor or recognised student of history . . . and some other third person qualified to examine documents and to weigh historical evidence'. De Valera promised to nominate three persons 'of the same character' and if these six could not agree on an impartial chairman, de Valera was prepared 'to invite the Bishops to nominate one of their body' to chair the proceedings. He himself was prepared 'to give evidence before this Commission, and Mr Cosgrave and Miss MacSwiney may both be my accusers, if they choose'. Historians — even if it would seem to threaten their livelihood — must regret that this novel proposal was rejected by Cosgrave. They will also ruefully note de Valera's offer at the time that 'the whole of the government archives' would be made available to the commission.[6] This seems somewhat incongruous coming from a politician who did so little to ensure that adequate records and minutes of meetings were taken, retained and, in time, made available to future researchers.

De Valera was sensitive to criticism. He was self-righteous about his own political record and was keenly aware of the potential damage being done to his party's political prospects by the hostile and antipathetic press accorded to those opposed to the Treaty. Hence his preoccupation from the end of the Civil War with buying or establishing a national newspaper. Antipathy and bias towards de Valera was not confined to Irish newspapers. In Britain in the 1930s he was a marginal figure, the subject of occasional press features but largely ignored, if not forgotten. When he came into office in 1932, the British political elite had no detailed knowledge of his party or personality; moreover, many of them had serious misconceptions concerning his policies and his essentially pragmatic instincts which were masked by his bellicose metaphors and rhetoric. The British perception of de Valera was that he was a bogeyman who, not content with being the wrecker of the Treaty settlement of 1921-2, was now determined to renegotiate it on the basis of a document which had never interested the British but one which the wiser heads in Whitehall presently realized was a document which would be well worth studying: Document No. 2.

Not that the advice available to the Dominions Office was very good. Their Irish desk had numerous informants but these lacked the empathy necessary for an understanding of the incoming Fianna Fáil government and its leader. Lord Granard, for instance, after an off the record talk with de Valera reported to London that he found the Irish leader 'a most curious personality' and 'certainly not normal'. His impression was that de Valera was

> on the border line between genius and insanity. I have met men of many countries and have been Governor of a Lunatic Asylum, but I have never met anybody like the President of the Executive Council of the Irish Free State before. I hope that the Almighty does not create any more of the same pattern and that he will remain content with this one example.[7]

Another informant R.S. Oldham, was principal medical officer of the British Ministry of Pensions at Leopardstown Hospital in Co. Dublin. He pressed his services on London as a possible intermediary in the Anglo-Irish economic dispute: he suggested that he had 'the medical knowledge which I deem essential for dealing with the psychological problem presented by Mr de Valera's mind'.[8]

Lloyd George added his verdict — from the backbenches in the commons — reminding his audience that he had some experience of dealing with de Valera: 'frankly', he had 'never seen anything quite like it'. De Valera was 'perfectly unique and I think this poor distracted world has a good right to feel profoundly thankful that he is unique . . .'.[9] This then was the context in which London publishers expressed an interest in having biographies written of the new Irish leader. The first three books here considered, Sean O'Faolain's *Life story of Eamon de Valera*, (1933), Denis Gwynn's *De Valera* (1933), and Desmond Ryan's *Unique Dictator: a study of Eamon de Valera* (1936) resulted from this interest.

Not much need be said about O'Faolain's first biography in 1933. He admitted to writing as an apologist: 'Heaven knows, the man needs an apologist — he has had his share of critics and even detractors . . .'.[10] The *Irish Times* described O'Faolain as a 'eulogist',[11] *An Phoblacht* complained of 'a popular write-up of a popular hero'.[12] The author some years later dismissed the book as 'arrant tripe': the book was written 'as shamelessly pro-Dev and pro-Irish propaganda at a time when all of us who had stuck by de Valera from 1916 onwards at last saw our hero coming into power and all our dreams and ideals — as foolishly and trustingly hoped — about to be realised.'[13] F.S.L. Lyons sums it up as 'Over-written, under-documented, hagiographical rather than historical . . . the ugly duckling among O'Faolain's works.'[14]

Gwynn's lack of sympathy for de Valera's character and personality was noted by contemporary reviewers of his biography. The *Irish Times* critic — in those days anonymous — suggested that Gwynn saw de Valera as a man

> whose origin is veiled in mystery, who has had greatness thrust upon him unexpectedly, favoured again and again by accident, a difficult person within his own political circle no less than with his nation's opponents, skillful in exploiting his opportunities, austere and cold, implacable, vain, remote and inaccessible . . . alternately the advocate of compromise and of steadfast refusal to compromise, mouther of moral dissertation, provoker of hatred, engineer of the civil war, pedantic, ingenious, plausible, conciliatory, now arrogant, now apparently sweetly reasonable . . . inspiring not only respect but also personal devotion.[15]

Dorothy Macardle — an active supporter of de Valera's and presently to be the author of *The Irish Republic* — reviewed Gwynn for the *Irish Press*. She found him guilty of both bias and prejudice, describing the book as

> a somewhat tedious compilation of the whole mythological cycle of the Ogre de Valera — cold and austere, incorruptible, pedantic, obstinate, egoistic, the despair of his colleagues, the scourge of a suffering people — the figure familiar to readers of the English press.

Of more interest in Macardle's review is her comments on the ideal relationship between biographer and subject. The *Irish Press* in introducing her review asks: 'By what authority' has Gwynn 'written a "life" of the Irish leader?' and returns the verdict 'None' from their reviewer. She sees the biographer's role as 'pursuing every clue to truth with a scientist's passion and an artist's obliviousness'. The biographer, she suggests, sometimes becomes 'a persecutor, remorseless in his demands on those who may be able to supply him with facts'. However, Gwynn's methods, she concludes, are not those of 'either artist or scientist. He leaves his subjects and their friends in peace . . . The publisher's announcement of a book by him on Mr. de Valera was the first information as to that undertaking which came to Mr. de Valera or anyone associated with him. It is a method which if it does not conduce to accuracy, saves labour for all concerned.'[16]

The implication in this seems clear: that de Valera's co-operation would be forthcoming if he were approached by an author engaged in writing a biography. Contemporary evidence from Desmond Ryan refutes this. The evidence is all the more interesting since much of it comes from an exchange of letters between Ryan and Frank Pakenham, who — as Lord Longford — was to be, thirty years later, entrusted with co-authorship of the 'authoritative' life. Ryan was a professional journalist and writer and was initially approached by a London publisher to write the biography. Among Ryan's private papers there is a sketch of 'E. de V.' which he marked 'suitable for obituary or general notice'. Internal evidence suggests that it was written in the early 1930s. 'Full evidence was lacking for a final judgement', wrote Ryan. 'An immediate failure he was, perhaps, but not an ignoble or final failure.' He also exonerated de Valera from being as his critics alleged 'self-seeking, bitter, or ambitious'.[17]

Ryan and his publishers wanted some co-operation from de Valera if possible. Ryan wrote to T.J. Kiernan, chief executive of Radio Eireann on 23 September 1935 asking for 'advice or hints' as to how to make an approach. Kiernan doubted 'very much' if de Valera would co-operate but it would be 'no harm to try'.[18] Ryan also sought help from Pakenham querying whether de Valera would be 'hostile' to a biographical project 'except from a member of his own party'?[19] Pakenham's response was spontaneous and generous and his advice was detailed. It would, he wrote, 'be splendid' if Ryan could write a biography. On the 'practical chances' of de Valera's help, Pakenham would 'guess as follows': firstly that it would be 'very hard to get permission for an *authorized* biography', de Valera being 'very cautious'. But if Ryan 'happened to strike lucky, it should not be difficult to get him to talk very freely about his past life, for which he has a very long memory. But I doubt whether he would have much or anything to give you in the way of documents. I think, however (I am going on my own experience) that in ad[ditio]n to get him to tell you what you want, you ought to be able to go to him with a skeleton draft.' Pakenham advised Ryan to 'make contact with Dev — get some kind of permit from him to go ahead; write a skeleton chapter' and 'get him to give you enough personal anecdotes to give the book news-value'. Pakenham hoped Ryan would write the book: '. . . I think almost anything except an *authorized* biography is possible'.[20] Ryan thanked Pakenham for his 'very careful and useful advice'. He added that in his approach to de Valera he had acknowledged 'all the objections and difficulties' which an official life entailed but thought that there was still 'room for a book for the general reader in England, impartial, but better than hitherto published . . .'. Moreover, he would be willing to submit his draft before de Valera made any final decision about co-operating. What he really wanted, he told Pakenham was 'de Valera's benevolence' possibly with a foreward or 'getting in touch with those who would really give the facts'. He already had 'quite a lot of material but I want some inside dope or at least a kind word. However, I must wait and see, banging away on my typewriter in the meanwhile.' Sean Moynihan, de Valera's secretary, had acknowledged his request which he would place before de Valera on his return from Geneva. Moynihan 'also pointed out that such requests had up till now been refused'.[21]

On 12 November Ryan wrote again informing Pakenham that de Valera had rejected the idea of an authorized biography 'on the pleas of lack of time for interviews and also reasons of public policy in the present circumstances'. He would therefore have 'to write the book on different lines and on my own. I have plenty of material and no doubt it is better to have a free hand.'[22]

To another correspondent in February 1936 Ryan reported that the book was

> shaping well. Once there is the right perspective and proper allowances are made, de Valera comes out very well. So much reckless and careless rubbish has been written by his friends and enemies that it is hard sometimes to check up all the details. They use up all their adjectives and are not very clear whether he wore a uniform in 1916 or not, where he was in the Civil War, and between the rhapsodies of Dorothy Macardle, the slap-dash sniffings of Gwynn, fishwife antics of Gogarty, the growls of Peadar [O'Donnell], the President is indeed a martyr for Ireland.

Ryan asked his correspondent to 'say nothing about this book of mine in Dublin for there is 'never any help from that quarter except obstruction and bunk'. He did not propose to visit Ireland — he was then resident in London — until the book was completed lest he 'should run into some hero-worshippers who would put me right off de Valera and I should need a year to recover.'[23]

In the book Ryan details 'the wonder and exasperation' which de Valera evoked in many contemporary journalists: 'They esteemed him personally . . . but the guard on the sanctuary amused and irritated them by turn. Communication was only possible through worshipful and eloquent acolytes who cultivated the art of saying nothing at length and handed out typewritten answers to questions borne reverently to the President. The typewritten answers were annotated with much casuistry . . .'.[24] Ryan did not entirely disapprove of this cautious, pedantic approach to the media by de Valera. He appreciated that it had been developed as 'a most effective dyke against the stunt Press and British propaganda . . .'. Later in 1938 when Ryan was criticised by an Irish newspaper editor — E.T. Keane of the *Kilkenny People* — for writing 'ballyhoo' about de Valera in the *Daily Herald*,[25] his defence revealed something of the factors which were at that time influencing his own writings on de Valera. If Keane read 'the poisonous and insulting rubbish' which the 'gossip-paragraphists' and 'certain Irish correspondents dish out to the English Press about de Valera', and if he wrote for an English paper, then Ryan was 'sure you would feel more tender towards him'. Indeed if Ryan found himself writing about Cosgrave in an English paper he confided: 'I should do my best for him, as I should feel that the great British public would be nearer the truth if a restrained and sympathetic account is given them than otherwise.' Ryan added that it was the 'yards and yards . . . of stale Ascendancy stuff' in the British press that explained the fact that 'we feel tender to Dev'.[26] Perhaps such an approach served a contemporary purpose but it also helps to explain why Ryan's *Unique Dictator* proves so disappointing half a century later.

In contrast Sean O'Faolain's second biography, the Penguin paperback, *De Valera*, published in 1939, is still of considerable interest. It presents one of the earliest critiques of de Valera's policy on Irish unity. O'Faolain complains that the south under de Valera is not 'deeply moved by what they consider an impossible situation, and they have been inclined to treat the matter as a sleeping dog.' De Valera's difficulty — a pretty commonplace observation but rare at the time from an Irish writer — was that 'the more he behaves as Nationalist, Gaelic-revivalist, anti-British, the more does he estrange the north'. O'Faolain cites pervasive clerical control in the south, the censorship and. the Gaelic revival movement, along with isolationist economic policy as being inimical to unity. In effect he is emphasising — although the term was not then current — the two political cultures in Ireland each 'in mutual derision or even contempt' of the other.[27]

O'Faolain, as Donal McCartney has written, 'was unable to take the angel in de Valera . . . the self-righteous one who had done no wrong and never could do wrong'.[28] A biographer, writes O'Faolain, demands at least 'no self-concealment'.[29] This book was liked — not surprisingly by one of de Valera's wartime adversaries, the American minister in Dublin David Gray. Near the end of his term of office in Dublin he wrote to O'Faolain expressing his amazement at the objectivity of the book.[30] O'Faolain in reply thought it 'needs revision badly'. Since it was written O'Faolain thinks de Valera has 'revealed himself in action, in ways not hitherto to be observed'. He doesn't see him any longer 'as a satisfactory nationalist symbol'. Rather, he believes that de Valera is now 'exposed as a man who was that, wishes to be that', but has become 'a cute kind of Tammany ward-boss posing as a national leader'. O'Faolain thinks him 'a sad figure, subconsciously aware that he has had to do too many tricky things (to keep power) to keep his bib clean'.

O'Faolain suggests that de Valera has made 'a very gradual change-over from Left to Right. I don't mind this, I mean I don't pass any priggish moral judgement, but I do think that he still kids himself and the public that he hasn't done it.' When writing about de Valera, adds O'Faolain, 'I naturally accept his premises. "Nobody can argue if he doesn't agree on the premises." My present view of de Valera is that he has abandoned his premises. His whole career leads up to an independent Republic . . . . He got power. He side-stepped it. He's been untrue to himself. He's just like Louis Napoleon . . .'. O'Faolain saw de Valera's career as a tragedy.

> He found he daren't pull it off. All this stuff about Gaelic, and new legations and paper constitutions is pure compensation. The state he should logically have created was blocked by the church and business; so he has produced a complete hotch potch which I personally consider corrupt and dishonourable in many ways. . . . De Gaulle will produce something much the same.

To Gray's suggestion that he should rewrite the book, O'Faolain replied: 'I'll recast that biography when the man dies, not before — if I outlive him, for he looks like hitting ninety'.[31]

In 1944 M.J. MacManus, a staff writer on the *Irish Press*, published his *Eamon de Valera*, written, according to the author from 'the standpoint of an admirer': he believed it to be an 'honest rather than an impartial account'. MacManus 'neither sought nor received any assistance' from de Valera himself who 'was not even aware that it was being written'.[32] O'Faolain in a celebrated and lengthy review in *The Bell* was dismissive of the new book but allowed that MacManus was writing under a disadvantage: 'One would not expect the Literary Editor of the *Daily Express* to be ironical about Lord Beaverbrook as long as the most important event in Lord Beaverbrook's life has yet, happily, to occur.'[33] MacManus took umbrage and in the pages of *The Bell* reminded O'Faolain of the view he had taken in his early de Valera biography. O'Faolain did not demur: that book he now considered 'arrant tripe'.[34] MacManus — and certainly de Valera — fared somewhat better from another reviewer, Henry O'Neill. He thought the new biography 'not quite a success, for personality is an elusive and complex thing but there does stand out from the book as a whole, a leader, tolerant, selfless, of steel-like strength, patient . . . of great prevision . . .'. One must add that 'Henry O'Neill' was one of the pen-names of de Valera's press secretary Frank Gallagher. O'Neill/Gallagher concluded his review with the comment that de Valera was 'lucky in his latest biographer': one may add that he was even luckier in his reviewer.[35]

Although widely welcomed as a useful biography — the first to include the war years — MacManus's book is now of little interest. Mary Bromage, an American academic and a frequent visitor to Ireland since the 1930s, had many interviews with de Valera, the first in 1936. She invariably found his emphasis was on the 'principles he deemed at work in the national destiny'. He 'did not allow his person to be singled out for comment'. At later meetings before and after the war, 'the man, though growing older and more burdened, remained unaltered in mind and thought.' If 'he guessed he was talking to a biographer, he gave no quarter in conversation. Always the cause and not the individual came to his lips'. De Valera may well have sensed that he was talking to a sympathetic witness. Earlier in her introduction Bromage writes of her initial 'commitment of respect' for de Valera 'and ultimately of devotion . . .'.[36] This shows through in the book. Two disparate contemporary verdicts fairly sum it up: *Newsweek* suggested that it amounted to 'The stirabout of modern Irish history seen through an admiring study of one of its chief mixers'.[37] Richard Crossman stated it was 'distinguished neither by style nor by critical acumen. She adores Dev and makes no attempt to write objectively about either his British or his Irish opponents.'[38]

The Bromage biography prompted one controversy concerning de Valera's opinion of Machiavelli. The book quotes Dick Mulcahy as saying that in 1921, de Valera had said to him: 'You are a young man going in for politics — I will give you two pieces of advice. Study economics and read *The Prince*.'[39] In the paperback edition which followed some time later, this story was omitted. Mulcahy complained. Bromage defended her position — plausibly — by stating that the paperback edition had been considerably abridged. As is clear from his private papers, Mulcahy was very keen to give the widest possible currency to this story: he thought it provided an important insight into de Valera's personality and intellectual make-up and he later suggested publicly that O'Neill and O'Fiannachta had, in their Irish language version of de Valera's official life, endeavoured 'to remove the suspicion of Machiavellianism' from their subject. Mulcahy wrote a detailed account of his encounter with de Valera in 1921 when 'in a fatherly way' he had advised him to read Machiavelli — which Mulcahy suggested was 'a gangster's manual'.[40]

The final book here considered is the joint work of T.P. O'Neill and Lord Longford, *Eamon de Valera*. It is the outstanding book of this collection: it supersedes all earlier attempts at a biography and is the best available life of de Valera. What one cannot be fully content about is its provenance. De Valera himself was, it is fair to say, midwife to this book. The authors in their foreward write:

> This book could not have been written without the co-operation of President de Valera himself. He has always steadfastly refused to write an autobiography, but once he had agreed to the suggestion that an authoritative biography be written he could not have been more helpful. The authors wish to express their gratitude to him not only for making his huge library of private papers freely available to them, but giving them the benefit of his personal recollections of the great events in which he has played so prominent a

part. But he made it clear at a very early stage that, if they ever found a discrepancy between his memory of events and contemporary documents, it was the documents that must be trusted. The authors would like to record that such discrepancies were almost non-existent.[41]

But Lord Longford, four years later in one of his volumes of autobiography, gives the sort of detailed information which should properly belong in the foreward of the book itself. Longford informs us that perhaps ten years before the book appeared Bob Lusty, managing director of Hutchinson's, 'had tried to persuade Mr de Valera to write his own biography and, failing that, to *nominate* a biographer . . . . Tom O'Neill, with the help of a considerable advance from Hutchinson's, worked for three years on Mr de Valera's papers in a room in his house'.[42] Longford himself joined the enterprise at a later stage: he is already on record as considering de Valera 'the greatest man' he had ever met.[43] Privately in a letter to Desmond Ryan in 1936 he had written: 'Dev. as you know is my only political hero and I am a jealous hero-worshipper. So that nothing that any one (least of all myself) writes about him satisfies me.'[44]

That this book was not described as an 'official' life, nor an 'authorised' life, but rather as an 'authoritative' life is merely proof that de Valera in his old age never lost his genius for the bespoke formula: might it be said perhaps that he worked in 'external association' with his biographers; or that the authors recognised 'the special position' of de Valera 'as the guardian of the (political) faith professed by the great majority of the citizens'? This is not to suggest that de Valera's role as midwife to the book is a defect: rather is it its central virtue, because in the absence of a volume of autobiography, or memoirs or contemporary diaries from de Valera himself, we have — given his intimate participation in the production of the book — the nearest thing possible to an autobiography, his preferred rationalization at the end of his career, his final self-justification, echoing what he had been saying at cross roads, chapel gates and in the Dáil for the previous half century. Holding this view, it must be added that a definitive life of de Valera has still to be written. This can scarcely be attempted until his own papers become available — ten years after his death — in August 1985. Although Longford and O'Neill enjoyed privileged access to these papers, it is difficult to assess — given their inadequate citing of references — the value of this collection.

It was surely, in any case, an error of judgement on de Valera's own part not to have made them available sooner: the arrangements leave, for instance, a 'sixty-four year rule' in operation on the critical events of 1921. What has happened, of course, is that much of de Valera's career is now being researched from British, American, German and Canadian archives and from other Irish collections. Writers, readers and de Valera himself must be the losers by this arrangement which he himself laid down in his will. Meanwhile however it is surely opportune that appropriate measures are taken to ensure that the papers are properly calendared and duly processed by a team of archivists. Moreover, since in the year of his centenary no public memorial to de Valera has yet been erected in Dublin, would it be opportune to suggest that a de Valera library be established — on the model of the United States Presidential Libraries, which are an integral part of the National Archives? This could be publicly funded but independently administered by professional archivists — provided the plan could be rendered compatible with the terms of de Valera's will and his contract with the Franciscans in Killiney, Co. Dublin, who are the custodians of his papers.

It may even be fair to call on de Valera himself as a supporter of such a suggestion. At the opening of the Manuscript Room in Trinity College in Dublin in 1957, he emphasised the importance of original documents for historical scholarship: some of the material he said in Trinity Library was available in facsimile, photostat or microfilm, or edited and published in printed form. 'But no earnest scholar, and I like to think of all scholars as enthusiasts will rest satisfied with the second hand if he can come and see and touch and examine the original. Here these originals are being safely stored catalogued and arranged so as to be readily accessible.'[45]

To which one can only add: Killiney papers please copy.

NOTES

1. The seven biographies considered are: Denis Gwynn, *De Valera* (London: 1933); Sean O'Faolain, *Life story of Eamon de Valera* (Dublin: 1933); Desmond Ryan, *Unique dictator: a study of Eamon de Valera* (London: 1936); Sean O'Faolain, *De Valera* (London: 1939); M.J. MacManus, *Eamon de Valera* (Dublin: 1944); Mary Bromage, *De Valera and the March of a Nation* (Dublin: 1956); Lord Longford and T.P. O'Neill, *Eamon de Valera* (Dublin: 1970). Although this is not an exhaustive list of the biographies of de Valera, these books were the most widely circulated during the course of de Valera's political career. Books published since such as T. Ryle Dwyer's short biography in the Gill's Irish Lives series, *Eamon de Valera* (Dublin: 1980) and the same author's, *De Valera's darkest hour: 1919-1932*, and *De Valera's finest hour: 1932-1959* (Cork: 1982) have not been considered.

2. Editorial, *Morning Post*, 22 February 1932.

3. John Bowman, *De Valera and the Ulster Question: 1917-1973* (Oxford: 1982), 110-14.

4. Quoted by U.K. High Commissioner (South Africa) to Dominions Secretary, 21 May 1932, Public Record Office, London (hereafter PRO), CAB 27,525 ISC(32)23.

5. Ramsay MacDonald to Abe Bailey, 22 July 1932, MacDonald papers, PRO 30/69/35.

6. Eamon de Valera, 'National discipline and majority rule', Fianna Fáil pamphlet, (1936) 25-7. See also exchange of letters between de Valera and Cosgrave in State Paper Office. Dublin, S.6295.

7. Granard, note of conversation with de Valera, 25 August 1934, PRO CAB 27/526, ISC(32)86, annex II.

8. R.S. Oldham, 'The Irish Free State Land Annuities', 17 July 1932, PRO DO 35/397/11111/261.

9. House of Commons debates, 17 June 1932.

10. O'Faolain, (1933), 95.

11. *Irish Times*, 25 March 1933.

12. *An Phoblacht*, 1 April 1933.

13. Sean O'Faolain, 'Principles and propaganda', *The Bell*, **10**:3, June 1945, 197.

14. F.S.L. Lyons, 'Sean O'Faolain as biographer', *Irish University Review*, 6:1, Spring, 1976, 95-6.

15. *Irish Times*, 25 March 1933.

16. *Irish Press*, 22 March 1933.

17. Desmond Ryan papers, UCD Archives Department, LA10/D/304/2.

18. Ryan to Kiernan, 20 September and reply 23 September 1935, *ibid.*, LA10/P/78/11-12.

19. Ryan to Pakenham, 20 September 1935, *ibid.*, LA10/0/121/6.

20. Pakenham to Ryan, 26 July 1935, *ibid*, LA10/0/121/7.

21. Ryan to Pakenham, 24 October 1935, *ibid.*, LA10/0/121/8.

22. Ryan to Pakenham, 12 November 1935, *ibid.*, LA10/0/121/9.

23. Ryan to Miss Kirwin, 2 February 1936, *ibid.*, LA10/P/76/5.

24. Ryan, (1936), 254-5.

25. E.T. Keane to Ryan, 17 January 1938, Ryan papers, LA10/8/77/1.

26. Ryan to Keane, 10 January 1938, *ibid.*, LA10/8/77/2.

27. O'Faolain, (1939), 153-62.

28. Donal McCartney, 'Sean O'Faolain: a nationalist right enough', *Irish University Review*, 6:1, Spring 1976, 85.

29. O'Faolain, (1939), 174.

30. Gray to O'Faolain, 5 May 1947, Gray papers, Franklyn Roosevelt Library, Hyde Park, New York State.

31. O'Faolain to Gray, 5 May 1947, *ibid.*

32. MacManus, (1944), 5-7.

33. Sean O'Faolain, 'Principles and Propaganda', *The Bell*, **10**:3, 190.

34. MacManus to O'Faolain, open letter, *ibid.*, 189-94.

35. Henry O'Neill, 'The life story of a statesman', undated press clipping, Sean Cullen papers, National Library of Ireland, MS 23,057.

36. Bromage, (1956), 11-13.

37. *Newsweek*, 21 January 1957.

38. R.H.S. Crossman, *The Charm of politics* (London: 1958), 34.

39. Bromage, (1956), 86.

40. Mulcahy papers, UCD Archives Department, P7/D/82-3.

41. Longford and O'Neill, (1970), xv.

42. Frank Pakenham, Earl of Longford, *The grain of wheat*, (London: 1974), 237.

43. Pakenham, *Humility* (London: 1969), 33-5, *Irish Press*, 30 August 1975.

44. Pakenham to Ryan, 5 June 1936, Ryan papers, LA10/0/121/10.

45. Maurice Moynihan (ed.), *Speeches and statements of Eamon de Valera:* 1917-1973 (Dublin: 1980), 578-80.

APPENDIX

A Methodological and Ideology-critical Note
on the Use of Concepts in the Socio-historical Sciences

Barend Pieter Strydom *

All scientific endeavour is characterised by a concern for conceptual clarity and precision. Beyond this general scientific principle the basic categories of science differ from one another in accordance with the manner in which they arrive at and the form taken by their respective concepts. In the natural sciences, clear and precise concepts are achieved by abstraction and generalisation, with the result that they assume the form of laws. In the socio-historical sciences, by contrast, the necessary clarity and precision can be achieved only by concepts which start from and render as univocal as possible, yet in principle remain bound to the linguistic procedures used in everyday life by the members of social groups to construct the meaning and normative reality of their social environment. As examples of the latter type of concept formation may be cited Max Weber's 'ideal types', Alfred Schutz's 'second level constructs' which are formulated in relation to 'first level (everyday) constructs', and finally Habermas' 'reconstructive concepts', as one may refer to them.

Whereas there exists a complete break between natural scientific abstraction and everyday experience of nature, the setting sun of the man in the street and the natural scientist respectively being two completely different matters, socio-historical concepts tie into reality, rendering its semantic structure clear and precise, and thus represent the conceptual level the members of society would attain were they able to conceptualise reality as clearly and precisely as possible. Concepts employed in the socio-historical sciences thus do not purport merely to describe but also to determine reality; they are not merely indicators of what they synthesise but also factors in it. They are not a simple reproduction or reflection of reality but represent what reality could possibly be. Social scientific and historical concepts are constructed from the perspective of a possible understanding of meaning and hence of possible action; they represent possible perspectives of self-interpretation and self-understanding of the members of society and as such form a horizon of action orientation.

Important implications flow from this peculiar nature of concept formation in the socio-historical sciences. It is vital to continually bear in mind and make clear the nature of socio-historical concept formation since the employment of these symbolic means is of decisive importance not only for scientific practice, be it historical sociology or historiography, but also for the historical consciousness of

---

* Mr. B.P. Strydom lectures in Sociology at U.C.C. He submitted this critique at the conference with reference to the use of the term 'charisma'.

contemporary society. On the one hand, socio-historical concepts remain dependent upon a general interpretation of the potential or even tendential synthetic character of socio-historical reality which can neither be proved nor be disproved by immanent empirical analytical criteria. On the other hand, the way we relate to our past through the use of socio-historical concepts has serious consequences in that we thereby establish that kind of attribution of responsibility which forms the collective identity. The latter is decisive, of course, not only for our interpretation of the past but also for the way in which we believe most appropriately to have to confront our future. The inappropiately entitled postulate of 'value-freedom' has its place in this context. Correctly understood, it asserts that it is incumbent on the sociologist and historian to declare the dependency of their fundamental theoretical assumptions upon normative presuppositions. In the case of the historian, these normative presuppositions pertain to his or her chosen interpretative framework which, over and above the unifying power of the context of life surrounding the historical event, determines the continuity of the narrative account. Of crucial importance here is the historian's interpretation or hermeneutic anticipation of the future which, although it does not enter substantively the narrated history itself, nevertheless forms the fundamental yet implicit basis of his or her choice of an interpretative scheme. In the case of the sociologist, in turn, the same situation applies insofar as he or she gets involved in historical sociology; in addition, however, the normative presuppositions of the sociologist's theoretical assumptions announce themselves also in his or her projection of as yet uninstitutionalised and perhaps even uninstitutionalisable structural possibilities which are arrived at by way of the rational reconstruction of social development and which serve as basis for the analysis and critique of the present.

To draw out the implications of the above, the concept of 'charisma' may serve as an example. Max Weber introduced the concept of charisma into sociology. To appreciate the nature and possible function of this concept we need to take into account the background against which he did so. Weber's overriding concern was with the progressively rational organisation of all spheres of life — from science, music, art and architecture, the press and periodicals, and institutions of higher learning to the state, bureaucracy, law and capitalism. Regarding 'rationalism' and the 'disenchantment' of the world as 'the fate of our times', he had a premonition of the contemporary world developing into a prison-house of future bondage, an 'iron cage', that is, a stage of cultural development characterised by 'specialists without spirit, sensualists without heart, . . . (a) . . . nullity (who) imagines that it has attained a level of civilization never before achieved'. Accordingly, he came to see the cultural problem of the present time as being the salvaging, in the face of the overpowering process of rationalisation, of any remanants of individual freedom of movement. Weber's own — inadequate and indeed objectionable — response to this problem in theoretical philosophy was introspectivism as against behaviourism, in practical philosophy decisionism as against the naturalistic fallacy, and in politics charisma as against submission: a headstrong leader with a predisposition toward wielding the instruments of power in both an authoritarian and 'rational' (in the sense of means ends rationality as distinct from communicative rationality) manner, a 'leader with a machine'.

In Germany, it should be noted, a connection is made between Weber and Carl Schmitt, the decisionist political theorist of the Third Reich. As regards the employment of the concept of charisma, therefore, we are compelled to take into account the consequences Weber's picture of a Caesar-like leader democracy had in the Weimar period. What aggravated these consequences was the fact that Weber, despite his limpid analysis of the ideal typical form of concept and theory formation, kept to the nominalism of his philosophical master, the Neo-Kantian Heinrich Rickert. The latter drew a sharp distinciton between concept and reality, reality being 'irrational', an 'extensive and intensive manifold' to which the content of concepts does not and in principle cannot correspond. This nominalistic position, which impressed itself on Weber, stands diametrically opposed to conceptual realism according to which the content of concepts is related to the content of reality itself and indeed such that a certain identity between concept and reality can be postulated. This latter position is common to Hegelian, Marxist, phenomenological and hermeneutical approaches, all of which assume that, in some sense or another, there is a reciprocal relation between the structure of consciousness and the structure of reality. Considered closely, in fact, it would seem as though there is a serious ambiguity in Weber's position on the ideal typical form of concept and theory formation. On the one hand, he maintains that the ideal type is a 'thought construct' (*Gedankenbild*) in the sense of an artificial or analytical construct. Here he manifests his conceptual nominalism. On the other hand, however, he suggests that the expression 'thought construct' must be taken in such a way that scientific concepts are regarded as starting from, linking up with, and remaining in principle bound to thoughts or ideas in everyday life. Here we witness Weber's tendency toward conceptual realism, that is, the view that concept and reality or the structure of consciousness and the structure of reality are related. While he shows in this latter sense that the ideal type rests on an assumption about the potential or tendential synthetic character of socio-historical reality, he retreats from the consequences of this conceptual realism of his to the safe harbour of nominalism. By means of this same strategy, moreover, Weber sought to circumvent the normative implications of his own position. While being aware of the fact that the socio-historical sciences are concerned with norms in the sense not only of studying them but also of relating to norms in order to constitute past human action as history, Weber nevertheless submitted that the evaluations which inform historical interpretation finally admit of irrational decision alone and thus elude intersubjective agreement. Scientific work is therefore bound to the rule that values, by virtue of their being in principle intersubjectively uncompelling, should be avoided at all costs. Weber took together this position of his under the title of the postulate of 'value-freedom'.

After a period of charismatic figures, including among them Hitler, we are no longer permitted to employ the concept of charisma in the same way as did Weber. Especially under contemporary conditions of economic and political instability, a nominalistic use of the concept is not merely naive but in fact tantamount to a dogmatism pregnant with political implications which is all the more dangerous to the extent that it is accompanied by the suggestion of being value-free. It may turn out to have undesirable consequences in that in the process of the formation of collective identity the public feels itself encouraged to take charisma as an appropriate political answer to present-day problems.

As against the possibility of a certain dismissive interpretation of the above, it must be pointed out that one need not assume a strictly Marxist position to arrive at this conclusion. In opposition to Weber, Marxism indeed rejects value-freedom in the sense of the avoidance of values in favour of explicitly choosing those values which allow the most comprehensive and fundamental disclosure of reality and thus declaring the normative presuppositions of scientific practice. But by identifying interests and knowledge Marxism not only obliterates the distinction between the freedom of scientific practice from the immediate pressure of the norms of practical action and its necessary relatedness to meaning constitutive norms; by the same token it also proves incapable of developing a philosophically cogent justification or grounding of the normative presuppositions of scientific practice. The most promising route today is offered by the transcendental pragmatics of the outstanding contemporary German philosopher, Karl-Otto Apel, which runs between Kant and Hegel, Weber and Marx.

Glossary

Ard-Fheis (lit.) supreme congress (Annual general convention of association or parties)

Bunreacht na hÉireann The Constitution of Ireland (1937)

Dáil Éireann House of Representatives

Gaeltacht The parts of Ireland where Irish is spoken as a native language

Seanad Senate

Taoiseach Chief, leader (Title of the head of Government)

Translations of Irish Phrases and Passages used in the Text

p. 8 *conas a réiteodh sé . . .* : 'how was he to resolve his obligation to declare his belief in the one true Church without doing injustice to minorities and without increasing difficulties.'

p. 12 *aisling*: vision, dream (as in Gaelic poetry)

p. 12 *cúis*: cause (especially the cause of Irish language revival)

p. 13 *ath-Mhaois*: a new Moses

p. 14 *ag coimeád cúil dúinn*: keeping, guarding goal for us

p. 55 *níor chlis sibh orm, a Ghaela*: My Gaelic people, you did not fail me.

p. 55 *Cailleach Bhéara*: the Old Woman of Beare

p. 67-8 *Ta ár dtír agus ár muintir . . .* : our country and our people are for a long time in servitude and bondage to our enemy. Today, we are breaking the bonds and nullifying the control, but the mark of the bonds and the servitude are [still] on her (the country). Work and commerce are the great arteries of the country. In those arteries goes the blood of the country, that blood which gives life and health to its body and which stirs its soul. They tend to be crushed and broken as a result of the servitude. The proper rhythm is not in the blood and because of that there are ugly swellings here and there on the body of the country, in the cities, in the towns and in the countryside itself. Those swellings are a sign to us of a disease which will increase and which will perhaps kill our country unless it is cured. If we want our country to survive, and to have it alive as well as liberated, we will have to save it. Let us do it correctly and skilfully. Let us understand exactly in that business what *is* our country — that Ireland which is a dream and a prophesy to every one of its children from their earliest youth. Let us understand that it is this land, beautiful as God made it, rich with the industry of its people, bright with their laughter, lovely with their joy, holy with their faith and goodwill. Let us understand that it is our people living joyfully and peacefully amidst the wealth that God has granted them, and working it for their sustenance.

p. 68   *Tuigimíd an droch-staid . . .:* We understand the poor condition of Ireland; she is impoverished, oppressed: everything has long been stolen from us by the enemy, and to-day the enemy is worse than he ever was . . . We'll have to fight that, there will have to be freedom in the people's livelihood as well as in the state; we will have to have freedom to export our own products . . .

p. 154   *A Dhia, Saor Eire:* O God, save Ireland

Contributors

JOHN BOWMAN	is a historian and broadcaster. He is author of *De Valera and the Ulster Question 1917-1973*.
T. RYLE DWYER	is author of *Eamon de Valera; Michael Collins and the Treaty; Irish Neutrality in the USA 1939-47;* and *De Valera's Finest Hour*.
RONAN FANNING	teaches history at University College Dublin and is author of *The Irish Department of Finance 1922-58*.
BRIAN FARRELL	lectures in political science at University College Dublin and is author of *Chairman or Chief? — The Role of the Taoiseach in the Irish Government* and *The Founding of Dáil Éireann*. He is a well known broadcaster.
DAVID FITZPATRICK	teaches history at Trinity College Dublin and is author of *Politics and Irish Life 1913-1921: provincial experience of war and revolution*.
DERMOT KEOGH	lecturer in history at University College Cork; has published *The Rise of the Irish Working Class* and *Romero: El Salvador's Martyr*.
JOHN A. MURPHY	is Professor of Irish History at University College Cork and author of *Ireland in the Twentieth Century*. He is co-editor of *De Valera and his Times*.
JOHN P. O'CARROLL	lectures in Sociology at University College Cork and has published articles in political and rural sociology. He is co-editor of *De Valera and his Times*.
JOHN O'CONNOR	lectures in Jurisprudence at University College Cork, is a member of the English Bar and has published articles on International Law and Relations, and the Irish Legal System.
GEARÓID Ó CRUALAOICH	lectures in Irish Folklore and Ethnography at University College Cork and has published articles on the continuity of native Irish tradition.

201

M.A.G. Ó TUATHAIGH   lectures in history at University College Galway, and is author of *Ireland before the Famine 1798-1848.*

RAYMOND J. RAYMOND   lectures in British and Irish history at the University of Connecticut.

MARYANN VALIULIS   teaches history at Lafayette College, Pennsylvania.

Authors Index

Subject Index

The following abbreviation is used throughout

E. de V.   Eamon de Valera

205